T0365678

FOR THE
LOVE OF WORDS

FOR THE
LOVE OF WORDS

RAY OROCCO-JOHN

ARCHWAY
PUBLISHING

Archway Publishing books may be ordered through booksellers or by contacting:

Archway Publishing
1663 Liberty Drive
Bloomington, IN 47403
www.archwaypublishing.com
844-669-3957

ISBN: 978-1-6657-7159-7 (sc)
ISBN: 978-1-6657-7162-7 (e)

Library of Congress Control Number: 2025900505

Print information available on the last page.

Archway Publishing rev. date: 1/24/2025

CONTENTS

Presented To:

_____

FOREWORD

In the vast canvas of life, words paint our stories, dreams, and deepest emotions. For the author, words have been more than mere tools; they are the essence of his existence, the lifeblood coursing through his veins. "For the Love of Words" is not just a collection of writings; it is a testament to the transformative power of language and the indomitable spirit of a man dedicated to the art of expression.

From a young age, the author discovered the magic of words. They were his companions in solitude, his solace in times of despair, and his wings in moments of joy. Through the written word, he navigated the complexities of the human experience, gave voice to the unspoken, and challenged the boundaries of understanding. Each sentence crafted, each paragraph penned, was an act of love transcending the mundane and touching the sublime.

"For the Love of Words" is a journey through life's storms, guided by the beacon of language. It celebrates the resilience of the human spirit and the enduring power of words to captivate, enlighten, heal, and inspire. It highlights the poet's unwavering dedication to his craft. As you turn each page, you are invited into the heart of a writer who has poured his soul into his work, facing the tempests of doubt and emerging with a powerful, profound voice.

The short stories delve into the intricacies of human love, the struggles of the Christian church, the temptations of the heart, the battles between hatred and forgiveness, the richness of traditions and customs, and the pain of unrequited love. The author has also crafted various types of poetry, including acrostics, cinquains, elegies, epitaphs, free verses, haikus, odes, sestinas, sonnets, villanelles, and other forms. A dedicated section captures love poems that warm the heart. Each piece of poetry speaks to love, hardship, disappointment, and happiness, giving voice to the voiceless and hope to the despairing.

May this book remind you of the beauty and strength that words can hold. May it inspire you to find your own voice and use it with courage and conviction. For it is through our words that we leave our mark on the world, touch the lives of others, and truly soar.

This book is the third in a series by the author. The first is titled "Of Sadness and Of Pleasure," and the second, "A Journey Towards Endless Light Out Of Pitiless Darkness."

DEDICATION

To my beloved brother, Arthur, who left us in July 2024, and to all the departed souls who have touched my life and shaped my journey. Your memories live on in my heart, and your influence continues to guide me. May your souls find eternal peace.

SHORT STORIES

1

A Love Against The Odds

Mansfield, Ohio, was a town steeped in tradition and conservative values. The streets were lined with quaint houses, each with well-manicured lawns and white picket fences. The residents prided themselves on their puritan lifestyle, often spurning those who didn't subscribe to their strict moral code. It was a place where appearances mattered, and any deviation from the norm would invite the crushing wave of reproach.

Fiona Mackeson grew up in this rigid environment, but her home life was anything but conventional. Her mother, Dorcas, was a woman whose beauty had long faded under the weight of her addictions. Her father, Gabe, was a man whose once-strong frame had been ravaged by years of alcohol and drug abuse. Despite their flaws, Fiona loved her parents deeply, clinging to the rare moments of tenderness they offered like a desert flower holding onto the morning dew.

Fiona's childhood was a chaotic whirlwind of broken promises and shattered dreams. The smell of alcohol and the sight of drug paraphernalia were constants in her home. Nights were filled with the sounds of arguments and the occasional crash of a bottle against the wall. Yet, amidst the turmoil, Fiona found solace in the small acts of kindness her parents sometimes showed. A gentle touch from her father, a rare smile from her mother—these fleeting moments were the threads that held her fragile world together.

At the tender age of thirteen, Fiona's world took a darker turn. Her mother, desperate to sustain her drug habit, introduced Fiona to prostitution. The first time was a blur of fear and confusion. Fiona's heart pounded in her chest as she was led into a dimly lit room and doused with perfume by her mother, whose whispered assurances did little to calm her nerves. The betrayal cut deep, and the innocence of her childhood was lost in that moment like a flower withered by a sudden frost.

Three years later, tragedy struck again. Fiona found her father lifeless on the floor, a needle still in his arm. The sight of his lifeless body was a wake-up call, a stark reminder of the destructive path her family was on. Though Gabe had been mostly drunk, their bond had been strong, and his death left a gaping hole in Fiona's heart. The grief was overwhelming, but it also ignited a spark of determination within her.

In the wake of her father's death, Fiona found the strength to defy her mother's attempts to prostitute her. She stood her ground, refusing to be a pawn in her mother's desperate game. The confrontations were fierce, but Fiona's resolve never wavered. Slowly, she began to persuade her mother to change her lifestyle. It was a long and arduous journey, filled with setbacks and moments of despair, but Fiona's unwavering love and determination began to make a difference—the light breaking through the storm clouds.

Despite the chaos at home, Fiona managed to navigate her way through high school. She was an average student, her grades reflecting the lack of parental support and the constant distractions of her tumultuous home life. But Fiona was determined to rise above her circumstances like a star shining through the darkest night. She studied late into the night, her textbooks illuminated by the dim glow of a bedside lamp. Her perseverance paid off, and she graduated, a small but significant victory.

College was a fresh start for Fiona. Away from the toxic environment of her home, she thrived. She threw herself into her studies, determined to make something of herself. The challenges were many, but Fiona faced them head-on, her resilience and determination driving her forward. She excelled in her nursing program, earning the respect and admiration of her peers and professors. When she graduated, it was with a sense of pride and accomplishment that she had never known before.

Fiona's career as a nurse brought her to Ohio Health Mansfield Hospital, where she met Justin Clapper, a charismatic and dedicated doctor. Their connection was immediate, a spark that quickly grew into a flame. Justin was captivated by Fiona's strength and compassion, while Fiona admired Justin's dedication and kindness. Their romance blossomed, bringing a sense of joy and fulfillment to Fiona's life that she had never experienced before. She told her friend that being with Justin was like being on a plane for the first time—thrilling and exhilarating, with every moment feeling like an adventure taking her to new heights.

Just as their relationship was reaching new heights, a dark shadow from Fiona's past threatened to tear them apart. At a party, Justin's wayward uncle, in a drunken stupor, revealed Fiona's past as a prostitute. He said,

"She and her mama were wild…" The words hung in the air like a toxic cloud, poisoning the atmosphere. Justin's face turned pale, his eyes wide with shock and disbelief.

"Is it true, Fiona?" Justin asked, his voice trembling with a mix of anger and hurt. "Were you really a prostitute?"

Fiona's heart sank, the weight of her past crashing down on her. "Justin, please, let me explain," she pleaded, her voice choked with emotion. "It wasn't by choice. My mother forced me into it. I was just a child."

Despite Fiona's heartfelt explanation, Justin felt betrayed. The revelation was too much for him to process, and he couldn't see past the stigma of her past—blinded by the shadows of her history. "I trusted you, Fiona," he said, his voice breaking. "But you kept this from me. I don't know if I can get past this."

Fiona's eyes filled with tears as she watched the man she loved walk away like sand through her fingers. The pain of losing Justin was a heavy burden, but Fiona knew she had to find a way to move forward.

The breakup with Justin left Fiona devastated, but she refused to let it define her. She channeled her pain into a fierce determination to improve herself. Every morning, she woke up with a renewed sense of purpose, her eyes set on a brighter future. She returned to school, immersing herself in her studies with a passion she had never known before. The long hours and sleepless nights were grueling, but Fiona's resolve never wavered. She graduated as a nurse practitioner, her heart swelling with pride as she held her diploma in her hands. It was a testament to her resilience and strength, a symbol of her journey from darkness to light.

With her new qualifications, Fiona secured a job at a hospital in Shelby, Ohio. The move marked a fresh start, a chance to leave behind the shadows of her past. She found a charming house about ten miles from the hospital, its cozy rooms filled with the promise of new beginnings.

The walls, once bare, soon adorned with pictures and mementos of her journey. Each morning, as she walked through the door of her new home, Fiona felt a sense of peace and fulfillment that she had long yearned for.

One weekend, while shopping at the local grocery store, Fiona's path crossed with Clyde Richter, a doctor who lived just two houses away. Clyde was immediately captivated by Fiona's mellifluous voice and piercing greenish-blue eyes, their depth hinting at the strength and resilience within her. "Excuse me," he said, a warm smile spreading across his face, "I couldn't help but notice your eyes. They're absolutely stunning."

Fiona blushed, a shy smile playing on her lips. "Thank you," she replied, her heart fluttering at the unexpected compliment. They struck up a conversation, discovering a shared passion for their work and a mutual appreciation for life's simple pleasures. By the time they reached the checkout, they had exchanged phone numbers, both eager to see where this new connection might lead.

On their first date, Fiona knew she had to be honest with Clyde about her past. She didn't want to make the same mistake she had with Justin. As they sat in a cozy corner of a quaint café, Fiona took a deep breath, her hands trembling slightly. "Clyde, there's something I need to tell you," she began, her voice steady despite the turmoil within her. "My past isn't something I'm proud of, but it's a part of who I am."

Clyde listened intently as Fiona painstakingly explained how she had been forced into prostitution by her mother and how she had fought to overcome the odds. Tears welled up in Clyde's eyes as he heard her story, his heart aching for the pain she had endured. "Your life has not been smooth, yet you persevered," he said, his voice filled with admiration. "I admire your strength, Fiona. And I promise to love and cherish you, if you'll open your heart to me."

Fiona's eyes glistened with tears of relief and gratitude. "Thank you, Clyde," she whispered, her heart swelling with hope. "I promise to do the same."

Fiona and Clyde's relationship blossomed, their love growing stronger with each passing day. They spent their weekends exploring the countryside, their laughter echoing through the fields as they shared stories and dreams. Clyde's unwavering support and understanding helped Fiona heal the wounds of her past, and she found herself opening up to him in ways she had never thought possible. They promised to love each other, their bond unbreakable—an unyielding fortress of love.

Six months later, Fiona and Clyde attended a fundraising ball where doctors from various hospitals gathered. Fiona looked radiant in a flowing gown, her arm linked with Clyde's like the interlocking rings of a chain, as they mingled with the guests. Everyone couldn't help but notice the pulchritudinous pair, their elegance and charm illuminating the room. As they moved through the crowd, Fiona spotted Justin across the room. He was stunned by her grace and beauty, the woman he had rejected now happily in another man's arms. Fiona, ever gracious, approached Justin and shook his hand. "Justin, it's good to see you," she said, her voice warm and sincere. "I'd like you to meet Clyde, my boyfriend."

Justin forced a smile, his heart heavy with regret. "Nice to meet you, Clyde," he said, his voice strained. As the night went on, Justin couldn't shake the feeling of loss. He watched Fiona and Clyde, their love evident in every glance and touch, and he realized how much he had let his uncle's derisive comments affect his love for Fiona. The regret gnawed at him, a constant reminder of what he had lost.

The grand hall was filled with the soft glow of chandeliers, casting a warm light over the elegantly dressed guests. The air buzzed with conversation and laughter, the atmosphere alive with celebration. Fiona and Clyde moved through the crowd, their hands intertwined, their smiles radiant. As the evening progressed, the master of ceremonies took the stage, calling for everyone's attention.

"Ladies and gentlemen, we have a special moment to share with you tonight," the MC announced, his voice echoing through the hall. "Please direct your attention to the center of the room."

A spotlight illuminated Fiona and Clyde, standing hand in hand. Clyde turned to Fiona, his eyes filled with love and determination. He dropped to one knee, pulling a small velvet box from his pocket. The room fell silent, all eyes on the couple.

"Fiona," Clyde began, his voice steady despite the emotion in his eyes. "From the moment I met you, I knew you were someone special. Your strength, your resilience, and your unwavering spirit have captured my heart. Will you do me the honor of becoming my wife?"

Tears welled up in Fiona's eyes as she looked down at Clyde, her heart overflowing with love. "Yes, Clyde," she whispered, her voice trembling with emotion. "Yes, I will marry you."

The room erupted in applause as Clyde slipped the ring onto Fiona's finger and rose to embrace her. Their kiss was a promise of a future filled with love and happiness, a testament to the journey they had taken together.

That evening, Justin trudged home, the weight of regret pressing down on him like a suffocating shroud. He collapsed onto his bed, staring blankly at the ceiling, his mind a whirlpool of self-reproach. How could he have been so foolish? His uncle's cruel, mocking words had wormed their way into his heart, poisoning his love for Fiona. Every flicker of the dim light seemed to taunt him, casting shadows of missed opportunities and the echo of her laughter, now lost to him forever.

Sleep was a distant dream, as Justin's thoughts spiraled deeper into despair. He could see Fiona's radiant smile and hear Clyde's tender words to her, a love so palpable it left a bitter taste in his mouth. The walls of his room seemed to close in on him, suffocating him with the realization that he had let his insecurities and someone else's venomous opinion rob him of the greatest love he had ever known.

As he lay there, paralyzed by the tormenting silence, the only sound that filled the room was the relentless ticking of the clock, each second a cruel reminder of the time he could never get back. His chest tightened with a sorrow so profound it felt like his heart was being squeezed by an invisible hand, and a tear slipped down his cheek. "Fiona," he whispered into the empty darkness, but there was no one to hear his broken plea.

In the weeks leading up to the wedding, Fiona knew she had to confront her past to fully embrace her future. She made the difficult decision to visit her mother, who had been receiving treatment and counseling for her drug addiction. The drive to her childhood home was filled with a mix of anxiety and determination.

When Fiona arrived, she found her mother sitting on the porch, her once gaunt face now showing signs of recovery. Dorcas looked up, her eyes filled with a mixture of hope and fear. "Fiona," she said softly, her voice trembling. "I didn't think you'd come."

Fiona took a deep breath, her heart pounding in her chest like a bass drum in a symphony. "Mom, I came because I need to forgive you," she said, her voice steady. "I need to let go of the pain and anger I've been holding onto. I want to help you, but you have to promise me that you'll continue to fight your demons."

Tears streamed down Dorcas's cheeks as she nodded. "I promise, Fiona. I'm so sorry for everything I've put you through. I want to make things right."

Fiona embraced her mother, the weight of years of pain and resentment lifting from her shoulders. It was a moment of healing and reconciliation, a step towards a brighter future for both of them.

The day of the wedding dawned bright and clear, the sky a brilliant blue. The ceremony was held in a picturesque garden, the air filled with the scent of blooming flowers. Fiona walked down the aisle in a stunning gown, her heart pounding with anticipation. Clyde stood at the altar, his eyes locked onto hers, a smile of pure joy on his face.

As they exchanged vows, their voices steady and filled with emotion, there wasn't a dry eye in the audience. "I promise to love you, to support you, and to stand by your side through all of life's challenges," Clyde vowed, his voice strong and unwavering.

"And I promise to cherish you, to be your partner in all things, and to love you with all my heart," Fiona replied, her eyes shining with tears of happiness.

When they were pronounced husband and wife, the crowd erupted in cheers, and Fiona and Clyde shared a kiss that sealed their commitment to each other. The reception that followed was a joyous celebration, filled with laughter, dancing, and the warmth of family and friends.

With Fiona's support and encouragement, Dorcas continued her journey to recovery. She attended counseling sessions regularly and worked hard to rebuild her life. The bond between mother and daughter grew stronger, their relationship healing with each passing day. Dorcas's full recovery was a testament to the power of forgiveness and the strength of the human spirit.

A year after their wedding, Fiona and Clyde welcomed a beautiful baby girl into their lives. They named her Cara, a symbol of their love and the new beginnings they had embraced. The first time Fiona held Cara in her arms, she felt a surge of love so powerful it brought tears to her eyes.

Clyde stood by her side, his eyes filled with pride and joy as he looked at their daughter.

"She's perfect," Fiona whispered, her voice choked with emotion. "Our little miracle."

Clyde kissed Fiona's forehead, his heart overflowing with love. "We are so blessed," he said softly. "I can't wait to see what the future holds for our family."

Meanwhile, Justin had moved on with his life, marrying Dora Silverstein, a successful realtor. Their wedding was a grand affair, filled with the trappings of wealth and success. At first, their marriage seemed perfect, a picture of happiness and prosperity.

As time went on, cracks began to appear in Justin and Dora's relationship. Dora became increasingly dissatisfied, her restlessness leading her to seek fulfillment elsewhere. She began having affairs with her real estate clients, her infidelity a stark contrast to the vows she had made. Justin, once confident and assured, found himself grappling with feelings of betrayal and inadequacy.

One evening, Justin could no longer ignore the signs. He confronted Dora in their living room, the tension between them palpable. "Dora, we need to talk," he began, his voice trembling with a mix of anger and hurt. "I've noticed the late nights, the secretive phone calls. Are you seeing someone else?"

Dora's eyes flashed with defiance, but she didn't deny it. "Yes, Justin," she admitted, her voice cold and unfeeling. "I've been seeing other people. I can't help it. I'm not happy with you."

Justin's heart sank, the weight of her words crushing him. "How could you do this to us?" he demanded, his voice breaking. "I thought we had something real. I thought we were building a life together."

Dora's expression remained indifferent. "Maybe for you, but not for me," she replied. "I've felt trapped, unfulfilled. You don't meet my needs, Justin. I need more."

"I can't believe this," Justin said, his voice barely above a whisper. "I gave up so much for you, and this is how you repay me? By making me feel inadequate, by betraying our vows?"

Dora shrugged, her indifference cutting deeper than any words. "I'm sorry you feel that way, but I can't change who I am."

Justin took a deep breath, trying to steady himself. "Maybe we should consider counseling," he suggested, his voice filled with a desperate hope. "We can try to work through this, to understand each other better."

Dora's eyes narrowed, her lips curling into a sneer. "Counseling? Really, Justin? I don't think that's going to fix anything. I don't want to be fixed. I want to be free."

Justin felt a wave of despair wash over him. He had hoped for a chance to salvage their marriage, but Dora's refusal left him feeling more alone than ever. "If that's how you feel," he said quietly, "then maybe we should consider a divorce."

Dora's expression softened slightly, but the resolve in her eyes remained. "Maybe we should," she agreed. "It's clear we're not meant to be together."

As Justin walked away from the conversation, he felt a profound sense of loss. The realization that he had let go of Fiona, a woman who had faced her past with courage and integrity, weighed heavily on him. His marriage to Dora, built on superficial foundations, had crumbled under the weight of deceit and dissatisfaction. Justin was left to reflect on his choices, the regret of lost love a constant companion.

In a quiet moment of reflection, Justin composed a sonnet to capture his predicament:

<u>My Regret</u>

In twilight's grasp, my heart does mourn its loss,
  For love once bright, now dimmed by past mistakes.
The path I chose has led me to this cross,
  Where sorrow's grip my weary spirit takes.
Her eyes, once filled with trust, now haunt my dreams,
  A mirror to the pain I've caused her soul.
Regret, like waves, upon my conscience streams,
  And in this storm, I struggle to be whole.
I let her go, deceived by whispered lies,
  Her strength and grace, I failed to recognize.
Now in the night, beneath the starless skies,
  I yearn for what I lost, my heart's demise.
Oh, fate unkind, to leave me here alone,
To mourn the love that once was mine, now flown.

Fiona and Clyde's love story continued to flourish. They faced life's challenges together, their bond growing stronger with each passing day. They watched Cara grow, her laughter filling their home with joy. Fiona's journey from a turbulent past to a life filled with love and happiness was a testament to her strength and resilience.

As they stood together, watching the sunset from their porch, Clyde wrapped his arm around Fiona. "We've come a long way," he said softly, his voice filled with pride.

"Yes, we have," Fiona replied, her eyes shining with tears of happiness. "And I wouldn't change a thing."

Their love had triumphed over adversity, and they knew that whatever the future held, they would face it together, hand in hand.

2

A Town's Reckoning

John Harris sat on the porch of his modest home in Spruce Pine, North Carolina, the weight of his checkered past pressing heavily on his shoulders like a yoke binding an ox. Once a respected police chief of this town, John had retired years ago, but the memories of his actions during his tenure haunted him daily. He had used his position to discriminate against people of other races, believing he was upholding some twisted sense of order. Now, in the twilight of his life, he was consumed by regret—a heavy cloak he couldn't shake off.

The town had changed over the years, becoming more diverse and vibrant as new migrants rebuilt once dilapidated buildings, reviving the local economy. Colorful murals adorned the walls, depicting scenes of unity and diversity, and the laughter of children playing in the streets filled the air. These were constant reminders of the world John had once tried to suppress. Now, he felt like an outsider in the community he once controlled.

Yet, as he watched the bustling streets, he couldn't help but notice the virtues the migrants had brought with them. The aroma of exotic spices wafted through the air, mingling with the scent of freshly baked bread. Food stalls lined the streets, offering dishes from around the world— savory empanadas, spicy curries, and sweet baklava. The town square, once a place of solemn gatherings, now echoed with laughter and music. Festivals celebrating different cultures were held regularly, filling the air with the sounds of drums, flutes, and joyous singing.

John saw families sharing meals on their porches, their conversations punctuated by bursts of laughter. Children played games he had never seen before, their faces alight with joy. The migrants had brought with them a sense of community and togetherness that had been missing for so long. They shared stories of their homelands, tales of struggle and triumph, and in doing so, they wove a rich tapestry of shared human experience. Their stories are not unlike the stories his grandparents told him about his ancestors; how they came to this land poor, but made the best out of their situation.

As he sat there, John realized that the migrants had not only rebuilt the town physically but had also breathed new life into its spirit. They had brought with them resilience, hope, and a boundless capacity for joy. And in their laughter and mirth, John found a glimmer of redemption, a chance to atone for his past by embracing the vibrant, diverse community that had blossomed around him.

John's health was failing; the doctors had given him a grim prognosis. It was this looming sense of mortality that had forced him to confront the darkness of his past. The weight of his actions pressed heavily on his conscience, and he knew he had to make amends. But the path to redemption seemed fraught with obstacles, each step more daunting than the last.

John's thoughts often drifted to Maria Lopez, a young woman of Hispanic descent who had been one of his victims—a casualty of his misguided crusade. Maria had grown up in the town, facing prejudice and hardship, much of it stemming from John's actions. Despite this, she had persevered and now ran a community center that provided support and resources to marginalized groups. John admired her strength and resilience, even as he felt the sting of his own shame. He remembered the day he had unjustly arrested her father and locked him up, the look of fear and confusion in her young eyes. That memory haunted him the most like a ghost lurking in the shadows.

Determined to seek forgiveness, John began writing letters of apology to those he had wronged. Each letter was a painful confession, a piece of his soul laid bare. He made anonymous donations to causes that supported racial equality and justice, hoping to balance the scales, even if only slightly. He donated to Maria's community center, local scholarships for minority students, and organizations that provided legal aid to those who had been wronged. But the guilt gnawed at him, and he knew that these gestures, while meaningful, were not enough. They were a drop in the bucket of misdeeds to a community he was trusted with leading.

John had two sons: Larry, who worked in the town's police force like his father, and an estranged son, David, who lived in a nearby city. David was unaware of the full extent of his father's past. Their relationship had been strained for years, with David feeling disconnected from the man who had raised him. John longed to reconcile with David, to explain his actions and seek his forgiveness, but he feared it might be too late. On the contrary, Larry, still a member of the town's police force, was his arrogant self, quietly espousing the racial hatred he had learned from his dad and had developed over the years. He kept close to very shady characters in the town whom he used to carry out his illegal actions, keeping his hands clean though in on most of their plans and ravages—a silent conductor orchestrating chaos from the shadows.

As the days grew shorter and the shadows lengthened, John felt the urgency of his mission. He had to find a way to make things right, to lift the dark cloud that hung over his conscience. But time was running out, and the path to redemption was anything but clear. Burdened by guilt and the weight of his past actions, John reached out to Maria. He remembered her as a young girl whose family suffered under his discriminatory practices and wrote her a heartfelt letter of apology, expressing his deep regret and desire to make amends.

Meanwhile, Evelyn Carter, a determined journalist, arrived in town to investigate its history of racial injustice. She heard whispers about John Harris, the former police chief, and his controversial past. Intrigued, she started to dig deeper, interviewing residents and uncovering stories of John's discriminatory actions. Evelyn's investigation gained momentum as she pieced together the impact of John's past on the community, like a seamstress stitching together a torn fabric.

John's health started to deteriorate rapidly. The urgency of his situation forced him to confront his past more directly. He decided that he must confess his actions to his estranged son, David, in the hope of finding some peace and perhaps helping David understand his own struggles with identity and purpose.

John wrote a long letter to David, detailing his past actions and expressing his deep regret. He recorded a video confession as well, hoping that seeing his face and hearing his voice would convey the sincerity of his remorse. He made plans to meet David in person to deliver the letter and recording, but his health continued to decline like a wilting flower.

Through an intermediary, the date was set, but before John could meet David, he passed away suddenly. It was a sad day for the Harris family, but not everyone shared this sorrow. Some people in the communities he had long oppressed had no sympathy for him. After all, he had unfairly targeted them, including jailing a few simply because of their race. On one occasion, he had beaten an African American boy with his baton, cracking a tooth in his mouth. His police report indicated that the boy had grabbed his baton, even though eyewitness accounts differed. John's death left many questions unanswered and his attempts at redemption incomplete, like a book with missing chapters.

David Harris stood in the faintly illuminated living room of his father's house, the air thick with the scent of old wood and memories. The house was eerily quiet, a stark contrast to the turmoil raging inside him. He had returned to Spruce Pine to handle his father's affairs, a task he approached with a mix of duty and dread.

As he sorted through John's belongings, David stumbled upon a stack of letters and a small video recorder. His hands trembled as he picked up the first letter, recognizing his father's handwriting. He sank into an old armchair, the weight of the moment pressing down on him.

David began to read, his eyes scanning the words that revealed a side of his father he had never known. The letters were filled with apologies and confessions, detailing John's discriminatory actions and his desperate attempts to make amends. David's heart ached with each word, torn between anger and sorrow.

He hesitated before pressing play on the video recorder. The screen flickered to life, and there was his father, looking frail and remorseful. John's voice, though weak, carried the weight of his regret.

John (on video): "David, my son, if you're watching this, it means I didn't get the chance to tell you in person. I've done terrible things, things I'm deeply ashamed of. I used my position to hurt people, to discriminate against them because of their race. I thought I was doing the right thing, but I was wrong. I was so wrong."

David's eyes filled with tears as he watched his father struggle to speak, the pain and regret evident in his voice.

John (on video): "I tried to make amends, to help those I wronged, but I know it's not... it's not enough. I hope you can find it in your heart to forgive me, and maybe, just maybe, you can help continue the work I started. I love you, son."

David turned off the recorder, his emotions a tangled mess. He was angry at his father for the harm he had caused, but he was also moved by his late efforts to seek redemption. He realized that his father had been trying to change, even if he didn't live long enough to fully achieve it.

Evelyn Carter, the detective of forgotten tales, met at the local library with Sarah Thompson, a passionate historian and librarian and lighthouse keeper of the past. Sarah, intrigued by Evelyn's quest, offered her assistance and access to the library's extensive archives.

Evelyn and Sarah sat at a large wooden table in the dimly lit archive room of the local library. The air was thick with the scent of aged paper and dust. Stacks of old records and documents surrounded them, each one a potential key to unlocking the town's hidden past.

Evelyn, her curiosity piqued, carefully opened a brittle, leather-bound book. "There's so much history here," she murmured, her eyes scanning the faded pages.

Sarah nodded, her fingers deftly sorting through a box of old files. "This town has many stories, some of them buried deep. We just have to find them."

As they worked, Sarah's hand brushed against a small, unmarked box tucked away in a corner. She pulled it out, her brow furrowing in curiosity. "What's this?" she wondered aloud, opening the box to reveal a diary, its cover worn, and edges frayed.

Evelyn leaned in, her heart quickening. "Let's see," she said, taking the diary from Sarah. She opened it to the first page, where the name Rebecca Harris was written in elegant script.

"John Harris's wife," Sarah whispered, her eyes widening. "I didn't know she kept a diary."

Evelyn began to read aloud, her voice soft and reverent. The entries revealed Rebecca's inner turmoil as she grappled with her husband's actions. She wrote about her love for John, but also her deep sorrow and disappointment over his discriminatory practices. She was also concerned about John's influence on Larry. Rebecca had tried to persuade both John and Larry to change, but her efforts were often met with resistance.

One entry stood out:

Rebecca's Diary: "June 15, 1995: Today, I spoke to John again about his treatment of the Lopez family. He dismissed my concerns, saying he was just doing his job. I can't stand by and watch this happen. I have to do something, even if it's in secret."

Evelyn and Sarah exchanged a glance, the weight of Rebecca's words settling over them. "She was trying to make a difference," Evelyn said, her voice tinged with admiration.

As they continued reading, they discovered more entries detailing Rebecca's covert efforts to help those John had wronged. She had provided financial support, legal advice, and emotional comfort to several families, all while keeping her actions hidden from her husband.

Rebecca's Diary: "August 3, 1996: I met with Maria Lopez today. She was so grateful for the help, but I fear what John would do if he found out. I must be careful. The town needs to change, and if John won't be the one to do it, then I will."

The diary painted a picture of a woman torn between her love for her husband and her moral duty to stand against his actions. It added a new layer to John's story, showing that Rebecca had been working against his harmful behavior from within their own home.

Evelyn closed the diary, her mind racing with the implications. "This changes everything," she said. "Rebecca's story needs to be told. She was a quiet hero in her own right."

Sarah nodded, her eyes shining with determination. "Let's make sure her voice is heard."

Despite the long hours and countless documents to review, Evelyn and Sarah remained indefatigable in their efforts to unearth the truth about the town's hidden past.

Larry Harris paced back and forth in his living room, the shadows dancing on the walls as the evening sun slowly faded into the night, the sword of Damocles hanging over his head. He had heard whispers about Evelyn and Sarah's research, and although they had not uncovered any documents specific to him, he was convinced that their investigation would eventually reveal his sordid past. His heart pounded with a mix of fear and anger.

On a brisk evening in the fall, Larry summoned his goons to his house—seasoned criminals, three of whom he had met while they were in jail for crimes they had committed. The air was crisp, and the leaves crunched underfoot as they approached. Larry's face was set in a grim expression as he laid out his plan.

"We need to stop them before they dig any deeper. Tonight, we set fire to the library. Make sure it looks like an accident, but leave no trace of our involvement," Larry said to his goons, his eyes scanning their faces.

"Are you sure this is what you want, boss?" asked one of the men, his face a mixture of doubt and curiosity.

"Yes. Get it done!" Larry responded emphatically, his voice rising.

His goons nodded, their faces reflecting a mix of loyalty and apprehension. As the night fell, they moved swiftly, dousing the library's exterior with gasoline and setting it ablaze. The flames licked the night sky, casting an eerie glow over the town.

The fire department acted promptly, their sirens piercing the quiet night. They managed to put out the fire before it caused major damage. The fire chief, after a thorough investigation, ruled that the blaze was caused by arsonists due to the flammable residues discovered at the scene.

The next day, the FBI was called to investigate the mysterious blaze at the library. Agents combed through the charred remains, collecting evidence and interviewing witnesses. It wasn't long before some of the perpetrators began to crack under pressure, like a cookie crumbling in a tight grip, their guilt weighing heavily on their consciences. They pointed their fingers at none other than Officer Larry Harris.

An arrest warrant was promptly issued, but Larry, sensing the noose tightening around his neck, went into hiding. A manhunt ensued, with law enforcement scouring the town and surrounding areas. They found him barricaded in an abandoned industrial complex about fifteen minutes from downtown.

A SWAT team was called in to apprehend him. As they surrounded the building, the tension was palpable. Inside, Larry was a man cornered, his mind racing with desperation. He knew his time was up. Just before the SWAT team could breach the perimeter, two gunshots echoed through the complex. Larry had fired his service revolver into his brain, ending his life in a tragic and violent manner.

The news of Larry's death spread quickly through the town, sending shockwaves through the community. It was a tragic end to a man who had terrified many members of his community.

The release of Evelyn's story and the tragic death of a corrupt police officer sent ripples through the town. Some residents were moved by John's efforts to seek redemption, seeing him as a man who tried to change despite his past. They believed his actions, though late, were sincere and should be acknowledged. Others, however, could not forgive the pain and suffering caused by John and his son, Larry. They argued that his attempts at redemption did not erase the harm he inflicted on the community.

The town became divided, with heated debates and discussions taking place in public forums, local cafes, and town meetings. Evelyn's article sparked a broader conversation about racial injustice, forgiveness, and the possibility of change.

David Harris, deeply affected by his brother's suicide, his father's letters and the revelations in Evelyn's article, found himself at a crossroads. He was torn between anger at his father's actions and a desire to honor his late efforts at redemption. After much reflection, David decided to continue his father's path of making amends.

He reached out to Maria Lopez, who was initially wary but willing to listen. They met at the community center, the air thick with unspoken tension.

David spoke, his voice laced with sincerity "Maria, I know my father caused you and your family a lot of pain. I can't change the past, but

I want to help make things right. I want to work with you to expand the community center, to create a space that supports marginalized groups and fosters dialogue and understanding." His eyes searching for concurrence from Maria's facial expressions.

Maria studied him for a moment, her eyes searching his face for sincerity. Finally, she nodded.

"I appreciate your honesty, David. If you're truly committed to this, then let's work together. This town needs healing, and it's going to take all of us because your father hurt many people."

Together, David and Maria started planning new programs and initiatives aimed at healing the racial divides in the town. Their collaboration became a symbol of hope and progress, showing that change is possible even in the face of a painful past.

In a town-wide event organized by David and Maria at the expanded community center, diverse speakers, performances, and activities designed to promote unity and understanding took place. People from all walks of life came together to celebrate their shared humanity and commit to building a more inclusive community. Maria penned a poem about the experience which read:

A Tapestry of Unity

In our town, where hatred once loomed,
We come as one, dispelling gloom.
Voices join in harmony's sung,
A band of hope, where once was none.

From different paths, we came to stand,
In hand and heart across this land.
Pains of our past, we can't erase,
As one we strive, to heal, embrace.

Our different colors, tongues we speak,
Are threads of bonds, unique and sleek.
Each story is a vital part,
Our future with love at its heart.

A dark cloud may linger ahead,
But our resolve is strong, we pledge.
Together we'll erase the pain,
As one, our town will rise again.

As David and Maria stood together on the stage, they looked out at the diverse crowd. The atmosphere was filled with a sense of hope and possibility. However, a dark cloud loomed on the horizon, symbolizing the ongoing challenges the town faced. The journey towards healing and reconciliation was far from over, but the event marked a significant step forward.

David felt a sense of peace, knowing that he was honoring both his parents' legacies in his own way. Maria, too, felt a renewed sense of purpose, inspired by the community's response and the progress they had made. Together, they vowed to continue their work, knowing that the path to true unity and understanding was a long and difficult one, but one worth pursuing.

3

Beneath The Austrian Skies

In the quaint town of Mondsee, nestled within the Austrian Alps, the beauty of the sunrise over the tranquil lake was ineffable, leaving anyone speechless and in awe of nature's magnificence. Here, Jonas Moser was born into a family that would forever shape his destiny. He grew up with two brothers, whose laughter once filled their modest home, and a younger sister, Carina, a beautiful young lady whose eyes sparkled like the pristine waters of Lake Mondsee. Their lives, though humble, were woven together with threads of love and resilience.

The family had been a picture of contentment, their days marked by simple joys and the unbreakable bond they shared. But fate's cruel hand struck a devastating blow one fateful winter. Their father, a seasoned hunter, ventured into the snow-covered wilderness in search of game. The mountains, silent and majestic, held a deadly secret beneath their serene facade. An avalanche, a roaring wave of snow and ice, cascaded down the slopes, swallowing him whole. He was gone in an instant, leaving nothing but a haunting silence in his wake.

The untimely death of their father cast a shadow over the Moser household, plunging them into a chasm of grief. Their mother, Laura, was left to shoulder the burden of raising four children alone. Laura, with her weary eyes and calloused hands, worked tirelessly to provide for her family. Each day was a battle against the encroaching despair, her strength the fragile thread that kept them from unraveling entirely.

The warmth of their home dimmed, replaced by the cold reality of hardship. The laughter of Jonas and his brothers grew quieter, their hearts heavy with the weight of loss. Carina's eyes, once bright and full of wonder, reflected the sorrow that now defined their existence. Despite the darkness that surrounded them, the family's bond remained unbroken, their love a flickering flame in the relentless storm.

Amidst this struggle, Jonas emerged as the family's beacon of hope. With a rifle slung over his shoulder and determination in his heart, he ventured into the dense forests that bordered their town. He hunted game, especially deer, to put food on their table, his sharp eyes and steady hands becoming essential to their survival. Jonas transformed from a boy into a masterful hunter, his skill with a gun unmatched.

But life demanded more than just survival. Jonas dropped out of high school, sacrificing his education to take on menial jobs, each task a brick in the wall that separated him from his dreams. One such job led him to a meat packing plant, a place filled with the scent of raw flesh and the drone of machinery. It was there he met Felix, a ne'er-do-well with a mischievous glint in his eye, his presence like a flicker of defiance in the monotony of the plant.

Felix, with his tales of adventure and mischief, quickly befriended Jonas, their bond forged in the shared drudgery of their work. Felix's laughter was infectious, a beacon of light in the otherwise bleak environment.

One evening, in the dimly lit confines of a local bar, Felix invited Jonas to join him for a drink. The air was thick with the scent of ale and the hum of conversation, a symphony of voices that drowned the silence of their thoughts. As they sipped their beers, their conversation turned to hunting, a topic that brought a spark to Jonas's eyes.

"I tell you, Felix," Jonas said, leaning back in his chair, "there's nothing quite like the thrill of the hunt. I've been doing it since I was a kid. Never missed a shot."

Felix listened intently, his gaze sharp as a hawk's. "You've got a real talent, Jonas. Not many can say that."

Jonas, with a touch of pride, bragged about his love for the hunt and his proficiency with weapons. The way he spoke about the forest, the stillness before the shot, and the exhilaration of the kill painted a vivid picture, like Picasso painting one of his masterpieces.

With a sly grin, Felix leaned in closer, his voice barely a whisper. "You know, there's more to hunting than just game. I've made quite a bit of money hunting... people."

Jonas's spine tingled, the words hanging in the air like a noxious cloud. "What do you mean?" he asked, his voice unsteady.

"I'm a paid assassin," Felix revealed, the admission dripping with danger and temptation. "It's not just about the thrill, Jonas. It's about power, control, and money. Lots of it."

Jonas, his mind clouded by the alcohol, dismissed Felix's overtures as drunken ramblings. "You're drunk, Felix. You don't mean that."

The following day, Felix rehashed his proposition with a sober mind. The plant's cold, mechanical hum was a stark contrast to Felix's heated words. He painted a picture of wealth and power, describing the lucrative nature of the job with a fervor that left Jonas unsettled.

"Think about it, Jonas," Felix urged. "We could be living the good life. No more struggling. No more scraping by."

Jonas found himself at a crossroads, torn between his need for financial stability and the moral teachings ingrained in him since childhood. His mind replayed the words of the commandment "thou shall not kill," a mantra that had guided him through life's darkest moments.

"Felix," Jonas said, his voice heavy with conflict, "I can't just kill people. It's wrong. It's a sin."

Felix's eyes gleamed with a predatory light. "Is it any worse than watching your family starve? Than living in poverty? These people I kill... they're scum, Jonas. They deserve it."

Jonas wrestled with his conscience, the weight of his religious upbringing pressing down on him like an iron shroud. He knew that taking a life, regardless of the circumstances, was a grave sin. Yet, the allure of money and the promise of a better life gnawed at him, whispering seductive promises of escape from poverty.

Despite his initial resistance, Felix's arguments and the prospect of financial gain began to chip away at Jonas's resolve. The idea of lifting his family out of their desperate situation became an overpowering force, an irresistible tide pulling him towards the darkness. He rationalized his decision, convincing himself that the people Felix targeted were despicable, deserving of their fate.

Three days later, Jonas was out in the forest hunting game. The crisp air filled his lungs, a stark contrast to the stifling tension that had plagued him. This time it was a bull; a huge caribou, its antlers stretching towards the heavens. It was quite large, so he got one of his brothers to help him carry it home. The meat would feed their family for at least six months, a reprieve from their constant struggle—an oasis in a desert of hardship.

Back at work, he told Felix of his kill, the size of the bull, and the thrill from hunting. "You should have seen it, Felix. The rush, the adrenaline... it was incredible."

Felix's eyes narrowed, a calculating smile playing on his lips. "That's the same thrill I get from hunting humans, Jonas. But the difference is, the cash ends up in my savings account."

Intrigued by the prospect of making huge amounts of money, Jonas set aside his religious convictions, his heart heavy with the weight of his choice. He agreed to become a paid assassin, stepping onto a path shrouded in shadows, where the line between right and wrong blurred into oblivion. Though the path he chose was dark and uncertain, he believed it was the only way to bring light into the lives of those he loved.

Jonas's first assignment was to kill a man who had stolen money from a group of ruthless rogues. This band of rogues had successfully pulled off a heist, yet one of their own had taken a large amount and fled, turning himself into a target. On the day of his engagement, Jonas was given a picture of the fellow and a possible spot he could be found.

The night was shrouded in a thick, suffocating fog as Jonas lay hidden in the underbrush, the chill of the earth seeping into his bones. The forest, usually a sanctuary, now felt like a prison, its shadows closing in around him. The picture of the man, worn and crumpled from Jonas's anxious grip, was the only clue in this deadly game of cat and mouse. The man's silhouette, barely discernible through the mist, moved with an air of nervousness, a rat caught in a maze of deceit.

Jonas's finger tightened around the trigger, his breath steady and controlled. He whispered a silent prayer, seeking some semblance of solace for the soul he was about to snatch from this world. The weight of the gun was a cold, unyielding presence in his hands, a stark contrast to the warmth of his childhood memories. With a sudden, thunderous crack, the bullet soared through the night, finding its mark with unerring precision. The man crumpled to the ground, life extinguished in an instant.

As Jonas stood over the lifeless body, a wave of conflicting emotions washed over him. Triumph and guilt intertwined, a venomous cocktail that left him hollow. The $20,000 reward felt like blood money in his hands, heavy with the weight of a life taken. The man's eyes, once filled with fear, now stared blankly into the void, a haunting reminder of the path Jonas had chosen.

For the next six months, Jonas and Felix moved through the shadows, their partnership forged in the crucible of death. They became ghosts, their presence felt only in the aftermath of their lethal deeds. Each assignment was a dance with death, a macabre ballet where the slightest misstep could spell their end. They executed their targets with ruthless efficiency, their actions as precise as clockwork.

Their bond, though born of darkness, grew strong. Jonas found solace in Felix's camaraderie, a twisted sense of brotherhood that eased the burden of their grim profession. The thrill of the hunt, once confined to the forest, now coursed through his veins as he hunted human prey. The adrenaline, once a fleeting rush, became a constant companion, a dark whisper that urged him forward.

But the dance could not last forever. One fateful night, under a moonless sky, Felix's aim wavered, his bullet missing its mark. The sharp crack of the gunshot echoed through the night, a harbinger of doom. The police, alerted by the gunfire, descended upon him like vultures, their sirens wailing a mournful dirge. Felix ran, his breath ragged and desperate, each step a frantic bid for survival. The terrain was unforgiving, the ground treacherous beneath his feet. A steep hill loomed before him, a cruel barrier offering neither cover nor escape.

Felix, unable to navigate the steep hill, stumbled, his movements growing more frantic. The night seemed to close in around him, the darkness a suffocating shroud. A police sniper, perched high above like a harbinger of death, took aim with deadly precision. The shot rang out, a single, thunderous crack that shattered the night. Felix crumpled to the ground, a crimson bloom spreading from his neck, the life draining from his body in a matter of moments.

Jonas's world shattered. The news of Felix's death hit him like a sledgehammer, the weight of their shared sins crashing down upon him. The bond they had forged in the crucible of death was severed, leaving Jonas adrift in a sea of guilt and despair. The thought of continuing without Felix was unbearable, the darkness of their profession now an insurmountable abyss.

Jonas's nights were haunted by visions of Felix, his friend's lifeless eyes staring back at him from the shadows. The guilt gnawed at him, a relentless specter that refused to be silenced. He wandered through his days in a daze, the weight of his choices pressing down on him like an iron shroud. The world around him seemed to blur, the colors fading into a monochrome landscape of regret.

The loss of Felix was a wound that refused to heal, a constant reminder of the darkness that had consumed them both. Jonas knew that he could never escape the shadows of his past, the ghosts of his actions forever haunting his steps. The path to redemption seemed distant and unattainable, a flickering light at the end of a long, dark tunnel.

He refused new assignments, the very idea of taking another life repulsive to him. Instead, he sought refuge in the material comforts his blood-stained money could buy, hoping to drown his sorrows in the trappings of wealth. But the solace was fleeting, the luxury a hollow echo of the life he had once known. The taste of opulence turned bitter, each indulgence a reminder of the price he had paid.

Later, desperation weighed heavily on Jonas, whispering that there was no turning back. He called his contacts, his voice trembling with a mix of resolve and regret, and resumed his work as an assassin.

His next target was the son of a judge, a young man marked for death to send a chilling message. The judge was presiding over a case involving a group of mobsters, and they wanted to make a statement by assassinating his son. Jonas had no idea who the boy was, only that he was a pawn in a deadly game of power and retribution.

The weight of the assignment pressed heavily on Jonas's soul, a cruel reminder of.the darkness he had embraced. As he moved towards his target, the echoes of his past and the shadows of his choices haunted him, each step a reminder of the path he had chosen and the price he would ultimately pay.

In the quiet stillness of the December night, Jonas crept through the darkened halls, each step heavy with the burden of his mission. The soft glow of candlelight flickered from beneath the door of his target's room, casting long, wavering shadows on the walls. The air was thick with the scent of pine and wax, a stark contrast to the cold steel of the gun hidden beneath his coat.

As Jonas approached, the murmur of a child's voice reached his ears, piercing the silence with an unexpected clarity. The voice was soft and earnest, filled with a sincerity that tugged at the frayed edges of Jonas's conscience. He paused, his hand trembling as it hovered over the door handle, straining to listen.

"What can I give Him, poor as I am? If I were a shepherd, I would bring a lamb..." The hymn's familiar melody transported Jonas back to his own childhood, to a time when he sat in Sunday school, his heart filled with innocence and faith. He recalled that the boy's words were from the hymn "In the Bleak Midwinter," a hymn he sang at Sunday school during Advent.

"...If I were a wise man, I would do my part. Yet what I can, I give Him. Give my heart." The boy's voice wavered with sincerity, and Jonas felt a pang of emotion. The prayer continued, and Jonas's breath caught in his throat as the boy mentioned a name that was all too familiar. "Lord, I have a confession to make. There is a young lady in my class, Carina, the one with the striking blue eyes. I would love nothing more for Christmas than for You to have her open her heart to me. Loving her does not mean I love You any less...."

Jonas's heart skipped a beat, the name tearing through the fog of his assassin's resolve. Carina—his sister. The boy's prayer, filled with yearning and innocence, stirred something deep within Jonas. His hand faltered, the cold steel of the pistol feeling like a weight too heavy to bear. Pushing the door open slightly, Jonas saw the boy, Elias, kneeling with his eyes closed, lost in his heartfelt supplication.

"Don't just stand there," Elias said, sensing a presence without turning around, "join me in prayer." Jonas quickly concealed his weapon and stepped into the room. The boy's prayer continued, "Lord, bless everyone today, including my friends and my parents. Amen."

As Elias finished his prayer, he opened his eyes, but Jonas was already gone. He had slipped out of the room and into the night, his mind a whirlwind of conflicting emotions. The darkness enveloped him, a suffocating shroud that mirrored the weight of his actions. Each step away from the house felt like a step deeper into his own despair.

That evening, as Jonas lay on his bed, the boy's prayer echoed in his mind, each word a needle pricking at his conscience. The room felt oppressive, the walls closing in around him as guilt surged through him, an unrelenting tide that threatened to drown him. The dim light from the lamp cast long shadows, transforming familiar surroundings into looming specters that mirrored his inner turmoil. The air felt thick, each breath a struggle as if the very atmosphere conspired to suffocate him.

He stared at the ceiling, his thoughts a chaotic storm of remorse and regret. Memories of his past actions played out in his mind, a relentless slideshow of violence and despair. Each face, each life taken, haunted him, their eyes accusing, their silent pleas for mercy echoing in his ears. The room seemed to shrink around him, the weight of his sins pressing down on him like an iron shroud.

The words from Elias' prayer, "give my heart," were echoing in his mind. Those simple, earnest words held a power that cut through the fog of his anguish. Jonas closed his eyes, the boy's voice resonating in the stillness of the night. Would Jonas give his heart to a higher power? Could he find redemption in faith, in surrendering to something greater than himself?

As he grappled with these questions, tears welled up in his eyes, blurring his vision. He felt a surge of emotion, a raw, unfiltered wave of guilt and longing. The darkness that had enveloped him for so long now seemed penetrable, the first glimmers of light breaking through. His soul ached for absolution, for a chance to make amends.

Jonas turned on his side, curling into a fetal position as if seeking to protect himself from the weight of his own conscience. His sobs were silent, his shoulders trembling with the force of his suppressed cries. He knew, with a clarity that cut through the fog of his mind, that he could no longer live this life. The path he had chosen had led him to the brink of despair, and now he stood at a crossroads, his future hanging in the balance.

The night stretched on, the minutes feeling like hours, each tick of the clock a reminder of the time slipping away. Jonas felt a shift within him, a tentative hope that perhaps he could find redemption, that the words of a child's prayer could guide him towards a new beginning.

The dawn broke gently, the first rays of sunlight filtering through the window, casting a soft, golden glow over the room. Jonas lay still, his mind quieter now, the storm of his thoughts easing into a tentative calm. The path to redemption would be long and arduous, but for the first time in a long while, he felt a flicker of hope, a light at the end of the tunnel.

With a renewed sense of purpose, Jonas rose from his bed, the resolve to change his life taking root in his heart. He would seek forgiveness, he would make amends, and he would give his heart to a higher power, finding solace in the faith he had once known.

That day, with a heavy heart, Jonas approached the mob. His voice trembled with remorse as he confessed that he could not kill a child. The mob's reaction was swift and unforgiving. Their eyes, once filled with trust, now burned with fury. They decided to eliminate Jonas, hiring an assassin code-named "The Sweeper" to end his life as punishment for his defiance.

The next day, The Sweeper came to Jonas's home to eliminate him, but he was ambushed by Jonas, who overpowered him, seizing his weapon. He spared The Sweeper's life and warned him never to return. The Sweeper, the mob's most trusted assassin, slipped away into the shadows with his pride shattered like glass.

Desperate to save himself and seeking a path to redemption, Jonas contacted the judge. His voice cracked with urgency as he revealed the mob's plans and the role he had played in their schemes. The judge, recognizing the gravity of the situation, acted quickly. The police were notified, and a series of arrests followed, dismantling the criminal network that had ensnared Jonas.

Jonas, his soul laid bare, repented for his past actions. He sought forgiveness for the lives he had taken and vowed to live a life of atonement. Each day became a journey towards redemption, each prayer a plea for absolution. He penned a poem about his experience, which read:

Atonement's Dawn

Through doubt and greed, my soul was lost,
    I tread the path of sin and pain.
With every step, my heart the cost,
    In quest for peace, I sought in vain.

A life once pure, now stained with guilt,
    The lives I took, a heavy toll.
My hands, with blood and sorrow built,
    Yet hope remains within my soul.

For in the night, a prayer's light,
    A boy's pure plea, my heart did stir.
His words of faith, a guiding sight,
    To seek a path where hearts confer.

Now in the light, I find my way,
    Atonement's road, though fraught with strife.
Each prayer, a plea, each dawn, a day,
    To mend the past, embrace new life.

In the months that followed, a sense of peace began to settle over Jonas. He watched from a distance as Elias and Carina grew closer, their bond a beacon of hope in the aftermath of darkness. Their laughter, once a distant memory, now filled the air with a melody of renewal. Ten years later, the day of their wedding arrived, and the cathedral was filled with light and joy.

The stained-glass windows cast vibrant patterns on the stone floor, the sunlight transforming the space into a sanctuary of colors. The air was thick with the scent of roses and lilacs, a fragrant reminder of new beginnings. As Elias and Carina exchanged vows, their voices steady and filled with love, Jonas stood at the back, his heart swelling with a bittersweet sense of fulfillment.

The ceremony symbolized a new beginning, not just for the newlyweds, but for Jonas as well. He watched as Elias placed a ring on Carina's finger, a symbol of their unbreakable bond, and felt a tear slip down his cheek. The path to redemption had been long and arduous, but with each step, he found solace in the knowledge that he had chosen the light over the darkness.

As they walked down the aisle, hand in hand, Jonas felt a weight lift from his shoulders. The cathedral's bells rang out, their joyous peals echoing through the town, a testament to the power of second chances. The light that filled the cathedral was not just a physical presence, but a spiritual one, illuminating the path forward.

Jonas knew that he still had much to atone for, but the wedding was a milestone, a moment of grace that marked the beginning of his journey. He had been given a second chance, and he was determined to make the most of it. The darkness of his past still lingered, but the light of redemption now guided his steps, offering a glimmer of hope for a brighter future, even for a former assassin.

4

Echoes Of Disillusionment: The Church's Struggle For Relevance

Growing up, my church's parish had a well-respected, middle-aged pastor named Reverend Williams. He wasn't just a preacher of the gospel but in various ways exemplified the teachings of Christianity. Though he was a stutterer, he was a man perceptibly enraptured by the Holy Spirit. Anyone privileged to be in his presence could feel his closeness with God, as if the divine light itself shone through him. His reverence for God knew no bounds. He was a faithful servant, a vessel of honor dedicated to living a life that God, the Maker, would be proud of. Humble yet appreciative, a truth-teller, a mentor to many in the community, and a spiritual healer, Reverend Williams was a beacon of hope and faith.

He frequently visited families in their homes, spreading the gospel and praying for them. Financially, he was a pebble on the shore, yet he didn't let his circumstances deter his love for God and the teachings of Christianity. Often seen sweating profusely under the hot, burning sun, he used public transportation to get around, visiting his parishioners and accomplishing parish missions, doing God's work with unwavering dedication—forging paths with celestial conviction.

One day, during a Bible class he led, we discussed the Ten Commandments. From the start, it appeared that he was sticking to rather strict interpretations of the word, not surprising for a man who treasured each written word of the holy book. He explained that the Sabbath day, set aside for rest according to the Bible's teachings, includes all activities, whether or not those activities are vital to survival or necessary for daily living.

For instance, he said that no commercial purchases should be made on the Sabbath, meaning that if your light bulb went out on the Sabbath and you had no replacements at home, you must remain in the dark or use a candle, but not attempt to purchase a replacement from a store. While I considered his interpretation of some biblical teachings impractical, a touch out of reality, I admired his genuine faith—a belief that would carry any soul through the toughest of storms. His genuine display of faith in God left a lasting impression on me and has guided my life for many years.

In contrast, modern servants of the cloth view their position as a pathway to riches, like wolves in sheep's clothing, hiding their true intentions. They prance around, not caring about the needs of their followers, but believing that everything about them is copacetic—their actions, speech, and thinking. Yet, this is far from reality.

In most instances, their behaviors run athwart the teachings of Christianity. They value things of the flesh like fancy cars, massive mansions with manicured lawns and attendants, private jets, book deals, custom-tailored suits and dresses, television shows, bodyguards, and servants. Of these, the most nauseating is their use of bodyguards, for it begs the question: What enemies can a servant of God make to the extent that he or she should require bodyguards?

It is as if they are knights fortifying a castle against imagined enemies. In my humble opinion, it conveys that these preachers of the word, whose lives are eternally under the divine protection of their Lord, do not believe in the word they purport to be spreading. Perhaps there are other sinister reasons—their unseemly associations or erstwhile malfeasance put them in peril, hence the need for physical protection.

Reverend Williams, with his humble demeanor and unwavering faith, stood in stark contrast to these modern-day preachers. His life was a testament to the true essence of Christianity—selfless, devoted, and pure. He was a man who, despite his stutter, spoke volumes through his actions, embodying the very spirit of the teachings he so passionately preached. His legacy is a reminder that true faith is not measured by material wealth or outward appearances but by the depth of one's devotion and the purity of one's heart.

In a spectacle that one could have never imagined, I attended a church service about ten years ago, honoring an invitation from a friend. It was a warm summer day, and the air was thick with anticipation, the kind that makes your heart beat a little faster. The sanctuary was packed with dedicated followers dressed in their Sunday best, their faces glowing with devotion. The music was superb, even heavenly, filling the church's dome with a symphony of praise. The harmonious blend of drums, guitar, and organ orchestrated the pastor's grand entrance, as if heralding the arrival of a king. The melodies seemed to lift the very roof, carrying the congregation's spirits to celestial heights.

When it was time for the pastor to take the pulpit, I witnessed a scene that left me astounded. The pastor, a flamboyant man, had a so-called servant by his side while he preached. The servant would periodically wipe the sweat off his face and head, a task that seemed both demeaning and unnecessary. On one occasion during the service, after the pastor himself had wiped the sweat from his brow, he threw the wet towel on the ground, and his attendant dutifully picked it up. It was a shocking spectacle that would have knocked even the Savior off his feet, for this action was not only demeaning but antithetical to what the Savior preached. The sight of the pastor's servant, head bowed in subservience, picking up the discarded towel, was a jarring image that clashed with the teachings of humility and service.

Disappointingly, this preacher was quite dynamic and charismatic, qualities that significantly attract and welcome people into the fold. He did not need the self-aggrandizing spectacles he frequently employed during that service. And guess what? His congregants were all in on his antics, exceedingly excited and often on their feet, claiming to be enraptured by the Holy Spirit. Yes, this is what Christianity in some parts of this country is perpetuating—a show of grandeur and spectacle rather than genuine faith and humility. The congregation's fervor, their eyes wide with what they believed to be divine inspiration, only deepened my sense of disillusionment.

For some church leaders, theirs is all about the transfer of wealth from unsuspecting parishioners to their coffers. Their services aim to coerce people into giving, using various tactics including shaming. Recently, Gloria, a close friend of mine, was asked by her pastor to give a testimony to her church during a Sunday service with the goal of enticing people to give more than they typically do. On that Sunday in Autumn, when the last rusty leaves were falling off the trees, and the aroma of Fall was at its peak, the congregation packed their sanctuary. Just as the pastor had requested, Gloria gave a testimony about her struggle with infertility and thanked God for finally blessing her family with a child. The congregation rose to their feet with shouts of "Alleluia" and "Thank you God." Then, following her testimony, the pastor scaled the dais and grabbed the microphone, telling his congregants that they must show their appreciation to God by putting more money in the offering plate. Most of them swiftly obliged. This was an example of a pastor taking advantage of a personal triumph over adversity by one of his members to exploit his congregation. The sight of Gloria, her face radiant with joy and relief, being used as a tool for financial gain, was a bitter pill to swallow.

Some churches have even installed teller machines within their buildings, making it quite convenient for congregants to retrieve their cash and turn it over to the pastor. Oh, how I wish the Savior could once more bring His whip to churches and overturn the tables of the dealers. The love of money has corrupted many Christian institutions, and by all accounts, it's only getting worse. The clinking of coins and the rustle of bills, once symbols of charity and goodwill, now seemed to echo with greed and exploitation within the church's walls.

These were a stark contrast to the humble and sincere faith I had known. The air, thick with the scent of incense and the murmur of prayers, seemed to mock the true essence of worship. The pastors' actions, a far cry from the teachings of humility and service, left a bitter taste in my mouth. It was a reminder that the true spirit of Christianity is not found in grand displays or material wealth but in the quiet, selfless acts of love and devotion. The true essence of faith, I realized, lies not in the grandeur of the service but in the simple, heartfelt acts of kindness and compassion that reflect the teachings of the Savior.

I am unsure whether Christians have fully atoned for the mortal sin of aiding and abetting the villainy of slavery. To this day, the remnants of those bygone years cast long shadows over the various denominations of Christians. Some have justified slavery by suggesting that if God truly abhorred it, He would not have given slave masters the upper hand over their slaves, failing to acknowledge that with slavery, humans succumbed to their worst instincts. Every Christian, in judging and reproving slavery faithfully from the onset, could have prevented its rise. Yet, at the time, many Christians did shrink from the contemplation of human suffering because they viewed slavery as a benefit.

Thomas Jefferson, often remembered as a founding father of this nation and author of the Declaration of Independence, penned the words "all men are equal." Yet, he owned slaves throughout his life, considering himself a Christian and often using biblical references to justify his actions. George Washington, a devout Anglican who attended church regularly, owned about three hundred slaves despite his devout beliefs. Confederate General Robert E. Lee, who claimed to be a devout Christian, also owned many slaves. John Newton, the famous hymn writer and composer of "Amazing Grace," was once a captain of a slave ship. These individuals, among many others, illustrate the complex and often contradictory relationship between Christianity and slavery, a sin that weighs heavily on the conscience of their souls.

One would be right to ponder how these people, who considered themselves devout Christians, could read the divine words of the Savior, receive the Holy Spirit, yet subject their fellow man to the horrors of slavery. Perhaps they were enchanted by a different spirit that defiled their conscience, one that espoused supremacy over shared ideals, segregation over camaraderie, avarice over magnanimity, dehumanization over exaltation. Whatever their rationale, the good book is quite clear: "A new command I give you: Love one another. As I have loved you, so you must love one another. By this, everyone will know that you are my disciples, if you love one another." The Savior beckoned. There is no ambiguity in the Savior's command. So, one would be right to ask, how some Christians lost their way.

The German Christian movement, a pro-Nazi faction within the Protestant church, sought to align with Nazi ideology and excluded Jews from the church while promoting a racially pure form of Christianity. Many Protestant churches and some Catholic leaders supported Hitler, believing that Nazism was compatible with Christian values. The church's involvement in slavery and the Nazis' treatment of the Jews severely undermined its moral authority. Even today, some churches continue to discriminate based on racial stereotypes. The contradiction between the teachings of love, equality, and compassion in Christianity and the brutal reality of slavery led to a crisis of credibility, affecting its ability to effectively function today. Its failure to unequivocally condemn slavery and Nazism, and its participation in the practice of slavery, tarnished its image and legacy.

As Christians, we believe that the Savior died on the cross for the sins of man. Believers need not put their fellow man in concentration camps or gas chambers, or tether them to trees and whip them into submission, or hang them on trees to instill fear and loathing in a particular segment of the populace, shedding their innocent blood, or unfairly profit from their labor. This dehumanization is antithetical to the teachings of Christ.

The echoes of chains and the cries of the oppressed still reverberate through the halls of history, a haunting reminder of the church's complicity. The blood-stained hands of those who preached love while practicing cruelty have left an indelible mark on the faith. The Savior's command to love one another stands as a beacon of hope and a call to repentance, urging believers to reconcile with the past and strive for a future where love, justice, and compassion truly reign.

I am grateful for the role Catholic institutions played in my early education. Their strict educational structure, with an emphasis on discipline and a focus on God, shaped my early years and has been a beacon in a world often plagued by dark paths and raging storms. The Catholic Church, more than others, has always ventured into forgotten areas of the world to meet the needs of the poor. There are many Catholic institutions making impactful changes in the jungles of Africa, in South America, and Asia.

Recently, I visited the Vatican in Rome while on a tour of Italy and saw firsthand the enormous riches of the Catholic Church on display. The grandeur of St. Peter's Basilica, with its towering columns and intricate frescoes, left me in awe. The Vatican Museums, filled with priceless artifacts and masterpieces by Michelangelo and Raphael, showcased the Church's dedication to preserving history and art. While I admire and understand the preservation of historical artifacts, I couldn't help but imagine how the displays could fetch millions of dollars that could be used to feed the poor in many parts of the world, including Italy.

A stone's throw from the Vatican's enclaves is Rome's Termini station, a main thoroughfare for buses and trains to and from many parts of Italy. At night, the exterior of that station's grounds is transformed into a graveyard for the homeless. Hundreds of Italy's homeless, wrapped in tattered sleeping bags, use that place for rest. The contrast between the opulence of the Vatican and the destitution at Termini station was striking. The golden glow of the Vatican's lights seemed to mock the dim, flickering streetlights under which the homeless sought refuge.

Meanwhile, many churches like Basilica di Santa Maria Maggiore, Basilica di Santa Maria degli Angeli e dei Martiri, and Santa Maria della Vittoria stand as huge edifices with enough space to shelter the homeless of Rome. Yet, this did not happen during my visit. Perhaps it is because of the role these edifices play in the business of tourism. Certainly, the churches may not want their prized Michelangelo paintings to be altered by the homeless. The thought of these grand spaces, echoing with the footsteps of tourists, remaining empty and unused at night while people slept on the cold, hard ground outside, filled me with a deep sense of sorrow.

As I walked through the streets of Rome, the scent of fresh bread from nearby bakeries mingled with the musty odor of the streets. I couldn't shake the image of the homeless at Termini station. Their faces, etched with lines of hardship, told stories of struggle and survival. The juxtaposition of their plight with the grandeur of the Vatican was a stark reminder of the work that still needs to be done. It is my fervent hope that Christian leaders in Rome and elsewhere will recognize that Christianity is not found in grand displays or material wealth but in the quiet, selfless acts of love and devotion. The Church, with all its resources and influence, must rise to this challenge and truly embody the teachings of Christ by extending a hand to those in need.

At home in the U.S., Christian churches continue to struggle with empty pews and church closures, a silent testament to the waning faith of their congregations. Many churches now spend more time wading into the murky waters of politics than seeking to save the lost souls yearning for spiritual guidance. They have become blind to the truth that Christianity cannot be dictated, legislated, or imposed on people. The Savior never resorted to such tactics; instead, He illuminated the virtues of Christianity through His prayers, gifts, and acts of service, inviting those with open hearts and minds to join Him.

The advent of the digital age, the divisive politics of organized religion, and the inability of Christians to view each other as equals continue to plague many churches. These challenges cast long shadows over the sanctuaries that once brimmed with life and hope. The essence of Christianity, rooted in love, compassion, and humility, seems to be overshadowed by the clamor for power and influence. Yet, amidst this turmoil, the true spirit of faith endures, waiting to be rekindled in the hearts of those who seek genuine connection and understanding.

Imagine a young boy or girl walking into a grand cathedral, the air thick with the scent of incense and the echoes of hymns reverberating off the ancient stone walls. The towering arches and stained glass windows bathe the space in a kaleidoscope of colors, creating an atmosphere of awe and reverence. Yet, amidst the opulence and grandeur, they feel a profound disconnect. The rituals and doctrines seem distant, relics of a past that doesn't resonate with their own lived experiences. The flickering candlelight casts long shadows, mirroring the doubts and questions that linger in their minds, like whispers in the dark.

For many young people, the scandals that have rocked religious institutions are like cracks in the stained glass windows, letting in harsh light that reveals the imperfections and hypocrisies within the church's walls. The stories of sexual abuse by priests are treacheries that cut deep, shaking their humble faith in these institutions. Each revelation feels like a betrayal, a wound that festers and refuses to heal. Additionally, they feel alienated by a religion that questions the rights of, and prejudges those with different sexual orientations and women's reproductive freedom, as if the church's doors are closed to them and their beliefs. The positioning of some Christian groups with extreme conservative agendas feels like a stumbling block, a wall that separates them from the inclusive values they hold dear.

In their search for authenticity, young people often find organized religion to be a maze of rules and doctrines that stifle their spiritual growth. They attend schools that are more diverse, yet their parents' congregations are still segregated. They are taught by both male and female teachers, yet some churches only allow men in the pulpit. They play sports that involve black, brown and white children of various backgrounds, yet some parents in church congregations wouldn't allow their children to mingle with kids of other races. These contradictions create a sense of disillusionment, as if the teachings of the church are out of step with the reality of their normal lives.

In essence, the departure of young people from organized religion is not a rejection of spirituality or community, but a search for a more authentic, inclusive, and meaningful way to connect with the divine and with each other. This desire for a more inclusive community must be explored by Christian churches to meet the needs of the young. For in doing so, Christians would ensure the future of their religion, a time when these same young people would assume the role of leaders.

The Christian journey of true compassion and justice is often a very lonely one. It is a path fraught with challenges and heartache, where the weight of the world's suffering can feel overwhelming. Often, Christians who fervently pray and read scripture find themselves reluctant to stand up for the truth, defend the persecuted, seek racial harmony, oppose political and economic oppression, or promote their faith. The fear of judgment, the risk of alienation, and the sheer enormity of the task can be paralyzing.

There is no expectation that all Christians will be actively engaged in the activities of the church in like manner. Each person's journey is a sacred awakening, unique to their soul, where no judgment casts its shadow. Every journey in faith is personal, every transformation a testament to grace. It is in the quiet, solitary moments of reflection and prayer that the true essence of faith is often found. However, one should expect that Christianity's most basic teachings must be embraced and exemplified by all Christians—love, compassion, forgiveness, and reverence for God.

Many Christians including myself have failed, sometimes exhibiting racism, supremacy, and an unwelcoming attitude to strangers. It is disheartening to see the church, which should be a sanctuary of love and acceptance, sometimes resemble an exclusive "country club." The pain of seeing such hypocrisy can be profound, leaving scars on the hearts of those who seek genuine connection and community.

Yet, amidst the failures and shortcomings, there is hope. The journey of faith is not about perfection but about striving towards the ideals that Christ taught. It is in the small, everyday acts of kindness and the courage to stand up for what is right that the true spirit of Christianity shines. It is in the embrace of diversity, the acceptance of all people, and the commitment to justice and compassion that the church will find its renewal.

As Christians, we must remember that our faith calls us to be beacons of light in a world often shrouded in darkness. We are called to love unconditionally, to forgive endlessly, and to welcome all with open arms. It is through these actions that we can truly embody the teachings of Christ and create a church that is a reflection of His love and grace.

Christians will be delusional to think that their future is bright amidst a highly fragmented church with numerous denominations.

This fragmentation within the Christian community is like a tapestry unraveling at the seams, each thread representing a different belief, a different interpretation, pulling away from the unity that once held it together. Perhaps it's time for the church to simply go back to its roots; one faith, one hope, and one Lord. This return to simplicity is not a step backward, but a profound leap towards the essence of what it means to be a follower of Christ.

The true essence of Christianity lies not in grand displays or rigid doctrines, but in the quiet, selfless acts of love and devotion that reflect the teachings of Christ. It is in the gentle touch of a hand extended in kindness, the whispered prayers for a stranger, and the unwavering support for those in need. These are the moments that define our faith, the moments that bring us closer to the divine.

It is in the embrace of diversity, the acceptance of all people, and the commitment to justice and compassion that the church will find its renewal. Imagine a church where the doors are always open, where every person, regardless of their background, is welcomed with open arms. A place where the beauty of diversity is celebrated, and the richness of different cultures and perspectives is seen as a gift, not a threat.

In this vision, the church becomes a beacon of hope and love, a sanctuary where the weary find rest and the lost find their way. It is a place where justice is not just preached but practiced, where the marginalized are uplifted, and where compassion flows like a river, touching every heart and soul.

As we strive towards this ideal, we must remember that the journey is not easy. It requires courage to confront our own prejudices, humility to admit our mistakes, and a steadfast commitment to the values that Christ taught us. But in this journey, we find our true purpose, and in this unity, we find our strength.

Let us then, as a community of believers, come together in this shared vision. Let us lay aside our differences and focus on what unites us—our faith, our hope, and our love for one another. For it is in this unity that we will find the true essence of Christianity, and it is in this unity that we will build a brighter future for the church and for the world.

As the young person leaves the cathedral, the echoes of hymns fading into the distance, they carry with them a hope for a church that truly embodies the love and inclusivity it preaches. A church that opens its doors wide to all, that listens and learns, and that walks hand in hand with its followers on the journey of faith. Only then will the pews fill once more, not just with bodies, but with hearts and souls united in a shared vision of a better world.

I penned this poem to capture the current state of the Christian church hoping for a better future.

The Christians' Delusion

The church is in dark delusion,
    Though Jesus Christ is Lord.
Through confusion and dissention,
    She blesses those with sword;
Enabling mean wars and menace,
    Against the Savior's will,
For all to live in joy and peace,
    Their precious lives fulfil.

Mid sad scenes of human conflict,
    She straddles the sidelines.
In scopes with bigotry's impact,
    She sought cordial confines.
Her courage darkened by this fact;
    She's drifted much astray,
From that which the Lord did instruct,
    To keep watch and to pray.

In bed with king and emperor,
    Their influence she craves.
While weak natives die of hunger,
    Her affluence makes waves.
She has in time all forgotten,
    Her purpose as laid out
By Him, the only begotten,
    To save the poor and lout.

In grief and utter suffering,
    Sad natives dwell with dread,
Her silence ever deafening,
    Their blood the tyrants shed.
She mocks His unsparing passion
    And dreadful agony,
For all to be in communion,
    In peace and harmony.

In trysts with many a despot,
    She's stained her radiant ray,
Darkened like the once dreadful spot,
    That shrouded Calvary.
Her light for all, ever His dream,
    Yet, her eyes marred to see.
Her temple once unveiled by Him,
    Now cloaked in secrecy.

To serve the restless natives well,
    She must to scripture turn;
Espouse the faith which clearly tell,
    Of the begotten Son.
Then shed her recent horrid way,
    Free natives from their pain,
And reclaim her once vivid ray,
    That she might shine again.

5

Echoes Of Love And Loss

John Armstead was only three years old when he joined the Galen family. The patriarch, Stephen, was a stern slave owner with a daughter, Sally, and a wife, Mary. They lived on a sprawling sixty-acre plantation where slaves toiled under the relentless sun, growing cotton and rice. The plantation was a complex of Victorian-style houses, with separate quarters for male and female slaves.

The Galen family resided in a grand two-story Victorian mansion, its white columns and ornate balconies a stark symbol of their wealth and power. Inside, the mansion was filled with luxurious furnishings, crystal chandeliers, and rich tapestries that whispered of opulence and privilege. The air was always cool, unlike the sweltering heat outside, and the rooms were filled with the scent of fresh flowers and polished wood.

In stark contrast, the slave quarters were small, cramped, and poorly constructed. The walls were thin, offering little protection from the elements, and the floors were bare dirt. The air was thick with the smell of sweat and toil, a constant reminder of the harsh realities of life as a slave. The quarters were overcrowded, with entire families sharing a single room, and the only light came from small, grimy windows that barely let in the sun.

John was given a small room near the rear of the mansion, a constant reminder of his precarious position. Though he was closer to the Galen family's world of comfort and luxury, he was always acutely aware of the thin line that separated him from the slaves in the quarters. The dichotomy between the grandeur of the mansion and the squalor of the slave quarters was a daily reminder of the brutal inequalities that defined his existence.

John was the son of David Armstead, a slave owner in the South and a close friend of the Galen family. His mother, Betty, was a slave owned by David. After John was born, David's wife, consumed by jealousy and rage, threatened to kill the innocent child. She couldn't bear the sight of a child born from her husband's indiscretions, especially with a slave. David, torn between his duty and his promise to Betty, sent John to live with the Galens, hoping to protect him from his wife's wrath.

A year after John was sent away, tragedy struck. David Armstead died suddenly in their home. Whispers of foul play spread like wildfire, with many speculating that David's wife had murdered him in a fit of rage after discovering his affair with another slave woman. The rumors were never confirmed, but the suspicion lingered. A week after David's death, Betty was found lifeless, her heart seemingly broken by the loss of her son and the man she loved. Some believed she had been murdered, silenced forever.

Mary Galen, though she loved John dearly, was torn. She questioned the wisdom of bringing a slave owner's love child into their home. She worried about the judgment of their upper-class peers, who often mingled with them at social gatherings. Despite her reservations, Mary's heart was kind. She loved her husband and her family fiercely and did her best to keep them together. Though they owned slaves, Mary was sympathetic to their plight. She often reminded Stephen to treat them with kindness, a sentiment born from her own past.

Mary had been raised by a slave woman from infancy. Her parents, always absent, had left her in the care of a nurturing slave who became her surrogate mother. Through this bond, Mary had grown to understand the slaves' struggles and desires for freedom. She had seen their pain and resilience firsthand, and it had shaped her into a compassionate woman.

John, despite his young age, felt the weight of his origins. He was a child caught between two worlds, neither fully accepted nor entirely rejected. The Galen household was a place of contradictions, where love and prejudice coexisted uneasily. As he grew, John would come to understand the complexities of his situation, the love that sheltered him, and the hatred that threatened to consume him.

John was quite handsome, with piercing eyes and beautiful skin that mirrored his father's features. Stephen often remarked how much John reminded him of his late friend, David. He would reminisce about their childhood, the times they spent growing up and attending a private school for the children of slave owners. Sometimes, Stephen would call John "David," a slip that revealed how deeply he missed his dear friend.

Stephen sent John to the best schools in town, and John, ever the astute pupil, excelled in his studies. He learned to play many musical instruments, including the fiddle and the piano. Moreover, he mastered the intricacies of Stephen's slave business, kept meticulous records, and later started constructing homes and buildings within the estate and beyond. John was trusted by Stephen, not as a son, but as a capable executor of his business. He became Stephen's confidante on matters pertaining to money, a role that brought him both respect and resentment.

Despite the privileges he enjoyed, John never forgot his roots. He often felt a deep, unspoken connection to the slaves on the plantation, sensing their silent suffering and shared history. This duality of his existence—privileged yet marginalized—shaped him into a man of quiet strength and profound empathy.

John played the piano frequently, his fingers dancing gracefully over the keys, much to the delight of Sally. She would often accompany him as a songstress, her voice blending harmoniously with the melodies he created. Their music sessions were a source of joy and connection, a shared passion that brought them closer. When the family hosted large gatherings, John would display his musical prowess, fiddling and playing pieces by Bach, Beethoven, Vivaldi, and other renowned composers on the piano. Guests were often mesmerized, with one even dubbing him "a maestro." Occasionally, John would be invited to play at the homes of other families, fulfilling their requests with his exceptional talent.

At eighteen, Stephen frequently asked John to drive Sally to the market and other events. Unbeknownst to him, a budding love was blossoming between the two teenagers. Only a few months apart in age, Sally found herself falling deeply in love with John, her feelings growing stronger with each passing day. She could hardly hide her affection, her heart racing whenever they were together. Her father, typically preoccupied with his slave business, and his frequent rendezvous with female slaves, especially teenage slave girls at the slave quarters remained oblivious to his daughter's emotions. On some occasions, when Sally yearned for John's company, she would cleverly trick her father into sending them on errands together, claiming she felt safer with John as her protector.

These moments on the road were precious opportunities for them to rendezvous, their love growing in secret.

By the time they were twenty-five, the love affair between Sally and John had fully bloomed. They often wrote poems to each other, expressing their deep affection and unwavering commitment. John, inspired by his love for Sally, composed a song that he would sing to her, his voice filled with emotion:

Unwavering love

My burning flame, my storms' anchor,
   My hope, my pleasure—steadfast will;
When fierce winds shake my very core,
   I will love you still.

Refrain:
In every breath, in every beat,
Through every joy and every thrill,
No matter what the world may bring,
I will love you still.

My guiding star in skies so vast,
   My shelter from the bitter chill;
Through every storm and shadow cast,
   I will love you still.

My moon's glow in my darkest night,
   My gentle rain, my soul's refill;
Through gales that seek to tear apart,
   I will love you still.

Their love was a beacon of light in a world filled with darkness and prejudice. Despite the societal constraints and the ever-present threat of discovery, Sally and John found solace in each other. Their love was a testament to the power of the human heart, capable of transcending boundaries and enduring even the harshest of storms.

One day, when they were alone in the house, John and Sally gave in to their passion. They were in bed together when Mary returned home unexpectedly. Though she did not catch them in the act, the sight of them together was enough. Mary, who had long suspected their love, felt a mix of understanding and fear. She scolded them, her voice trembling with concern. "If your father finds out about this, he will be furious," she warned, her eyes filled with worry. She was mostly concerned about John, fearing Stephen's wrath would fall heavily upon him.

About two months later, Stephen, acting on a tip from one of his paid workers, rummaged through Sally's room. There, he found love letters John had written to Sally, including one she'd kept underneath her pillow, where John expressed his undying love. His fury was palpable, but he preserved his anger, a storm brewing beneath the surface. He approached Mary with the letters, his face a mask of controlled rage, but she was equally furious at him for going through Sally's personal belongings.

"This is my house," he declared, his voice like a thunderclap. "I can search anything and anywhere." His voice cut through the quiet like a sharp blade. "So you knew about their affair all this time?" he accused, his eyes narrowing.

"It's not an affair. They are deeply in love," Mary replied vehemently. "Had you spent more time trying to understand your daughter instead of savoring the female slave quarters, you would have seen that she loves him, and he loves her dearly too."

"You approve of their affair?" Stephen's voice rose, incredulous.

"Why should it matter? He loves her and makes her happy, unlike you," Mary said, her tone dripping with sarcasm.

"That is not true! I love my daughter dearly, and this negro boy must pay for his deceit. In a few hours, he will be begging for his life," Stephen retorted adamantly.

"So what of your commitment to his father; to love and protect his son. Is that of no consequence?" Mary inquired, her voice steady.

Stephen paused, his face contorted with conflicting emotions. "He'll understand, besides he is dead nonetheless. Don't you realize that this negro boy has tarnished our daughter forever? She would gain no gentleman's affection now, after the son of a slave has defiled her." he said, bewildered.

"Defile her?" Mary questioned. "Why would she need another man when they are deeply in love?" she said, trying to justify the lovers' actions to her husband. The irony was not lost on Mary. Her husband who frequently slept with and sometimes raped young slave girls is now claiming that his friend's son of mixed race has defiled his daughter.

"This negro boy has hurt me badly, and I am going to teach him a lesson," Stephen vowed.

"He did not hurt you, only your vanity is hurt," Mary replied, her voice filled with quiet defiance.

That weekend, Stephen sent Sally on a trip about three hours away. When Sally requested John's escort, her father refused, stating that John had a building project to complete. As soon as Sally departed, Stephen had John bound by some of his paid workers. The slaves watched from a distance, shivering in tears and shrinking in fear as John was stripped naked, tethered to a tree, and whipped mercilessly by the plantation's henchmen.

For the next few hours, John called for Sally, his love, singing to her with tears streaming down his cheeks despite his pain. The beating was brutal. His flesh was splattered all over the tree and on the ground while his blood flowed freely into a shallow nearby ditch. Some of the onlooking slaves shed their torrent tears. Although John had few interactions with them, he cared about their well-being and treated them kindly on the few occasions he was allowed to mingle with them.

The sight of John's suffering left a deep scar on the hearts of those who witnessed it. His cries for Sally echoed through the plantation, a haunting reminder of the cruelty and injustice that pervaded their lives. Despite the agony, John's love for Sally remained unbroken, a testament to the strength of their bond.

Sally, while on her way to her father's assignment, felt a gnawing sense of unease. It was unlike her father to send her on a trip alone. As she drove, her mind raced with possibilities, each more sinister than the last. After several hours, unable to shake the feeling that something was terribly wrong, she turned the car around and headed back home.

As she pulled into the driveway, a chilling sound reached her ears—John's voice, calling for her. Panic surged through her veins as she raced towards the source of the cries. She found John tethered to a tree, his body a canvas of pain and suffering. The men whipping him tried to restrain her, but she broke free and ran into the house, her heart pounding with fear and anger.

"What have you done, Father?" she demanded, her voice trembling with rage. Stephen's response was swift and brutal—a slap across her face that left her reeling. "You have disgraced your family," he spat, his eyes blazing with fury.

Recovering from the blow, Sally's eyes filled with tears. "I love him, Father. I am pregnant with his child—your grandchild. Does this change your mind now?" she pleaded, her voice breaking.

"It is of no consequence. He deceived me," Stephen replied, his voice a mixture of shock and anger.

"You are heartless! You are heartless!" Sally cried, her voice echoing with despair as her father remained indifferent to her pleas.

Meanwhile, the men continued their merciless torture of John. His death was slow and agonizing. Mary, unable to bear the sight, locked herself in the master bedroom, crying and praying for divine intervention.

Desperate and driven by a fierce protectiveness, Sally raced to the living room, her breath quick and shallow. The living room was dimly lit, shadows dancing eerily on the walls. The knightly dagger, glistening in the faint light, hung as a silent witness to her turmoil. With trembling hands, she seized the cold, ornate handle, its weight a strange comfort in her grip.

As she approached Stephen from behind, her heart thundered in her chest, a wild drumbeat of fear, anger, and resolve. The air was thick with tension, her mind a whirlwind of the horrors she'd endured. She saw him turn, his eyes widening in surprise and confusion, but before he could utter a word, she plunged the dagger into his chest, the blade sinking deep with a sickening thud.

Once. Twice. Each thrust was a release of her pent-up fury and sorrow. Stephen gasped, his face contorting in pain and disbelief as he crumpled to the floor. The life drained from his eyes, and in the heavy silence that followed, Sally leaned close and whispered, her voice trembling yet resolute, "This is for taking my heart."

In that moment, a torrent of emotions surged through her—relief, grief, and a bittersweet satisfaction. The henchmen, alerted by Stephen's agonized cries, thundered up the steps towards the mansion. The sound of their heavy boots echoed ominously, yet Sally stood her ground, the dagger still clutched tightly in her blood-stained hand, ready to face whatever came next.

Sally then ran to the tree where John lay, barely clinging to life with the bloody dagger still in her hand. Though weak from blood loss, he recognized her and whispered, "In life and death, never apart." With tears streaming down her face, she responded, "I will love you still." A tribute to the song he always sang to her. John breathed his last breath, and Sally, overcome with grief, took the dagger and drove it into her own heart, dying beside her love.

Mary, though she had loved her husband, detested his indiscretions with the female slaves. She had long seen him as a rapist, a man who abused his power and inflicted pain on those who had no means to defend themselves. The realization of his true nature had been a slow, agonizing process, but the recent tragedy had shattered any remaining illusions she held about him.

In the aftermath of the tragedy, Mary was consumed by grief and guilt. She buried Sally and John next to each other in a secluded part of the estate, a place where the sun filtered gently through the trees, casting a serene light on their final resting place. She chose a simple yet poignant inscription for their vault: "In life and in death, they love each other still." As she stood by their graves, tears streaming down her face, she whispered a prayer for their souls, hoping they had found the peace and happiness in death that had been denied to them in life.

The days that followed were a blur of sorrow and reflection. Mary wandered through the empty halls of the mansion, haunted by memories of laughter and love, now replaced by an oppressive silence and an overwhelming sense of loss. Each room echoed with the ghosts of happier times, their absence a constant reminder of what had been taken from her.

She found herself drawn to the places where Sally and John had spent their happiest moments—the music room where their melodies once intertwined, filling the air with joy and harmony. Now, the piano keys lay untouched, gathering dust, a stark contrast to the vibrant life they once brought to the space. In the garden, where Sally and John had stolen secret glances and whispered sweet nothings, the flowers seemed to wilt in mourning, their colors fading as if in sympathy with Mary's grief.

Determined to honor their memory and make amends for the wrongs committed by her husband, Mary took decisive action. She gathered the slaves, her heart heavy with the weight of her decision. With a voice choked with emotion, she announced their freedom. The words felt both liberating and terrifying, as if she were releasing a part of herself along with them. Some of the slaves, befuddled, did not know what to do.

"We is free!" One of them shouted, starting a celebration amongst the gathered throng. The air filled with cries of joy and disbelief, a cacophony of emotions that brought a glimmer of hope to Mary's heart. She gave them land to start their new lives, a small but significant gesture of restitution. The joy and disbelief on their faces brought a glimmer of hope to her heart, a sign that perhaps some good could come from the ashes of tragedy.

Mary sold fifty acres of the plantation, a place that had become a symbol of pain and oppression, and distributed some of the money to the former slaves. She hoped this act would help atone for the sins of her husband and bring some measure of justice to those who had suffered under his rule. It was a small step, but it was a start. The land, once a source of sorrow, now held the promise of new beginnings and a chance for redemption.

In her quiet moments, Mary often visited the graves of Sally and John. She would sit by their vault, reading the inscription over and over, finding solace in the words. The cold stone beneath her fingers was a stark reminder of their absence, yet the act of visiting their resting place brought her a sense of peace. She would speak to them, her voice barely a whisper, sharing her hopes and fears, seeking comfort in the belief that they could hear her. The garden around their graves, once a place of secret glances and whispered sweet nothings, now became a sanctuary of reflection and remembrance.

She wrote a poem to encapsulate the recent events in her life, a way to process her grief and honor the love that had been so tragically cut short:

Echoes Of Love and Loss

In murky shades, where sorrow lies,
    A tale of love and pain unfolds;
Beneath the stars and silent skies,
    A heart once warm, now bitter cold.

A daughter's love, a father's wrath,
    Two souls entwined, yet torn apart;
In secret whispers, hidden paths,
    They found their love, they lost their hearts.

The cruel hand of fate did strike,
    With lashes fierce and blood so red;
A love so pure, a bond so tight,
    Now broken, shattered, left for dead.

Yet in the darkness, hope remains,
    A flicker in the coldest night;
For love endures through all the pains,
    And finds its way to morning light.

In mem'ry of the love they shared,
    A mother's tears, a silent plea;
May freedom's song be ever heard,
    And hearts be bound in unity.

Mary's poem became a testament to the enduring power of love and
the hope for a better future. It served as a reminder that even in the
darkest times, love could light the way and bring healing to wounded
hearts. Later, Mary married a gentleman who was quite successful in the
railroad industry. They lived happily together, and she often pondered
the promise of the love between her daughter Sally and her dearest love,
John, a love that was cut short far too soon.

6

Harmony In Discord

In the embrace of May's tender warmth, my friends Stella and Theo, and I found ourselves drawn to the vibrant heart of Cleveland, Ohio. Stella, ever the sagacious guide, proposed a stay in Independence, a township founded in the 1800s, where history whispers from every corner, and modernity's conveniences are interwoven with the fabric of a bygone era. Her suggestion was a stroke of genius, allowing us to immerse ourselves in the city's grandeur while discovering the quaint allure of its suburban secrets.

As the sun kissed the plants, its rays dancing on the surface of the lake, and the wind a gentle touch of spring's enduring bliss, our first day unfurled like the petals of a blooming flower in downtown Cleveland. We stood by the lake, a tranquil guardian of the city's memories, and let our laughter mingle with the breeze. In a park by the lake, the "Cleveland" sign rose before us, a proud sentinel, as we captured moments that would linger long in our hearts. The beach pulsed with life, a mosaic of joyous souls basking in the sun's lingering kiss.

In downtown Cleveland, the iconic silhouettes of football and baseball stadiums and the Rock and Roll museum etched themselves against the skyline. We wandered through the west side, where the splendor of the city was undeniable, with stately homes boasting emerald lawns and windows winking at the lake's expanse. It was as if the neighborhood itself was in a state of blissful serenity, untouched by time's relentless march.

Our journey's crescendo was a lakeside dining experience at Pier W, a restaurant that transcended mere sustenance. On the elevator's descent into the main dining room, we heard the inducing sounds of a piano. The pianist, an artisan of harmony, crafted a symphony of notes that enveloped the room in aural splendor with ballads that stirred the soul— tributes to the legends Streisand, Houston, Jackson, Ritchie, McCartney, Wonder and Carmen. Each note was a thread in the evening's fabric, each chord a memory etched in melody. The ambiance was a cocoon of warmth, and the patrons, a gallery of contented spirits, each basking in the glow of shared humanity.

The culinary delights at Pier W were nothing short of extraordinary. Each dish was a masterpiece, a symphony of flavors that danced on the palate. The lobster bisque with buttered croutons, rich and velvety, was a warm embrace on a cool evening, while the salmon, perfectly seared, flaked apart with the slightest touch, revealing its tender, succulent heart. The oven-roasted, cedar-planked walleye, my favorite, was a revelation, its delicate flavor enhanced by a subtle blend of herbs and spices. Theo indulged in some oysters Rockefeller with creamed spinach and Parmesan cheese and chargrilled wild striped bass, while Stella had some spiced grilled swordfish with roasted corn and jalapeño salad.

But it wasn't just the food that made the evening unforgettable. The view from the restaurant, overlooking the serene expanse of Lake Erie, was nothing short of breathtaking. As the sun sank into the twilight, the sky was painted in hues of pink and gold, casting a magical glow over the water. The city skyline, twinkling in the distance, added a touch of urban elegance to the natural beauty of the scene. It was a sight that stirred the soul, like a breathtaking sunset that made every bite taste even more exquisite.

The ambiance of Pier W was a perfect blend of sophistication and comfort. The soft lighting, the gentle hum of conversation, and the attentive, yet unobtrusive service created an atmosphere that was both intimate and inviting. It was a place where time seemed to stand still, where every moment was savored, and every detail was appreciated. The combination of exceptional food, stunning views, soft piano music and a warm, welcoming atmosphere made our evening at Pier W a truly unforgettable experience.

As night's velvet curtain descended, we retreated from the west side's embrace, our spirits alight with the day's symphony of experiences. The city had bestowed upon us a treasure trove of moments, each more precious than the last, and we carried them with us, a trove of emotional riches, as we returned to the quiet charm of Independence.

With the dawn of a new day, we set our sights on the unexplored vistas of Cleveland's east side. Theo and Stella, though hesitant, embraced the spirit of adventure, their curiosity piqued by the unknown. As we ventured forth, the cityscape transformed before our eyes, disclosing a panorama of existence, depicted in vividly distinct and contrasting tones that illustrate the diverse facets of life.

The east side, a mixture of forgotten splendor, lay before us like a canvas of contrasts. Buildings that once echoed with the laughter of families now stood silent, their stories slowly being erased by the relentless embrace of nature. Ivy tendrils clung to crumbling walls, a verdant reclaiming of man-made structures, as if the earth itself was whispering secrets of a time long past.

Amidst this backdrop of abandonment, the true heart of the community pulsed with an irrepressible vitality. African American children, the embodiment of resilience, wove through the streets on their bicycles, their laughter a defiant chorus against the silence. They were the unexpected blooms in a garden of concrete, their spirits undimmed by the shadows that loomed around them.

As we descended a hill, a ghostly tableau emerged—a vast estate of boarded-up homes, the remnants of a bygone era's aspirations, now assuming the role of quiet watchers to history's capricious winds. Stella's diligent research revealed the bittersweet truth: this relic of communal hope had been bartered away to the hands of progress—real estate investors.

A stone's throw from this monument to the past, the future reared its head in the form of gleaming new residences. Expensive apartments and townhomes rose like phoenixes from the ashes of history, their very existence a stark reminder of the chasm between those who are remembered and those who are overlooked.

Our journey took a turn towards Little Italy, a vibrant enclave where the proud colors of the Italian flag adorned every storefront. The air was rich with the scent of authentic cuisine, and the streets thrummed with the energy of people reveling in the joy of shared heritage.

The day's odyssey culminated at University Circle, an oasis of enlightenment amidst the desert of despair. Here, the prestigious Case Western Reserve University stood as a beacon of progress, its hallowed halls promising a future bright with possibility. The Cleveland Medical Center and the Cleveland Museum of Art lent their luster to the area, creating a constellation of cultural and intellectual wealth.

In the span of ten miles, we had traversed worlds within a single city. One, a silent witness to the relentless march of time, the other, a vibrant testament to the boundless potential of human endeavor. The dichotomy was profound—a city divided not just by geography, but by the very essence of hope and despair.

At Mitchell's, a stone's throw from Case Western University, we surrendered to the sweet allure of high-quality ice cream, a sanctuary of flavor in a world too often bitter. Each taste was not just a symphony but an opera of sensation, a crescendo of artisanal mastery that danced upon our tongues with the grace of a prima ballerina. We indulged in samples, each a prelude to the main performance, and then cradled two generous scoops of our chosen delights. The creamy richness was a fleeting comfort, a tender embrace that melted away all too quickly, leaving behind a poignant yearning for more.

As we journeyed back to Independence, our minds were awash with the stark contrasts of east Cleveland. The vibrant life of the city streets gave way to the muted tones of neglected avenues. We found ourselves lost in contemplation of life's profound inequities, the joy of our indulgence now a bittersweet memory against the backdrop of harsh reality.

Theo wondered aloud, his voice a whisper of concern in the quiet of our car, "The pockets of poverty we just witnessed, where will they go once the giant wave of gentrification approaches?" His question hung in the air, a specter of the future looming over the present.

I paused to think, my heart heavy with the weight of his words. The young kids on bicycles, their laughter the kindling flames amidst dying embers, were a stark reminder that these are our children too. They are the forgotten verses in the grand narrative of our nation.

Did 'E Pluribus Unum'—out of many, one—include a clause exempting consideration of these children? Or have we, as a society, chosen to redact such passages, leaving them to fade like the last notes of a song, unheard and unheeded?

In the end, the ice cream was but a momentary solace, a sweet distraction from the enduring questions that linger long after the taste has faded. It is in these moments of reflection that we find the true essence of our humanity, the shared sweetness and the collective sorrow that bind us all.

Late that night, moved by the experience, Stella, ever the skilled wordsmith, penned a poem capturing the stark dichotomy of East Cleveland:

Cleveland Mosaic: A Tale Of Two Faces

In Cleveland's heart, where bright lights gleam,
Lie vibrant townships, quaint, serene.
A place steeped in history's embrace,
With modern touch, holds a dual face.

In Cleveland's soul where skies unfold,
By lakeside signs, memories took hold.
The stadiums stood proud and grandiose,
And westward homes in trimmed repose.

A lakeside feast, with music sweet,
Old ballads—our hearts skipped a beat.
The charmed crowd in dusk's soft caress
Awed our hearts of west side's finesse.

Yet eastward bound, a different scene,
Where time's vile hand swept the slate clean.
Abandoned homes—nature's retake,
A canvas stark, some dreams forsake.

The children's laughs, midst ruins' sprawl,
A strength of hope that conquers all.
Their virtue—light in shadows cast,
Wading through streets that hold them fast.

The war-time homes, now empty rows,
An era lost, renewal grows.
New buildings rise where wreck once dwelt,
A tale of two, its heart has felt.

As the sun rose to kiss the morning sky, we embarked on a new chapter of our Cleveland odyssey, setting our compass towards Parma. This quaint suburb, nestled just a heartbeat away from Independence, welcomed us with open arms, its streets a vibrant quilt of Ukrainian culture. State Road, a lifeline of the community, stretched before us, inviting exploration and discovery.

The air was rich with the scent of tradition, each storefront a proof of the enduring spirit of those who had crossed oceans and continents to find a new beginning. The Ukrainian churches, architectural jewels set against the azure canvas, stood proudly, their golden domes catching the sunlight in a silent hymn of glory. St. Josaphat and St. Vladimir, more than mere structures of worship, were pillars of a community's faith, symbols of hope and resilience that had weathered the storms of history.

Driven by a longing that tugged at our souls, we sought the comfort of familiar flavors in a local Ukrainian eatery. It was a place where every dish told a story, where the Borscht soup's deep crimson spoke of the land's rich bounty, and the Chebureki's savory embrace evoked memories of family gatherings in faraway homes. Each bite was a journey through time and space, a bridge between the old world and the new.

It was here, amidst the warmth of shared meals and the clinking of spoons against bowls, that we met Ivan and Katiya. Their love, a beacon amidst the tempest of geopolitics, shone with a brilliance that transcended borders and conflict. Ivan's eyes, reflecting the blue of the Ukrainian flag, met Katiya's gaze, which held the depth of the Russian steppes. Together, they wove a narrative of unity, a poignant reminder that love knows no nationality, no allegiance other than that of the heart.

Their story, a succinct embodiment of the broader human narrative, resonated with us deeply. In the simple act of breaking bread together, we found a shared humanity, a common thread that bound us all, regardless of the lands we called home.

Their marriage, a demonstration of the enduring power of love, had begun in 2005, far from the turmoil that now gripped their native lands. Ivan, a beacon of innovation in a software company, and Katiya, a guardian of health as a registered nurse, had found each other in a Cleveland that once celebrated the mingling of Russian and Ukrainian spirits. But the war had cast a shadow over these once-joyous gatherings, chilling the warmth that had fostered countless friendships. The couple's lives were now punctuated by harrowing messages from their brothers—Mykola, fighting valiantly in the Ukrainian army, and Yuri, conscripted into a war he did not choose. Their stories, relayed across miles and tears, spoke of a reality too cruel, of towns erased and hopes besieged, of the relentless pursuit of survival amidst the thunder of guns. Yet, in their shared struggle, Ivan and Katiya found strength, their love a quiet rebellion against the forces that sought to divide them.

Ivan and Katiya, bound by love yet divided by heritage, found themselves grappling with the incomprehensible war between their motherlands. "It's a mockery," Ivan lamented, his voice laced with scorn as he recited the Lord's Prayer in Russian, 'Otche nash, susthiy na nebesah.' "They pray to the heavens, yet unleash hell on earth." The couple, once regulars at the nearby Russian church, now faced a spiritual rift as wide as the geopolitical one. Since the invasion, Ivan's heart had hardened, and he could no longer bear to sit in the pews, his soul in turmoil.

As the conflict raged, Ivan's anger simmered like a relentless flame. An incursion on a Ukrainian border town by the Russian army killed members of his family, including an uncle, who had helped raise him. Meals were forgotten, replaced by the bitter taste of peanuts and the hollow comfort of beer. Each message from the front lines, each tale of horror relayed by his brother, stoked the fire within him. Katiya watched helplessly as her husband became a shadow, haunted by the war's cruel specter. "I felt like the enemy," she whispered, her gaze fleeting across Ivan's tormented face. "As if I were the very embodiment of the war that sought to claim his brother's life." Their home, once a sanctuary, echoed with silence, the distance between them a painful reminder of the war's reach.

The night Yuri was conscripted, Ivan drowned his sorrows in the company of friends, leaving Katiya to face the chilling news alone. Upon his return, the alcohol-fueled bitterness spilled forth. "What do you want?" he slurred, his words like daggers. "Go on, take my life too. You've already taken so many." Katiya retreated, the sting of his accusations lingering in the air, heavy with the scent of spirits. Alone in her room, she reached out the only way she could, her text message a beacon in the night: 'Yuri has been conscripted into the Russian army.'

Morning light brought clarity to Ivan, the words on his screen a stark reminder of their shared plight. A realization dawned, softening the edges of his resentment. They were not adversaries but allies, entwined in a love that the war sought to unravel. He apologized to Katiya, pledging his undying love for her, assuring her that he would not allow the ravages of war to affect their relationship again. In a moment of profound reflection, Ivan penned a poem he shared with us, a vessel for his anguish and hope:

A War of Hearts

In our dear home, where love once danced,
A war has crept, with silent glance.
Two hearts that beat as one now fray,
As Russia and Ukraine betray.

The pray'r, "Otche nash" so divine,
Now booms hollow, midst the war's line.
A church that housed us, side by side,
Stands void—our faith begins to slide.

Katiya, my dear, you bear no blame,
For war that seeks to maim and shame.
Your brother fighting not by choice,
His voice now lost, midst the gun's voice.

Let not this war our walls divide,
Our love provides safe place to hide.
From east to west, our hearts restore,
And be a haven from the war.

And as we left the eatery, the flavors of Ukraine lingering on our tongues, we carried with us not just the satisfaction of a meal well enjoyed, but also the profound understanding of the power of love to bridge the greatest of divides. The tastes lingered—of borscht and pampushki—a culinary metaphor for the bittersweet blend of joy and sorrow, of unity and separation, that defines our existence. Katiya said to us in Ukrainian, "Berezhy vas Boh," and we replied, "God bless you too."

Upon our return from Cleveland, the myriad of our experiences was rich and complex, interlaced with strands of discovery, disparity, and the enduring human spirit. The city had revealed itself to us in layers, each one telling a story of its own. We had witnessed firsthand the stark dichotomy of a metropolis split into two halves—each a mirror reflecting a different facet of society.

The heart of our journey, however, was the unexpected encounter with Ivan and Katiya. Their love story was a powerful narrative that transcended the physical and societal borders that divided their ancestral lands. In the midst of Cleveland's own split identity, they stood united—a testament to the fact that love can flourish even when it seems the world itself is split in two. Their shared history, now marred by the conflict of nations, only strengthened their bond, making it clear that the heart knows no boundaries, no politics, no war.

As we reflected on our time in Cleveland, it became clear that the city was a living lesson in contrasts and unity. The experience of gentrification and the dichotomy of east Cleveland were not just local phenomena but global truths, echoed in the lives of Ivan and Katiya. Their resilience and unity in the face of division were a profound reminder that, while landscapes and cities may change, the human capacity for love and connection remains constant, a bridge over the chasms of change.

7

Her Final Words

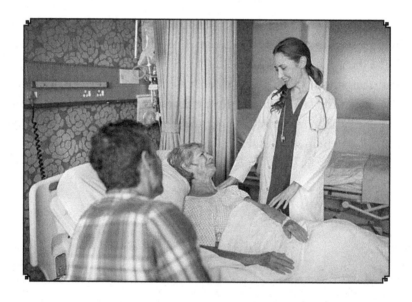

Tarsha was her mother's only daughter, the spitting image of her. Among five siblings, she was cherished by her brothers, who guarded her like sentinels at a maximum-security prison—sometimes bordering on overprotectiveness. During her teenage years, she shared a remarkable closeness with her mother. She donned her mother's clothes, shoes, jewelry, and makeup, and they exchanged intimate secrets. She often sought her mother's advice on the young boys who sought her company.

Her father's passing when she was quite young left her mother to raise the family alone. Despite the challenges, her mother's unwavering love made her the favorite child—a status she was well aware of. After graduating high school, she landed a job at a produce facility. The position offered good pay, a blessing considering her limited experience and education. Her earnings became a pillar of support for the household, contributing to food, gasoline, and other necessities. Moreover, her generosity extended to her siblings, particularly her brother Peter, with whom she shared a special bond.

Tarsha's life was flourishing, except in the realm of romance. Her high school sweetheart, once believed to be her destined partner, left her for someone else. Adhering to tradition, Tarsha had envisioned her first love becoming her lifelong spouse, yet reality unfolded differently. Afterward, she encountered Marc Telson, who adored her deeply. However, the spark was absent for Tarsha, leading to the relationship's end.

Later, Tarsha found love with a man significantly her senior. This relationship initially dismayed her mother, who feared the age gap might lead to undue influence. John, Tarsha's partner, was a respected businessman in Bexley, Ohio, known for his jovial and affectionate nature. Despite her initial reservations, Tarsha's mother eventually recognized the depth of their bond and came to accept their union.

John and Tarsha's wedding was a lavish affair, a true celebration of love and commitment. The grand ceremony was held in a stunning venue, adorned with elegant floral arrangements and soft, ambient lighting that created a romantic atmosphere. Approximately three hundred and fifty guests were in attendance, a testament to the couple's wide circle of friends and John's extensive business network.

The air was filled with the soulful melodies of a jazz band, their rhythmic tunes setting the tone for the evening. As the night progressed, a renowned disc jockey from a popular local radio station took over, spinning a mix of classic hits and modern favorites that had everyone on the dance floor.

The joyous occasion marked the beginning of a new chapter for the couple. Not long after their nuptial celebration, they welcomed their first child, a bundle of joy that brought even more happiness into their lives. Two years later, they were blessed with a second child, further completing their family.

John and Tarsha's children were the epitome of excellence, attending prestigious private schools in the vicinity. Their education was a priority for the couple, ensuring their offspring had access to the best learning opportunities.

John, a father figure of unwavering dedication, extended his love and support not only to his children with Tarsha but also to his two children from a previous marriage. He seamlessly blended his responsibilities, ensuring all his children received equal affection and guidance.

Their life was a portrait of contentment, with each family member thriving in their own right, and their home a haven of warmth and happiness. The couple's journey together was marked by milestones of joy, and their love story continued to inspire those around them.

John's business prospered until around 1997. His standard practice involved supplying inventory to partners and receiving payment in subsequent quarters. Unbeknownst to John, several of his partners' businesses were struggling financially, and some were failing. His friend, Moses declared bankruptcy, unable to fulfill his financial commitments to John, followed by James Pinkston, who owed John's company a staggering $365,000 and also declared bankruptcy. Neither Moses nor James could repay John. Consequently, John had to lay off many employees due to payroll constraints.

The next year, John managed to keep his business afloat, frequently tapping into his savings to support his household and those who had long relied on his generosity. Tarsha, having resigned from her job after the birth of their second child, was now a full-time mother. Facing severe financial challenges, the family sold all their real estate assets, but for an old house John leased to a couple. This provided temporary relief but was ultimately unsustainable. In their time of need, they turned to Tarsha's mother, Mavis. Having lived alone since the passing of her second husband five years prior, Mavis readily suggested that the entire family move in with her. Despite Peter, Tarsha's brother, expressing concerns based on his own challenging experience of hosting his mother-in-law, the family decided to move in with Grandma Mavis.

Grandma Mavis cherished her role as a grandmother, often rising at dawn to prepare breakfast for her grandchildren. Whenever the children were disciplined by John, Mavis would intervene, much to John's frustration. He had specific ideas about parenting and saw Mavis's involvement as an obstacle. Despite this, they managed to coexist. Mavis frequently contributed financially from her retirement funds to assist John and Tarsha. John perceived this as Mavis's attempt to exert influence over his wife and children, which troubled him. His discomfort with the living arrangement and its impact on his ego led to a confrontation with Tarsha about her mother's behavior, even threatening to leave if the situation didn't improve. Tarsha endeavored to maintain focus on their marriage, reassuring John of her commitment.

One afternoon, John's son, Brian, returned from school and found himself in a heated debate with his father over a math assignment. This incident added yet another layer to the family's complex dynamics. Normally, such a disagreement wouldn't have escalated, but this time, Grandma Mavis intervened, chastising John for his strictness with the children. It seemed John was projecting his frustrations from his floundering business onto his kids, and Mavis's confrontation only fueled his anger.

In the past, their moments of disdain and anger were often brushed aside, leaving their relationship strained and the issues unresolved. However, this altercation was different. Mavis's voice was sharp as she accused, "You're robbing the cradle by marrying my young daughter!"

John's retort was equally biting. "And what of your husbands? All deceased, and all wealthy before they met their untimely ends. One might wonder if you had a hand in that."

Amidst the chaos, Tarsha walked in, fresh from the grocery store, and was met with the uproar. "What's happening?" she inquired, her eyes wide with confusion.

Brian somberly responded, "Dad and Grandma are at odds again."

Before Tarsha could probe further, the argument between John and Mavis reignited with a fury. "You orchestrated a meeting between my wife and another man!" John accused, his finger pointing accusingly at Mavis.

Unable to bear the toxic environment, John declared his intention to leave Mavis's home. "I can't stay here any longer," he announced, his voice resolute.

Tarsha, bound by marriage, followed suit. "We need to leave, for our own peace," she whispered to John.

They packed their belongings and relocated to an old house owned by John, leading to a deterioration in the relationship between Tarsha and her mother. Despite the tension, Tarsha occasionally visited Mavis to assist with household tasks.

During one such visit, Mavis's words were laced with unspoken blame. "You know, I gave you shelter when you needed it most," she said, her gaze fixed on Tarsha.

Tarsha felt the weight of her mother's words. "I know, Mom. And I'm grateful," she replied, her voice barely above a whisper.

Mavis, though never stating it outright, held Tarsha accountable for her husband's disrespect, believing she had provided them shelter in their time of need.

Mavis continued to support Tarsha financially, especially for the children's needs. Then, in a cruel twist of fate, John was taken from them. His death left a void in Tarsha's life, a chasm of sorrow that seemed insurmountable. In this dark time, the support of her mother and brother, Peter, became her anchor. They stood by her, a steadfast presence amidst the turbulent waves of grief. Mavis, with a heart both broken and resilient, enveloped Tarsha in a love that knew no bounds, a love that whispered of strength in the face of despair.

As the days passed, the bond between Tarsha and her mother wove itself back together, thread by delicate thread. The visits to Mavis became a balm to Tarsha's wounded soul, as she watched her children bask in their grandmother's affection. Mavis, despite her own fading health, doted on them with treats and money for school lunches and other essentials, her generosity a testament to her unyielding spirit.

The children's laughter became a light in the darkness, a reminder that life, though fragile, still held moments of pure joy. And in those moments, Tarsha felt John's presence, a gentle reminder that love, once shared, never truly leaves us.

Suddenly, Tarsha stopped visiting her mother. It was as if a switch had been flipped; she neither called nor visited. The children, now grown, would occasionally sneak in to see their grandmother, but Tarsha remained absent. Three years later, Mavis' health declined, leading to a two-month hospital stay. Tarsha, deeply involved with a Pentecostal group known for claiming divine visions, traveled extensively with her fellow members but avoided the hospital. Her brother, Peter, made numerous attempts to reach her, to no avail. Kevin, another brother, encountered Tarsha at a grocery store and urged her to call their mother, but she refused.

After Mavis was discharged to a rehabilitation center, Peter persisted in his attempts to connect the two, but Tarsha never answered her phone. During his visits, Mavis frequently inquired about Tarsha. Once, she expressed a dying wish to Peter: to hold Tarsha's hand one last time. Despite Peter's best efforts, Tarsha remained unresponsive. The reasons for her avoidance were speculative: divine instruction, unresolved grievances, or perhaps a cruel intention to inflict pain by withholding her presence. Regardless, Mavis' longing to see her daughter was both literal and profound.

Mavis waited patiently for Tarsha, her memories fueling her hope to see her daughter again. One evening, she asked Peter to call Tarsha multiple times. As Tarsha repeatedly ignored the calls, Mavis transitioned from attentive and talkative to a dazed state, silently resigning to the possibility of never seeing her daughter again.

As Mavis lay on her deathbed, she revealed to Peter that she had written a letter to Tarsha years ago, explaining her actions and expressing her deepest regrets and love. This letter, hidden in a family heirloom, was meant to be read by Tarsha when the time was right. However, Mavis never had the courage to give it to her.

Three weeks later, the doctors convened a meeting with Mavis' family to discuss her deteriorating condition. Peter reached out to Tarsha, conveying their mother's dying wish to see her. At the hospital, Peter dialed Tarsha's number so Mavis could talk to her, but Tarsha did not answer. That night, Mavis' health sharply declined, marking what might have been her final chance to hear her daughter's voice.

As the sun set, Mavis' strength waned. Tarsha's absence at her bedside was a stark testament to the chasm between intention and action. The family gathered, enveloping Mavis in a tapestry of care, guardians of her final journey. In a moment of clarity, Mavis' frail voice was a beacon of forgiveness, her love reaching out to Tarsha across the miles.

Tears traced the lines of Mavis' face, each one a testament to unmet dreams and unsaid farewells. As life's threads frayed, her whispers of "Tarsha, Tarsha, Tarsha…" became a haunting lullaby, a mother's love etched into the echoes of eternity.

Peter captured the interaction between Tarsha and their mother in a poem:

A Mother's Wish

Her final wish could not be had,
    In spite of all she pled;
A daughter's heart by rashness bound,
    A reunion deterred.

Perhaps her mum's past deeds transformed,
    Their once tight, budding bond;
No pain or anguish could defend,
    Deeds of a vengeful mind.

As she lays dying on her bed,
    Her cries for love, unheard,
By such intransigence of mind,
    Quite crippling and unkind.

A mother's love will e'er extend
    A hand for kids to hold;
From toddler days to her death bed,
    It must ne'er be unheld.

On the solemn day of Mavis' farewell, Tarsha made her way through the chapel doors, her daughter's hand clasped in hers. The air was thick with unspoken grievances, as many averted their eyes, their hearts heavy with the unfulfilled promise that Tarsha would be the solace in her mother's final moments. Peter, the peacemaker, whispered words of caution, urging the family to embrace compassion over confrontation.

Tarsha stood before the gathering, her voice trembling as she gave a myriad of excuses, each more puzzling than the last. She spoke of an ailment, vague and shadowy, that barred her from her mother's bedside—a condition shrouded in mystery that left the family grappling for understanding. Her words fell like pebbles into a still pond, causing ripples of confusion and hurt.

In the quietude of the service, Peter held onto a secret—a message from Mavis brimming with tenderness and absolution. Yet, he tucked it away in the silent chambers of his heart, fearing that its revelation might fracture the fragile threads holding them together, unraveling the memories of their shared history.

Mavis's yearning for Tarsha and her unmet dream of reconciliation was a profound ache that permeated her every waking moment. The pain of her daughter's absence was a constant, gnawing sorrow, a wound that refused to heal. Each unanswered call, each day without a visit, deepened the chasm of longing in Mavis's heart. Her dreams were filled with memories of Tarsha's laughter, her touch, and the bond they once shared. The nights were the hardest, filled with silent tears and whispered prayers for her daughter's return.

After Mavis's passing, Peter found the letter while sorting through her belongings. Torn between respecting his mother's wishes and the potential to heal the rift between his sister and their mother, Peter decided to give the letter to Tarsha.

Tarsha, initially resistant, finally read the letter. In it, Mavis poured out her heart, recounting their shared memories, her reasons for certain decisions, and her unwavering love for Tarsha. The letter ended with a plea for forgiveness and a hope that Tarsha would find peace and happiness.

Reading the letter, Tarsha was overwhelmed with emotions. The realization of the depth of her mother's love and the pain she had endured struck her deeply. Overcome with grief, Tarsha wept bitterly, tears streaming down her face uncontrollably. The weight of her emotions proved too much, and she fainted, collapsing onto the floor. Her family rushed to her side, reviving her with gentle words and cool cloths. As she regained consciousness, she whispered, "I was foolish," recognizing her mistake in not seeing the love her mother had always had for her.

Later, Tarsha in a moment of reflection, penned a sonnet about her foolish attitude towards her mother which read:

Bitter Light of Late-Regret

When youthful pride blinded my heart and mind,
    I turned away from love that knew no end.
In selfish shadows, reasons I did find,
    And failed to see my truest, closest friend.
For years, I walked a path devoid of grace,
    With memories of warmth lost in the mist.
I spurned her outstretched arms, her loving face,
    Ignoring all the moments that I'd missed.
Now, tears do wash away my foolish scorn,
    As sorrow blooms where arrogance once grew.
Her tender words, a beacon, brightly shone,
    Reveal the love I never truly knew.
Forgiveness late, yet heart will now confess,
Her love endured, my mother's sweet caress.

Despite the hurt and the silence, Mavis's love for her daughter remained unwavering. It was an enduring love, a beacon of hope that shone through the darkest of times. Her love was a testament to the unbreakable bond between mother and child, a love that persisted even in the face of heartache and separation. Mavis's final wish to hold Tarsha's hand one last time was a poignant reminder of the depth of her maternal love, a love that sought to bridge the distance and heal the wounds of time.

8

Hidden Connections

In the quaint coastal town of Cape May, known for its serene beaches and mysterious fogs, the story began. The fog rolled in from the sea, shrouding the town in a mystical veil each morning and evening, creating an atmosphere of both beauty and melancholy. The cobblestone streets, lined with Victorian houses painted in pastel shades, added to the town's charm and history. The sound of waves crashing against the shore was a constant, soothing background to the residents' daily lives, blending with the distant calls of seagulls and the occasional toll of a lighthouse bell.

Lila Andrews was a talented painter with a mysterious past. She had recently moved to Cape May to escape her troubles, seeking solace in its tranquil beauty. Lila was a reserved yet passionate artist, often seen with paint-splattered clothes and a distant look in her eyes, hinting at the memories she was trying to outrun. Her long auburn hair was usually tied back in a loose bun, and her eyes had a chatoyant quality, shifting in color from green to gold as the light changed, mesmerizing everyone who looked into them. Yet they reflected a world of untold stories and unhealed wounds.

Logan Cole was a charming writer, haunted by the death of his first love, who lived in Cape May. Logan was charismatic and kind, with a disarming smile that hid his deep-seated grief. He had a rugged, handsome appearance, with dark hair that fell messily over his forehead and eyes that carried the weight of lost love. He spent his days writing in a small café by the beach, drawing inspiration from the sea and its ever-changing moods. The café, with its wooden floors and walls adorned with local art, had become a sanctuary where he could pour his heart into his stories.

Lila, hoping to make a fresh start, decided to participate in a local art gallery exhibition. The gallery, a quaint building with large windows overlooking the ocean, was known for showcasing the works of both renowned and emerging artists. Its white walls were adorned with a mix of contemporary and classic pieces, creating a vibrant yet serene atmosphere. On the night of the opening, the gallery was abuzz with chatter and the clinking of glasses. Soft jazz music played in the background, mingling with the laughter and conversations of the guests. Lila stood nervously by her paintings, her heart pounding, eyes scanning the crowd.

Logan, intrigued by the new artist in town, wandered into the gallery, drawn by the allure of fresh creativity. He was instantly captivated by Lila's paintings—vivid depictions of the sea, each canvas filled with raw emotion. The colors were bold and intense, capturing the tumultuous beauty of the ocean during a storm, the gentle caress of waves at sunrise, and the haunting silence of the fog-covered shore. As he moved closer to one particular piece—a stormy seascape that seemed to mirror his own inner turmoil—he felt a presence beside him. Turning, he found himself face-to-face with Lila.

Their eyes met, and there was an immediate, inexplicable connection between them, as if their souls recognized each other from a past life. Lila's initial nervousness melted away as she met Logan's gaze, seeing in his eyes a reflection of her own hidden pain. Logan was struck by the depth of emotion in Lila's eyes, the unspoken stories that seemed to echo his own. In that moment, surrounded by the beauty of art and the gentle hum of conversation, their connection began to form, setting the stage for a love story intertwined with healing and discovery.

After their initial introduction, Logan complimented Lila on her work, and they quickly fell into an easy conversation about art and literature. The gallery's soft lighting cast a warm glow on their faces as they spoke. Lila's cheeks flushed slightly at his praise, a rare smile playing at her lips. They discovered a shared passion for expressing emotions through their respective crafts. Logan's writings often explored themes of loss and love, weaving intricate tales of human resilience, while Lila's paintings captured the haunting beauty of the sea, each brushstroke echoing her internal battles and longings.

They started spending more time together, visiting art galleries, bookshops, and cafes. The quaint bookshop, with its overstuffed shelves and the scent of aged paper, became one of their favorite haunts. They shared their favorite books, often picking out passages to read aloud to each other, voices hushed in the cozy corners of the shop. Over steaming cups of coffee in a seaside café, they discussed the nuances of their artistic expressions, finding common ground in their mutual appreciation for the beauty of the mundane and the depth of human emotion.

Lila often painted scenes inspired by Logan's stories, infusing her canvases with the raw emotions his words evoked. The paintings depicted not just the sea, but also the stormy inner landscapes they both navigated.

Their bond deepened as they inspired each other to create new works. They spent hours together, not just talking, but also creating—Logan tapping away at his typewriter, the rhythmic clacking of keys a comforting sound, while Lila stood at her easel, lost in the world of colors and forms. The sound of the waves, ever-present, provided a soothing backdrop to their creative endeavors, harmonizing with the soft murmur of their conversations.

On their six-month anniversary, following a dinner date at a seaside restaurant, Logan read a love poem he had penned for Lila, which went:

Brushstrokes Of Love

Your eyes, a light in twilight's hues,
    A canvas touched by ocean's grace,
Your laughter clears my darkest glooms,
    In you, my heart has found its place.

Beneath the stars, our spirits soar,
    Through whispered dreams, our love ignites,
Together, we shall evermore,
    Create a world of pure delights.

Your brushstrokes paint my soul anew,
    With colors bright, our love revealed,
Each moment spent, our bond renew,
    In passion's light, our hearts are healed.

As waves sing softly to the shore,
    Our love's sweet symphony unfurls,
In every kiss, I love you more,

My muse, my heart, my precious girl.

With this heartfelt poem, Logan entwined his love in verses, sealing their bond with the ink of his devotion. Moved by his words, Lila rested her head on his chest, and they sealed the night with a kiss.

One evening, as they walked along the fog-draped beach, Lila felt the weight of her secrets pressing down, a heavy burden she could no longer bear alone. The cool mist clung to their clothes as they walked hand in hand, the moonlight casting an ethereal glow on the sand, transforming the beach into a silver dreamscape. The rhythmic sound of the waves crashing against the shore created a soothing symphony, yet it did little to calm the storm brewing inside her.

She stopped, turning to face Logan, her eyes reflecting the shimmering moonlight and the deep pain she had carried for so long. "I need to tell you something," she began, her voice trembling with the intensity of her emotions. Logan squeezed her hand, silently encouraging her to continue.

Lila's gaze drifted to the horizon, where the sea and sky melded into an indistinguishable blur. "I moved to Cape May after a tragic accident in my hometown," she confessed, her voice barely above a whisper. "An event I feel responsible for." She took a deep breath, the salty air filling her lungs. "I lost my former fiancé, James, in that accident. We had quarreled a week before his death, and I was told he died in a car crash soon after." Her words hung in the air, heavy with sorrow and regret.

Tears glistened on her cheeks, mingling with the salty breeze. "The guilt has haunted me ever since," she continued, "driving me to leave my old life behind in search of peace." Each word seemed to drain her, leaving her feeling exposed and vulnerable.

Moved by Lila's vulnerability, Logan shared his own painful story. He looked into her eyes, his eyes filled with a mix of empathy and pain. "I understand more than you know," he said softly. "I write to cope with the loss of my first love, Emily, who died in a mysterious accident." He paused, the memory of Emily's death still a raw wound. "Emily was my muse, my greatest inspiration, and her sudden death left a void in my life. I moved to Cape May to escape the memories and to find solace in my writing. I figured the vastness of the Atlantic would drown out my sorrows, its view a comforting balm in my torrent of pain."

The pain was palpable in his voice, his eyes reflecting the depths of his grief. "I spent countless nights staring at a blank page, unable to capture the essence of my loss in words," he confessed. The weight of their shared sorrows formed a bridge between them, a connection forged in the crucible of their pain.

The pain of their respective losses created a deeper bond between Lila and Logan, as they found comfort in each other's understanding and shared grief. They held each other close, the sounds of the ocean a testament to the ebb and flow of life and loss. The warmth of their embrace provided a stark contrast to the cool mist enveloping them, a beacon of hope in the fog.

Later, Logan read his latest poems to Lila, his voice steady yet filled with emotion. She listened intently, her eyes reflecting the understanding and solace she found in his words. His poems, drenched in melancholic beauty, resonated deeply with her. One evening, Logan read a sonnet he had penned, which went:

Love And Loss

Beneath the twilight's gentle, fading light,
    A dance of shadows, hearts entwined as one.
Your eyes, like stars, with silent secrets greet,

Reflecting loss and love, where dreams begun.
The sea, our constant muse, its whispers cold,
  Carries the echoes of our pasts away.
Yet in its depth, new tales of love unfold,
  As waves of sorrow softly wash to gray.
With every line I pen, your tears I trace,
  Each brushstroke you create, my soul you see.
In stormy skies, your art finds soft embrace,
  And through your hues, the sun returns to me.
Together, we heal wounds that time once tore,
In love's pure light, our hearts shall ache no more.

In this small town shrouded in mystery and beauty, two souls found each other, drawn together by their shared love for art and their haunted pasts. Their journey of healing and discovery began, intertwining their lives in unexpected and profound ways.

Despite the weight of their pasts, Lila and Logan found their love growing stronger with each passing day. They spent countless hours walking along the fog-draped beaches of Cape May, visiting local galleries, and sharing intimate conversations over coffee in cozy seaside cafés. Their favorite café, with weathered wooden floors and large windows offering a perfect view of the sea, became their refuge.

Their connection deepened as they found solace in each other's presence, slowly healing the wounds left by their previous losses. They laughed together, finding joy in small moments—sharing a croissant, reading passages from their favorite books, or simply watching the sunset paint the sky with hues of orange and pink.

Lila and Logan inspired each other creatively, their combined talents flourishing in this serene setting. Logan's stories took on new layers of emotion, infused with the colors and textures of Lila's paintings. Meanwhile, Lila's art captured the essence of Logan's words, each brushstroke a testament to their shared journey.

Their love, born from the ashes of their pasts, became a testament to the healing power of connection and creativity. Each moment they shared was a step towards mending their fractured hearts. In each other, they found not just solace but a renewed sense of purpose and hope, ready to face whatever the future might bring together.

Logan introduced Lila to his favorite spots in Cape May—places that held special meaning and had been his sanctuary during times of sorrow. The old lighthouse stood tall and proud, its light cutting through the fog, a beacon of hope and guidance. They climbed to the top, where the panoramic view of the town and the endless sea took Lila's breath away.

Next, Logan took her to a secluded cove, a hidden gem known only to him. The sound of the waves gently lapping against the rocks created a peaceful ambiance, perfect for reflection and creativity. It was here that Logan often came to write, the natural beauty of the cove inspiring his words. They sat together on a large rock, the sun setting behind them, resembling molten gold spilling onto the shimmering sea.

They also visited a charming bookshop owned by a kind elderly couple, the Mastersons, who had become like family to Logan. The shop was filled with the scent of old books and fresh coffee, the creak of wooden floors adding to its cozy charm. The couple greeted them warmly, their smiles and stories a comfort to both Lila and Logan. It was a place where time seemed to slow down, allowing them to savor each moment.

In turn, Lila invited Logan into her world of colors and canvases, allowing him to watch her paint and even inspiring some of her new works. Her studio, with its large windows and view of the sea, became their creative haven. The walls were lined with her paintings, each one a testament to her emotions and experiences. Logan sat nearby, his typewriter at the ready, the rhythmic clacking of keys a comforting sound, as Lila lost herself in her art. In the midst of their work, they shared a passionate kiss while watching the ocean waves. Their connection felt as timeless and boundless as the sea before them, an unspoken promise of their shared journey ahead.

As they grew closer, they discovered a mutual appreciation for the simple joys of life. They laughed together over shared memories and inside jokes, their laughter a melody that lightened their hearts. They shared secrets in hushed tones, their trust in each other growing with every revelation. Their love was a balm for their broken hearts, mending the pieces with each tender moment they shared.

However, amidst their blossoming love, strange coincidences began to surface. One rainy afternoon, Lila was organizing her art supplies when she stumbled upon an old letter tucked inside one of her art books. The envelope, yellowed with age, was addressed to James from someone named Emily. The letter was filled with affection, hinting at a close bond between them. Curiosity piqued, Lila started to investigate further, wondering about the connection between James and Emily.

Logan, too, found unsettling clues. While rummaging through a box of Emily's old belongings in his attic, he discovered a journal filled with her thoughts and experiences. The entries mentioned a dear friend named James, whose relationship with Emily seemed to run deeper than he had ever known. The words on the pages stirred a mix of emotions in Logan, making him question what he knew about Emily's past.

Both Lila and Logan were struck by the eerie similarities in their discoveries, though they had yet to share their findings with each other. As they delved deeper into their respective pasts, they uncovered old photographs, letters, and journals that revealed connections that linked James and Emily. It became clear that their lost loved ones were childhood friends who shared a significant history, their lives intertwined like threads in a tapestry, creating a pattern that Lila and Logan had never envisioned.

On their second anniversary, Lila and Logan decided to celebrate with a romantic dinner at the Seaside Deck, a quaint oceanfront restaurant. The restaurant, with its candlelit tables and view of the moonlit ocean, provided the perfect backdrop for their celebration. The meal was exquisite, each course a delightful experience, but it was the conversation and shared glances that made the evening truly special.

After the meal, they sat by the shore, watching the moonlight dance on the waves. The gentle sound of the ocean and the cool night air created a serene atmosphere. Lila decided it was time to share her discovery with Logan. She pulled out an old photograph she found of James and a woman, both smiling brightly. The image was worn but clear, capturing a moment of happiness.

She explained that she found the picture among James' belongings and had been trying to piece together its significance. As if he had seen a ghost, Logan's eyes widened in recognition as he took the photo from her, his hands trembling slightly. "That's Emily," he said, his voice filled with a mix of shock and sorrow. "She was my first love." The revelation left them both silent, the weight of their discoveries settling over them like the fog that so often blanketed Cape May.

In that moment, they realized that their pasts were more intertwined than they ever imagined, their fates linked by the loves they lost. The pain and the mystery of their shared history deepened their bond, bringing them closer as they navigated the complexities of their intertwined lives.

Logan shared with Lila that he recently found Emily's diary, which hinted at a deep secret about her death. The entries suggested that Emily and James were involved in a car accident together, the same one that led to their deaths. The revelation that their loved ones died in the same accident was both shocking and heartbreaking. Emily's delicate handwriting described the events leading up to the fateful night, revealing a sense of foreboding that she never had the chance to escape.

As they compared notes and pieces of evidence, Lila and Logan realized that Emily and James were together on the night of the accident. The discovery deepened their connection, as they found themselves bound not only by their love but also by the intertwined fates of their lost loved ones. The diary entries were filled with intimate details and shared dreams, painting a picture of a deep bond between Emily and James that Lila and Logan hadn't fully understood until now.

Determined to uncover the full truth, Lila and Logan delved deeper into the circumstances surrounding the accident. They unearthed evidence suggesting that the crash might not have been an accident, but rather a deliberate act by someone with a grudge against James and Emily. The clues pointed to Mark Daghemmer, a prominent local figure and wealthy businessman with a long-standing vendetta against them. Old newspaper clippings and witness statements began to paint a sinister picture of Daghemmer's involvement. His relentless money-making schemes had long drawn the town's attention, as he often seemed more interested in accumulating wealth by any means possible.

Lila and Logan gathered enough evidence to confront Mark Daghemmer. They learned that Daghemmer, who had a personal and professional conflict with James, orchestrated the accident to eliminate them. Daghemmer had been trying to cover up the truth for years, using his influence and resources to keep the real story hidden. The knowledge of his malicious actions fueled their determination to seek justice.

Realizing the danger they faced, Lila and Logan decided to hire Bert Kelly, a private detective to help them gather irrefutable proof against Daghemmer. Bert was a seasoned investigator with a reputation for uncovering hidden truths. His sharp mind and keen sense of justice made him the perfect ally in their quest. They met Bert in a dimly lit diner, the smell of coffee and the low hum of conversations creating an atmosphere of covert urgency.

As Bert delved deeper into the case, he uncovered critical evidence that could expose Daghemmer's crimes. Bert's meticulous research and tenacity revealed a trail of corruption and deceit that Daghemmer had left behind. However, just as he was about to meet with Lila and Logan to share his findings, his lifeless body was discovered near a stream. It was clear he'd been murdered to keep him silent.

The scene of Bert's death was haunting. The stream, usually a peaceful place with water trickling over smooth stones, now held a macabre stillness. Bert's body lay partially submerged, his eyes staring blankly at the sky, a testament to the ruthless lengths Daghemmer would go to protect his secrets. The area was cordoned off by the police, the flashing lights of their cars reflecting off the water, casting an eerie glow over the tragic scene. Lila and Logan arrived, their hearts sinking at the sight. The loss of Bert, who had become a trusted ally and friend, weighed heavily on them.

Shaken but undeterred, Lila and Logan resolved to continue their quest for justice. They realized that their own lives were now at risk, but they were determined to honor the memories of Emily and James by exposing Daghemmer's heinous deeds. The fear in their hearts was palpable, but so was their resolve. They gathered all the evidence Bert had managed to collect, determined to finish what he started.

The journey towards justice and healing continued as they navigated the shadows cast by their pasts and confronted the present threats. Their love, now forged in the fires of shared grief and the pursuit of truth, became their greatest strength. The sound of the waves, ever-present, reminded them of the continuous flow of life, even in the face of death and danger. Together, they stood strong, ready to face whatever came next, knowing that their love and determination would guide them through the darkness.

As the evidence against Mark Daghemmer mounted, Lila and Logan realized the danger they were in. Daghemmer, desperate to keep his secrets buried, grew increasingly threatening. One fateful evening, Lila made the heart-wrenching decision to confront Daghemmer alone, hoping to protect Logan from harm.

Lila arranged a meeting with Daghemmer under the guise of negotiating silence. She drove to an isolated warehouse on the outskirts of Cape May, armed with the damning evidence and a resolve to end his reign of terror. Logan, unaware of her plan, found a note from Lila explaining her intentions and pleading with him to stay safe.

At the warehouse, Lila faced Daghemmer. The dimly lit space echoed with the sound of dripping water and the distant hum of machinery, creating an atmosphere thick with tension. Daghemmer's eyes were wild with desperation, his movements erratic as he realized the gravity of his situation. The confrontation quickly turned dangerous as Daghemmer's desperation turned to violence. Despite her bravery, Lila was tragically overpowered and fatally wounded. Her last thoughts were of Logan, hoping that her sacrifice would ensure his safety and bring justice. As she lay on the cold, hard floor, her vision blurred, and she whispered Logan's name, a tear slipping down her cheek.

The authorities, alerted by Logan who found the note and rushed to the scene, arrived in time to apprehend Daghemmer. The flashing lights of police cars illuminated the warehouse, casting long shadows that danced eerily on the walls. The officers moved swiftly, securing the area and taking Daghemmer into custody. They uncovered his involvement in the deaths of Emily, James, and Bert Kelly, in addition to Lila.

The news of Mark Daghemmer's arrest and the revelation of his heinous crimes sent shockwaves through the community. Cape May, a town known for its serene beauty and close-knit community, was rocked by the scandal. Residents gathered in small groups, whispering in disbelief about the man they had once respected and trusted. The local newspaper ran headlines detailing the shocking turn of events, and the story dominated conversations in cafés, shops, and homes.

Later, Daghemmer was sentenced to life in prison for his heinous crimes. The families of James and Emily finally got the peace they had sought for so long, knowing that justice had been served.

Logan was devastated by Lila's death. The loss of Lila felt like a cruel twist of fate, compounding his grief from losing Emily. He struggled with the emptiness left by her absence, the silence of his home a constant reminder of the love he had lost. The memories of their time together haunted him, each corner of the town holding a piece of their shared history. Yet, he found solace in knowing that Lila's actions had brought justice and peace to their loved ones. Logan immersed himself in his writing, using it as an outlet for his sorrow and a way to honor Lila's memory. His words flowed with a new depth of emotion, each sentence a tribute to her courage and love.

Determined to preserve Lila's legacy and keep her spirit alive, Logan opened an art gallery in her memory. The gallery, named "Lila's Echoes," showcased her paintings and told the story of her life, love, and ultimate sacrifice. Logan curated each exhibition with care, ensuring that Lila's passion for art and her courageous spirit continued to inspire others. The gallery became a haven for those seeking solace and inspiration. Artists, writers, and visitors from all walks of life came to see Lila's work, drawn by the poignant story of her love and bravery. Logan's own writings, dedicated to Lila, accompanied her paintings, creating a powerful narrative of love that transcended loss.

"Lila's Echoes" became more than just an art gallery; it became a beacon of hope. Logan's dedication to preserving Lila's memory touched the lives of many, reminding them that even amidst tragedy, love could create eternal echoes that resonated through time. The gallery stood as a testament to the enduring power of love and the impact of one person's courage and sacrifice.

Logan found a sense of purpose in his work, and though he carried the weight of his grief, he also felt a profound connection to Lila. Her spirit lived on in the art and stories that filled the gallery, offering comfort and inspiration to all who visited. The legacy of their love continued to shine brightly, casting a hopeful light even in the darkest of times.

Through their journey, Lila and Logan's love story became a timeless tale of resilience, sacrifice, and the enduring power of love.

9

Lacking The Will To Let Go

"I am going to marry him regardless of what you think or feel about him," Jenny declared, her voice trembling with a mixture of defiance and desperation.

Her grandmother, eyes filled with a lifetime of wisdom and worry, responded softly, "My child, I have lived long on this earth and have seen people come and go—some with good intentions and others, not so much. I tell you, that boy is no good! He is poorly raised, comes from a disreputable family, and you will never find happiness with him. Mark my words! Marriage is a lifetime commitment between two people who love each other. While you may love him dearly, he doesn't love you. I'm pleading with you not to marry him," her voice breaking, tears pooling in her eyes.

"The only reason you don't like him is that he isn't from a wealthy family," Jenny replied, her voice rising like a storm brewing on the horizon.

"No, my dear. Can't you see he is a bully, respects no one, and only loves himself?" her grandmother asked, holding back tears as her heart ached for her granddaughter.

"But I love him, don't you understand? Why can't you understand?" Jenny persisted, her voice cracking with the intensity of her emotions.

Grandma wasn't the only one opposed to Jenny and Tom's tumultuous, somewhat one-sided relationship. Jenny's entire family was disturbed by it. Her uncle, Haden, said to Jenny, "You have been like a daughter to me since childhood, and I have watched you grow into an exceptionally fine lady with consistent discipline and great morals. You have everything going for you—a good job, beauty, intelligence. However, you are about to risk it all if you marry this young man. You may love him, but he certainly does not love and respect you. He is arrogant and takes counsel from no one. Can't you see that he is using you?"

"No, Uncle, he loves me, and I plan to marry him."

Jenny's heart was like a fortress regarding her unqualified love for Tom, impenetrable by even the most rational advice or admonishment. It was as if he had her under a spell, a bewitching charm that clouded her judgment and entranced her soul. Reluctantly, to please Jenny, both her grandmother and Uncle Haden gave their blessings, their hearts heavy with unspoken fears.

Jenny had an uneasy childhood. Her father left her mother when she was seven years old, although he maintained contact with Jenny. She grew up with her mother and grandmother, who did their utmost to raise and shape her. She is intelligent, often topping her classes in school, and was a great cook, adept at teaching those who lack culinary skills the intricacies of creating a great meal. Yet, she was quite naïve when it came to matters of the heart. Tragically, Jenny lost her mother ten years ago. She was her best friend and confidante, probably the only one who could have dissuaded Jenny from marrying Tom.

Now, Jenny stood at the precipice of a decision that could shape her entire future. The love she felt for Tom was like a wildfire, fierce and consuming, but potentially destructive. Her family's warnings echoed in her mind, but the pull of her heartstrings drowned them out. As she prepared for the life-altering step of marriage, the weight of their concerns lingered, casting long shadows over her path ahead.

The memory of her mother's gentle voice and comforting embrace haunted her, a bittersweet reminder of the guidance she had lost. She longed for her mother's wisdom, a lighthouse in the stormy seas of her emotions. But now, she was adrift, navigating the tumultuous waters of love and loyalty on her own, clinging to the belief that love would conquer all.

Tom was a tall, dark man from a fractured family, the epitome of solipsism. Born from one of his father's numerous extramarital affairs, he carried the weight of a broken lineage. His haughty demeanor was matched by appalling hygiene and manners, a stark contrast to the grace and kindness that Jenny embodied. Tom's arrogance was only surpassed by his penchant for bullying others, lacking even a trace of empathy. His voracious appetite for food often saw him consuming in one sitting what most would eat over a day, a gluttony that mirrored his insatiable pride and vanity.

Jenny was like fresh spring water, pure and refreshing, while Tom was a raging fire, consuming everything in his path. Perhaps Jenny's yearning for companionship stemmed from the absence of her father and the loss of her mother. Nevertheless, Tom quickly exploited Jenny's innocence, pressuring her to prove her love for him. He took advantage of her youthful grace with his arrogance and repulsive charm, often boasting about how much control he had over her. Eventually, they married, and the problems began almost immediately.

Jenny, a dedicated pharmacist employed by a prominent pharmaceutical company, supported Tom both emotionally and financially during his period of unemployment. When Tom secured his first job, it was short-lived; he was terminated after a few months due to conflicts with management. Eventually, he landed a stable position, which revealed a shift in his behavior. No longer dependent on Jenny's income, he began returning home late, often after nights spent drinking and socializing. Despite his inebriation, Jenny would faithfully reheat his meals, though he scarcely acknowledged them. Tom's habitual floccinaucinihilipilification of his wife's efforts often made her sad and discontent, significantly affecting her morale.

The couple's relationship was further strained by Tom's mistreatment of Jenny, especially during her pregnancy. The physical and psychological abuse took a heavy toll on her, culminating in multiple miscarriages. Yet Jenny persevered and was expecting once again.

The betrayal was deepened by an incident during Jenny's pregnancy. Jenny stood in the doorway, her hands trembling as she clutched her coat. The scene before her was a visceral blow, the kind that steals the breath and numbs the mind. There, on the kitchen floor she had so lovingly cleaned just hours before, lay Tom and Janice Kelly, a former high school peer of Jenny's and the ex-wife of Tom's acquaintance, entwined in a betrayal that scorched her soul.

"Tom?" Jenny's voice was a whisper, a feeble attempt to deny the reality that sprawled before her eyes.

Tom's head snapped up, his expression morphing from shock to a sneer. "What? Surprised to see me enjoying some company?" he jeered, his words slicing through the thick silence.

Jenny's heart raced, her pulse thundering in her ears. "How could you?" she managed to choke out, the pain evident in her voice.

Janice, with a smug look, rose to her feet, smoothing her skirt. "Oh, honey, if you satisfied him, we wouldn't be here, now would we?" she taunted, her eyes gleaming with malice.

Tom stood up, brushing off his clothes with a nonchalance that stung. "You're always so busy, Jenny. Always at the doctor, always working. Did you really think I'd just wait around for you?" he snarled.

Jenny's eyes filled with tears, a mixture of anger and sorrow. "I'm carrying your child, Tom. Our daughter," she said, her voice breaking.

Tom shrugged, a cruel smirk playing on his lips. "And? That was your choice, wasn't it? I never asked for a kid."

The words were a physical force, pushing Jenny back as if she had been struck. She had endured much, but this was a new depth of cruelty.

"I loved you, Tom. I loved you with everything I had," she whispered, the finality of her realization settling in like a winter frost.

Tom's laugh was harsh, echoing off the walls. "Love? That's your problem, Jenny. You're too emotional. It's all just a game, and you played it poorly."

With those words, Tom turned his back on her, on their life together, leaving Jenny to grapple with the shards of her shattered dreams. He left

Jenny and their unborn daughter for Janice, the echoes of his betrayal lingering in the empty spaces of their once-shared home.

Meanwhile, Jenny's half-brother Jay, a compassionate man, deeply cared for his sister, whom he affectionately regarded as his "little" sibling despite their minor age difference. Their bond was a tapestry woven from shared childhood memories and mutual support, enduring despite the different fathers that shaped their lives. Jay was a steadfast protector, often stepping in as a silent guardian, providing financial assistance and essentials during Tom's unemployment. Regrettably, work commitments in Aruba prevented him from attending Jenny's wedding, but his genuine support for her never wavered.

Years ago, Jay and Tom were classmates. Jenny, Jay's sister, felt a strong connection to Tom simply because he shared classes with her brother. However, Jay, ever aware of his sister's tendency towards naivety, sternly warned her to steer clear of Tom. He cited Tom's arrogance and unwarranted self-importance as clear red flags, despite Tom's lack of notable achievements. To Jay, Tom was nothing more than an empty vessel of charm, a façade with no substance.

In a particularly intense discussion, Jay bluntly called Tom a "giant head," alluding both to his physical appearance and his inflated ego. Jenny, taking offense to this portrayal, accused Jay of jealousy. Stung by her hurtful retort, Jay vowed to withdraw from discussing her romantic affairs, still convinced that she deserved better. He often remarked that his sister had overlooked many of his accomplished and attractive friends for someone he considered unworthy.

Jay, quite perturbed by his sister's unyielding devotion to a man he knew did not truly love her, penned this poem, pouring his fears and frustrations into each line:

Blind Grasp Of Love

In love's blind grasp, you wander lost,
A heart of gold, by shadows crossed.
Your eyes, so bright, now dim with pain,
For fleeting love, you chase in vain.

His empty charm, a hollow boast,
In him you see a loving host.
Yet I, who've seen his darker shade,
Fear for your heart, so kind, betrayed.

You were the light, in childhood days,
My little star, my sister's gaze.
Now tangled in a web of lies,
I watch you fall, I hear your cries.

Oh sister, dear, why can't you see?
The truth in love, not misery.
Break free from chains, and lift your veil,
Find love that's pure, where hearts prevail.

Through this poem, Jay hoped to reach Jenny's heart, to make her see
the truth obscured by her love for Tom. His words were a heartfelt plea,
a brother's cry for his sister's happiness and well-being.

In those quiet moments of reflection, Jay's love for Jenny burned bright,
an unwavering beacon of hope and protection. He longed for the day
when she would break free from the illusions of false love and embrace
the genuine warmth and respect she truly deserved.

As the seasons changed, Jenny found herself anchored to the past, her
heart tethered to the ghost of a marriage that never was. The leaves
turned from vibrant green to the fiery hues of autumn, mirroring the
tumult within her soul. Meanwhile, Tom sailed through life's waters

with the ease of a ship in the wind, basking in the adoration of many. He seemed to float effortlessly, carried by the currents of his own charm and arrogance.

Jenny's dreams were filled with visions of a life together, a harmonious union that remained just out of reach. Her nights were haunted by images of a future that could have been, a beautiful mirage that dissolved with each morning's light. Despite Tom's cold indifference and the neglect that spilled over to their daughter, Jenny remained ensnared by the illusion of his charm. It begged the question: What magic did Tom possess that held her so captive? Love, in its labyrinthine complexity, often blurs the lines between deep affection and mere attachment, sometimes dwelling silently within the heart, unrecognized.

When fate dealt Tom a cruel hand, leaving him comatose from a neurological affliction, Jenny's resolve did not waver. She abandoned her professional duties without a second thought, rushing to his side like a moth drawn to a flame. There, amidst the sterile hum of hospital machinery, she became his unwavering sentinel, coordinating with the medical team and tending to his every need. The antiseptic smell of the hospital and the rhythmic beeping of monitors became the backdrop of her life, a testament to her unyielding devotion.

During this vigil, she crossed paths with faces from the past—Tom's former flames, including those who had once celebrated their union. Each encounter was a dagger to her heart, a bitter pill to swallow, yet Jenny's spirit did not falter. She stood tall, her love for Tom a steadfast lighthouse in the stormy sea of betrayal and heartache.

Upon his miraculous awakening, Jenny stood before Tom, a portrait of hope and forgiveness. Her eyes, still brimming with love, searched his face for any sign of recognition, any glimmer of the man she believed he could be. She extended an olive branch, an invitation to mend what had been broken and to forge a new beginning. Yet, Tom, ever the embodiment of pride and arrogance, turned away from her outstretched hand. His refusal was a silent echo of the void that had grown between them, a chasm too wide to bridge.

Tom's rejection was the final blow, shattering the last vestiges of the dream Jenny had clung to for so long. She realized that love alone could not save what was already lost. The image of her future, once so vividly painted in her mind, faded like a forgotten sunset, leaving behind the cold reality of a love unreciprocated.

In that moment, Jenny understood the true nature of her captivity. It was not Tom's charm that held her; it was her own heart, shackled by hope and blinded by love. She knew then that to heal, she had to let go, to untether herself from the ghost of what could never be. As the days grew shorter and winter's chill set in, Jenny began the arduous journey of finding herself again, of rediscovering the strength that had lain within her all along. The question remained: did she have the will to recover?

Jenny's inability to let go of the past could stem from various factors: perhaps guilt over defying her family, a desire to change Tom and validate their love to the world, or fear of loneliness after enduring a tumultuous relationship. Her mind was a labyrinth of regret and hope, each corner hiding shadows of what could have been. Despite her emotional turmoil, Jenny expertly concealed her depression, though it occasionally manifested in outbursts of frustration over her past choices. The façade of normalcy she wore was a mask, hiding the storm within.

One day in 2014, feeling the weight of her burdens too heavy to bear alone, Jenny reached out to her brother Jay, who had recently returned to the U.S. from Aruba. She needed someone to confide in, someone who had seen her through the highs and lows of life. Jay, ever the attentive sibling, was open to discussing anything except matters concerning her husband, Tom. Despite this, Jenny broached the subject, her voice trembling like a fragile leaf in the wind.

She shared her distress over the numerous warnings she'd ignored from their grandmother and Uncle Haden regarding Tom. Her eyes filled with tears as she recalled the painful argument with her grandmother, during which she had spoken harshly, leaving the elderly woman in tears. The memory of her grandmother's sorrow was a thorn in her heart, a constant reminder of her missteps.

As Jenny confessed her realization of having made a grave mistake in marrying Tom, Jay listened with a mix of shock and skepticism. His eyes narrowed as he tried to gauge her resolve, and he asked pointedly, "So, when are you divorcing him?" Jenny's silence spoke volumes. The unspoken words hung in the air, heavy with unfulfilled promises and lingering attachment. Jay surmised that despite her remorse over past actions, her feelings for Tom lingered like a persistent ghost.

In time, with the family's encouragement, Jenny sought counsel from her pastor, opening up about her depression and the loss of the love she once cherished. The guilt of not heeding her grandmother's advice and the hurt she caused while defending Tom's misdeeds weighed heavily on her, a burden too great to carry alone.

Amidst the turmoil, their daughter Emma remained an overlooked figure, a silent witness to the unraveling of her parents' relationship. A striking and determined young woman, Emma shared a special bond with her Uncle Jay. Currently immersed in her medical residency, she displayed none of her father's lack of ambition. With impressive speed, intellect, and discipline, she excelled through her academic journey, authoring two widely celebrated books with plans for a third post-medical school.

Emma had long attempted to forge a connection with her father, but his disinterest in her life was palpable. He neglected to visit during her college years and offered no financial support. Each rejection was a stab to her heart, yet she remained resolute. Eventually, Emma reached her limit and distanced herself from him. She had even urged her mother to do the same, to no avail. Jay recently remarked on Emma's resilience in handling her father's indifference, saying, "she has handled her dad's intransigence quite well."

Jenny's journey was a testament to the complexities of love and family, a mosaic of choices and consequences. Through it all, she held on to the hope that one day, she would find the strength to break free from the past and create a new future for herself and her daughter. The road ahead was uncertain, but with the support of her family and the resilience she had cultivated, Jenny knew she could face whatever challenges lay ahead.

Emma would often write poems in her spare time, pouring her emotions into the verses as a way to cope with the complexities of her family life. One evening, she sat by her window, the moon casting a silvery glow over her desk as she wrote a poem about her father's arrogance:

The Perhaps Of Paternity

Perhaps, I should beg you to be,
    A father to your kid.
Perhaps, I should pray that you'll see,
    The hurts your hubris did.

Perhaps, your ego will never,
    Let you see past your pride.
Perhaps, you will never sever,
    Those deeds that oft deride.

Perhaps, you won't share the spotlight
    With any of great mind;
Perhaps, the contrast will highlight,
    Of shallow mind, your kind.

They know not why I say perhaps;
    Like me, they don't know you.
Although unsure, say I; perhaps,
    Your hubris defines you.

The act of writing provided Emma with a measure of solace, her words a cathartic release of the pain and disappointment she felt. Each line was a testament to her resilience, a way to make sense of the emotional turmoil her father's neglect had caused.

Two years later, the inevitable happened: Tom filed for divorce from Jenny. Upon receiving the papers from the court, Jenny's hands shook as she dialed her brother, Jay, seeking his steady voice to calm her stormy heart. When he answered, she poured out her anguish, her voice cracking with the weight of her emotions.

Jay listened, his heart aching for his sister. "Sometimes one only sees murky skies, even though their sun is shining. Your sun has always been shining, yet you've allowed murky skies to dominate. His petition for divorce brings you closer to healing. So, trust in God and move on," he gently advised, his words like a balm for her wounded spirit.

Six months later, Jenny and Tom were officially divorced. The legal end to their tumultuous marriage was both a relief and a sorrow, a bittersweet conclusion to a chapter filled with hope and heartbreak. Jenny continued to receive counseling from her pastor, following Jay's wise suggestion. Each session was a step toward reclaiming her sense of self, a journey through the dark valleys of her soul towards the light of healing.

Jay, ever the supportive brother, often reflected on Jenny's progress. "I'm not sure she will ever completely let go of him, for reasons unknown to me, but with prayer and God's help, she will overcome," he mused, his faith in her resilience unwavering.

Through it all, their daughter Emma remained a pillar of strength. Her bond with Uncle Jay was a source of comfort, a reminder of the love and support that still surrounded her. Emma's focus on her medical residency was unrelenting, her achievements a beacon of hope and pride for the family.

Three years after Jenny and Tom were officially divorced, at a funeral repast attended by Jay and other family members, the air was thick with the scent of lilies and the murmur of subdued conversations. When it was time to leave, Jay passed by one of his nephews, Walker, who was chatting with Tom. Tom reached out and shook Jay's hand. Tom was almost unrecognizable, a shadow of his former self, though he still wore his traditional evil grin. Jay's eyes narrowed, and his jaw tightened as he exchanged a few words before walking away.

Later that week, Walker called his uncle, Jay, recounting that Tom had mentioned during their conversation at the repast, "Your uncle Jay is scared of me." Upon hearing the comment, Jay smiled, the corners of his mouth lifting slightly as he said, "True to form. Really true to form." The smile was tinged with a mix of bemusement and resignation, a recognition of the unchanged nature of Tom's malice.

As the seasons continued to change, Jenny, Emma, and Jay navigated their way through the aftermath of Tom's absence. The sun that Jay often spoke of began to shine more brightly in their lives, burning away the murky skies that had once obscured their vision. With each passing day, they moved closer to a future filled with hope, love, and the promise of new beginnings.

10

Melodies Of The Heart

The small coastal town of Millsboro, Delaware is a hidden gem, known for its picturesque sunsets that paint the sky in hues of orange and pink, and its serene beaches where the gentle waves whisper secrets to the shore. Emma, a passionate artist, finds endless inspiration in the town's natural beauty. The Indian River, which borders Millsboro, offers a tranquil escape for boating, fishing, and crabbing enthusiasts, its waters reflecting the ever-changing moods of the sky.

Millsboro's delightful downtown is a tapestry of charming antique stores and quaint restaurants that serve up hearty American dishes and fresh seafood, often accompanied by the soft strains of local musicians and the vibrant colors of street art. The town is a haven for those who appreciate the finer things in life, where every corner holds a story waiting to be discovered.

Emma Watson's family has called Millsboro home for over fifty years, and her heart is deeply entrenched in this quaint town. The memories of her childhood are woven into the fabric of Millsboro's streets and shores. Following her college graduation, Emma opened an art center with seed money from her parents, a testament to their unwavering support and belief in her dreams. The art center quickly became a cornerstone of the community, a place where creativity flourished, and connections were made.

Emma's success is not just measured by the thriving business she built, but by the smiles of the children who attend her art classes, the joy of the tourists who discover her gallery, and the pride of her parents who see their daughter's dreams come to life. Each day, as she walks through the town, Emma feels a profound sense of belonging and purpose, knowing that she is contributing to the vibrant tapestry of Millsboro.

Emma's closest friend is Sophie Angelino. They were classmates in high school and even shared an apartment while studying at the University of Delaware. As Emma's best friend, Sophie is a spirited and supportive confidante. Sophie runs the Nectar Café, which is owned by her older brother. She offered to manage the business as a way to prepare for her chance at establishing her own café, one she plans to open after saving enough money. The Nectar Café, with its delicious food, live music, and creative ambiance, is quite the attraction for single people looking to mingle.

On a sunny Friday afternoon in May 2010, the sun's rays hovered over the blooming flowers, casting a golden hue that signaled the blossoming of life. The air was filled with the sweet scent of freshly cut grass and the vibrant colors of spring in full bloom. Sophie and Emma were seated at a quaint café, savoring oysters and corn chowder, the aroma of the rich broth mingling with the earthy scent of the nearby flowerbeds.

The door chimed softly as Liam Helmsley, a musician with dreams of making it big, walked in. His presence seemed to draw the room's attention, a subtle magnetism that made heads turn. Emma's eyes followed Liam as he approached the counter to pick up his order. His confident stride and easy smile made him stand out, a beacon of charm amidst the everyday hustle.

As Liam walked by their table on his way out, he greeted Sophie with a playful grin. "Hello Sophistic," he joked, a playful variation on her name he often used because of her smarts and high level of cultural awareness, capturing the sophisticated nature of her spirit. His voice was smooth, like a melody that lingered in the air.

"Hello Liam," replied Sophie with a smile, her eyes twinkling with warmth. Meanwhile, Emma was spellbound, totally captivated by Liam's looks and warmth. She was in awe, her mouth so wide open that one could stick the entire contents of her plate in it. Her heart raced, each beat a drum echoing her captivation.

After he left, the ladies chatted about him on the surface, their words light and casual. Yet, beneath the veneer of their conversation, a silent understanding lingered. Their true feelings about Liam were never discussed, although it was clear that Emma was completely enraptured by him. Her eyes sparkled with a newfound light, a silent testament to the impact Liam had made.

Liam's parents had moved to Millsboro from Smyrna, Delaware several decades ago. After finishing high school, Liam decided to pursue his dreams in the music industry, frequently playing with his friends at bars, restaurants, and cafés. Sophie also liked Liam but thought she merited something more. She had higher aspirations and was unsure whether Liam's free spirit complemented her drive and dedication.

That evening, after Emma got home, she couldn't stop thinking about Liam. She recalled his chiseled jawline framing a face that exuded confidence and charm, his high cheekbones accentuating his piercing blue eyes, which seemed to hold a depth of wisdom and kindness, his thick, dark hair perfectly styled, with a few strands rebelliously falling across his forehead, adding a touch of effortless allure. She put a blank canvas on an easel and started to paint the man who had heightened every emotional string in her heart. After she was done, she stared at the painting for a while before going to bed.

The next morning, no longer able to withhold her feelings for Liam, Emma called Sophie to explain her predicament. Sophie encouraged Emma to pursue her feelings for Liam, offering her unwavering support.

Meanwhile, each morning, Alex Caruso would stop at the Nectar Café. He was quite charming and was described by a former girlfriend as having a chiseled body with well-defined lips that often curled into a warm, inviting smile, revealing a set of pearly white teeth. His smooth, tan skin glowed with health, and a subtle dimple appeared on his left cheek when he laughed, adding to his boyish charm. He was interested in more than just his regular cup of coffee; his eyes were on Sophie. In his mind, she would make a perfect wife. In a conversation with a colleague at his job, he described Sophie quite admiringly, saying, "Her presence exudes a sense of peace and stability, making those around her feel cherished and valued. She is intelligent and thoughtful, always ready to engage in meaningful conversations or offer wise advice. Her laughter is a melody that brings joy to those who hear it, and her compassionate heart is evident in her actions, always putting others before herself." Sophie started to notice Alex; however, she was hesitant to pursue a new relationship due to a past heartbreak. Yet, encouraged by Emma, Sophie decided to give Alex a chance.

About a month later, Emma decided to hold an event at the art gallery to showcase her talents. She shared the idea with her deputy, Sarah, who was excited about planning the entire event. "The showcase will include music, food, and a chance for people to meet and learn more about the talented artist, Emma Watson," she mused. Sarah, a meticulous planner, scheduled the event on a day in autumn, prior to Thanksgiving.

On the day of the showcase, the air was crisp and cool, carrying the faint scent of fallen leaves and distant woodsmoke. As the sun rose, it cast a golden glow over the Indian River, where the water reflected the vibrant hues of the season. The trees along the riverbank were a riot of color, with leaves in shades of red, orange, and yellow, creating a breathtaking tapestry against the clear blue sky. In the heart of Millsboro, the downtown area was bustling with activity. The antique stores and quaint restaurants were adorned with autumn decorations, from pumpkins and gourds to wreaths made of dried leaves and berries. The aroma of freshly baked pies and roasted coffee wafted through the air, inviting locals and visitors alike to pause and savor the moment. Sarah ensured that every single detail in her plan was executed. The art pieces, including the painting Emma had made of Liam, were set up under special lighting to accentuate their beauty. Emma was brimming with pride, scanning the galaxy of her work when suddenly she heard a voice say, "Hello, I'm Liam Helmsley. I will be providing the music tonight," extending his hand towards her. "Hello," Emma hesitated, her hands shaking, still in awe of Liam. "Glad to have you," she blurted out.

As Liam scanned the art pieces, he noticed that one of the portraits had an uncanny resemblance to him but didn't make a fuss. He complimented her work and started playing his music. That evening, Emma and Liam fell for each other, and their romance started almost immediately. Meanwhile, Alex continued his romance with Sophie, frequently spending time with her at the café, at music shows, and outdoors. On one occasion, they took a trip to New York City, and Sophie had "the time of her life," an experience she later described to her friend Emma.

Emma and Liam's relationship grew as they spent more time together, sharing dreams and creating art. In their quiet moments, he would serenade her with songs he composed specially for her, and she loved every bit of them. A year later, Liam got an opportunity to move to New York to pursue his music career. Emma was torn between supporting his dreams and fearing the distance would break them apart. Moreover, she preferred the quaintness of Millsboro to the bright lights of New York City. Seeing this new engagement as a once-in-a-lifetime opportunity, Liam left Millsboro and the blossoming love between him and Emma. During Liam's farewell party, he and Sophie shared a moment that sparked unexpected feelings between them. This was strange since they were seeing other partners. Was it was because they had known each other for quite a long time, or was there something more between them?

Liam left for New York City and did his best to stay in contact with Emma. As months passed, the distance took its toll on Emma and Liam's relationship. Misunderstandings and missed calls became frequent. Meanwhile, Sophie bought an old building in Northern New Jersey which she plans to refurbish and open a café, fulfilling her dream to own her own business. The relationship between her and Alex had been a bit rocky, but they had promised to make it work. However, the busy life of running her new café put a strain on their relationship, and as time went on, they grew further apart.

About a year later, Emma visited Liam in New York, hoping to rekindle their connection, but found him growing closer to Sophie, who had been visiting him as well. It turned out that Liam had been playing music with his friends at Sophie's café in New Jersey, and the bond between him and Sophie was growing stronger. Emma was furious at Sophie for what she considered the ultimate betrayal. On a bright day in her café in New Jersey, Emma confronted Sophie, who confessed her feelings for Liam.

"How could you do this to me?" Emma asked, her voice a mixture of anger and disappointment. "How could you? I loved you as my sister and shared my secrets with you, and this is how you repay me? I will never forgive you. You are a heartless soul!" she snarled, her eyes widening.

Sophie's eyes filled with tears as she shook her head. "Emma, I—"

"Don't," Emma interrupted, her voice trembling with emotion. "I don't want to hear your excuses. You knew how much he meant to me, and yet you still went behind my back."

Sophie took a deep breath, trying to steady her voice. "Emma, it wasn't like that. I never meant to hurt you. Liam and I... it just happened. We didn't plan for this."

Emma's face flushed with anger. "Didn't plan for this? How convenient. You expect me to believe that you just accidentally fell in love with him?"

Sophie's voice broke as she replied, "I'm so sorry, Emma. I never wanted to come between you two. But the more time we spent together, the more I realized how much I cared for him."

Emma's eyes narrowed. "Cared for him? You betrayed me, Sophie. You betrayed our friendship. How can you stand there and justify what you did?"

Sophie's tears spilled over, her voice barely a whisper. "I'm not trying to justify it. I know I hurt you, and I hate myself for it. But I can't change how I feel."

Emma's hands clenched into fists at her sides. "You've changed everything, Sophie. Our friendship, my relationship with Liam... it's all ruined because of you."

Sophie stepped forward, reaching out a hand. "Emma, please, let's talk about this. We can find a way to make things right."

Emma recoiled, her voice cold. "There's nothing to talk about. You made your choice, and now you have to live with it. I will never forgive you."

With that, Emma turned and walked out of the café, slamming the door behind her.

Upon her return home, Emma, disappointed by the actions of her lover and a once dear friend, found solace and inspiration in the beauty around her. Often she'd set up her easel near the river. The gentle rustling of leaves and the occasional call of a bird provided a soothing soundtrack as she painted. Her brushstrokes captured the essence of the season, the way the light danced on the water and the vibrant colors of the foliage.

As days progressed, the sun's warmth gave way to a cool breeze, and the sky took on a deeper, more introspective hue. The vibrant colors of autumn leaves began to fade, replaced by the muted tones of late fall. Emma found herself spending more time outdoors, seeking solace in the natural beauty that surrounded her. The gentle rustling of leaves and the occasional call of a bird provided a soothing soundtrack as she painted by the river, her brushstrokes capturing the essence of the changing season.

During this time, Alex Caruso, Sophie's former boyfriend, became a source of comfort for Emma. His presence was a balm to her wounded heart, and their bond deepened with each passing day. They would often take long walks along the riverbank, sharing stories and dreams, their conversations filled with laughter and understanding. As they spent more time together, Emma's anger over her dear friend's betrayal began to subside. She found herself drawn to Alex's warmth and kindness, his ability to make her feel cherished and valued.

Yet, as her feelings for Alex grew, so did her inner turmoil. After all, she was now in love with Alex, once a lover of the same dear friend who had betrayed her. Would it be considered a betrayal knowing that Alex was once Sophie's intimate lover? Many thoughts ran through her mind as she pondered the intricacies of love. She questioned the fairness of her own actions, wondering if she was repeating the same mistakes that had caused her so much pain.

Emma often found herself lost in thought, contemplating the complexities of human relationships. She realized that love was not always straightforward; it was a tangled web of emotions and connections. Sometimes, one cannot help but give in to their deep affections, and perhaps that's simply what Sophie did. Maybe Sophie had meant no harm, and her actions were driven by the same powerful emotions that now guided Emma's heart.

As Emma and Alex's relationship blossomed, she began to see the situation from a different perspective. She understood that love could be unpredictable and uncontrollable, and that sometimes, people were drawn together by forces beyond their control. This realization brought her a sense of peace, allowing her to forgive Sophie and move forward with her own life.

Emma's paintings during this period reflected her emotional journey. The vibrant colors and bold strokes of her earlier works gave way to softer, more introspective pieces. Her art became a mirror of her soul, capturing the beauty and complexity of her experiences. Through her creativity, she found a way to heal and embrace the new chapter of her life with Alex.

One day, as the streets of Millsboro were filled with the sounds of laughter and conversation as people gathered to enjoy the seasonal festivities, Emma and Alex were among them. The children played in piles of leaves, their joyful shouts echoing through the town, while other couples strolled hand in hand, taking in the beauty of the day.

As evening approached, the sky was painted with the rich, warm colors of sunset. The town was bathed in a soft, golden light, and the Indian River glowed with the reflections of the setting sun. There, at the edge of the river, Alex proposed to Emma, who sweetly said, "Yes, I will." It was a moment of serene beauty, a perfect end to an autumn day in Millsboro and the perfect icing on the cake of two loves whose simple pleasures of life were being celebrated and cherished.

As time went on, Liam's music career flourished, and he found inspiration in his relationship with Sophie. Their love bloomed, and they got married in Times Square in New York City. Six months later, Emma and Sophie had a difficult but honest conversation, realizing that their paths had diverged and agreed to support each other's happiness despite the initial hurt.

Later, the small coastal town of Millsboro, Delaware, was transformed into a winter wonderland for Emma and Alex's Christmas wedding. The air was crisp, and a light dusting of snow covered the ground, adding a magical touch to the already picturesque setting. The Indian River glistened under the soft winter sun, its surface reflecting the twinkling lights strung along the riverbank.

The wedding took place at Emma's art center, beautifully decorated for the occasion. Evergreen garlands adorned with red ribbons and twinkling fairy lights framed the entrance, welcoming guests into a warm and festive atmosphere. Inside, the scent of pine and cinnamon filled the air, mingling with the soft strains of holiday music.

Emma walked down the aisle in a stunning white gown, her bouquet a mix of red roses, holly, and baby's breath. Alex, looking dapper in a classic black tuxedo, waited for her at the altar, his eyes filled with love and anticipation. The ceremony was intimate, with close family and friends gathered to witness their vows. The officiant, a dear friend of the couple, spoke of love, commitment, and the joy of finding a soulmate. Emma and Alex shared their first dance as husband and wife to a classic Christmas song, their movements graceful and filled with emotion.

Sophie, Emma's best friend, gave a heartfelt toast, sharing memories and expressing her joy for the couple. Liam, now a successful musician, played a special song he wrote for the occasion, adding a personal touch to the celebration. The song went:

Tides Of Love

In this small town by the sea,
Where the sunsets set us free,
We found love in simple things,
In the joy that each day brings.

Chorus:
Tides of love, they ebb and flow,
Through the highs and through the lows.
In your hearts, a light will shine,
Guiding you through all of time.

Emma's art, a world so bright,
Alex's love, a guiding light.
Together now, your paths entwined,
A perfect match, by fate designed.

May your days be filled with laughter,
And your nights with dreams so sweet.
In each other, find your shelter,
In each other, be complete.

As the seasons come and go,
May your love forever grow.
In this town where dreams take flight,
May your hearts be ever bright.

Chorus:
Tides of love, they ebb and flow,
Through the highs and through the lows.
In your hearts, a light will shine,
Guiding you through all of time.

Outro:
So here's to love, and here's to you,
To the life you'll build anew.
With each other, hand in hand,
May your love forever stand.

As the evening progressed, guests stepped outside to enjoy a surprise snowfall. The town's Christmas lights twinkled in the background, creating a magical backdrop for photos and memories.

A year later, at Emma's art studio, her exhibit featured a painting titled "Echoes of Yesterday," capturing the essence of their intertwined lives and lost love, symbolizing acceptance and moving forward. Emma, Alex, Sophie, and Liam attended the exhibit together, their friendships and relationships stronger than ever.

11

Roots Of Belief

The Oroko tree stands majestically at the heart of the village of Axum, its presence both commanding and serene. Its trunk is thick and gnarled, with a rough, textured bark that tells tales of centuries past. The bark is a deep, earthy brown, interspersed with patches of moss and lichen, giving it an ancient, almost mystical appearance. To Trekson Tookah, this tree is not just a natural wonder but a living entity with supernatural powers.

The tree's canopy is vast and sprawling, providing ample shade to those who seek refuge beneath its branches. The leaves are a vibrant green, shimmering in the sunlight and rustling softly in the breeze. Each leaf is broad and heart-shaped, with intricate veins that catch the light, creating a delicate lacework of shadows on the ground below. Trekson believes that these leaves whisper secrets of the divine, and he often sits beneath them, feeling a sense of connection to something greater.

The branches of the Oroko tree twist and turn in a seemingly chaotic yet harmonious pattern, reaching out in all directions. Some branches are thick and sturdy, capable of supporting the weight of a person, while others are slender and flexible, swaying gently with the wind. The roots of the tree are equally impressive, sprawling out from the base and burrowing deep into the earth. They form a network of natural pathways and small alcoves, where small animals and insects find shelter. Trekson is convinced that the tree's roots are channels of mystical energy, grounding the tree's supernatural powers.

In the spring, the Oroko tree bursts into bloom, its branches adorned with clusters of delicate white flowers. The blossoms emit a sweet, subtle fragrance that fills the air, attracting bees and butterflies. As the seasons change, the flowers give way to small, round fruits that dangle from the branches. These fruits are a deep, rich purple, and are said to have medicinal properties, adding to the tree's mystical reputation. Trekson often collects these fruits, believing they hold the key to the tree's divine intervention, including a source of male fertility.

As people walked by the Oroko tree, the susurrus of its leaves created a soothing, almost magical ambiance, making them feel as though they were in another world. The belief that the Oroko tree possesses supernatural powers is reinforced by its striking appearance. At night, the tree takes on an otherworldly glow, as if illuminated from within. This ethereal light is faint but unmistakable, casting a soft, enchanting glow on the surrounding area. Villagers often speak of feeling a sense of calm and clarity when they sit beneath the Oroko tree, as if the tree itself is imparting wisdom and peace. Some villagers, believing in the tree's medicinal attributes, use its bark to make concoctions for curing diseases. Trekson, however, sees more than just a glow; he perceives the tree as a guardian spirit, watching over the village and guiding those who seek its counsel.

Trekson's unwavering belief in the Oroko tree stems from a pivotal moment in his life. One evening, as the sun faded into the night, casting a golden glow over the village of Axum, Trekson sat beneath the tree, his heart heavy with longing. He closed his eyes and prayed fervently for the tree's divine intervention. He was deeply in love with a young lady in the village and yearned for her hand in marriage. With every whispered word, he poured his heart out to the Oroko tree, believing that its supernatural powers could grant his wish.

As he sat there, the air around him seemed to hum with energy. The leaves rustled more intensely, as if responding to his plea. A gentle breeze caressed his face, carrying the sweet scent of the blossoms. Trekson felt a warmth envelop him, a comforting presence that seemed to assure him his prayers were heard. In that moment, he felt a profound connection to the Oroko tree, as if it were a bridge between the earthly and the divine.

The next day, Trekson woke up early for a trip to nearby Sambi, a rural town in the north, known for farming, to purchase fertilizer for his farm. He boarded the bus just before sunrise, reached his destination without incident, and completed his transactions with the suppliers. On his way back, the bus stopped to pick up some passengers, and there in the distance was the Oroko tree. Trekson was certain it was the same Oroko tree from his town that had traveled to Sambi. He was sure of it; same look, same height, and width. After all, he had spent a lot of time at the tree in his hometown. Upon returning home, he rushed to see that the Oroko tree was still standing. This confirmed his belief that the tree could move and that only those who believed in its mystical powers would recognize this.

Days turned into weeks, and Trekson continued his visits to the tree, each time feeling more attuned to its mystical aura. One evening, as he sat beneath the tree, the young lady he loved approached him. She had heard of his devotion to the Oroko tree and was moved by his sincerity. They spoke for hours, sharing their dreams and hopes under the tree's protective canopy. It was as if the tree itself had brought them together, weaving their destinies with its ancient roots.

Their bond grew stronger with each passing day, and soon, the village of Axum celebrated their union. The Oroko tree stood as a silent witness to their love, its branches swaying gently in approval. Trekson knew that the tree's supernatural powers had played a role in their happiness, and he vowed to honor it for the rest of his life. The Oroko tree remained a symbol of hope, love, and divine intervention, its presence a constant reminder of the magic that exists in the world.

Despite the skepticism of many villagers, Trekson's devotion to the Oroko tree inspired a small but growing group of followers who share his belief in its supernatural abilities.

One sunny afternoon, a well-known man in the village, who did not share the same devotion to the tree as its followers, was walking past the tree when he suddenly collapsed and died. Trekson and others who believed in the tree's powers spread news that the man met his fate because of his lack of reverence for the tree. Although the coroner later revealed that the man had died of a heart attack, this revelation did not dissuade the tree's followers.

Unbeknownst to Trekson, he had a condition that caused him to see the world differently. His dyslexia, undiagnosed and misunderstood, led him to misinterpret the changes around the Oroko tree. Whenever he returned to the tree and noticed objects moved or shifted, his mind interpreted these changes as evidence of the tree's movement. To him, the tree was alive, a mystical entity that responded to his presence and prayers. This belief only grew stronger with each visit, as his dyslexia continued to blur the lines between reality and his perceptions.

The villagers of Axum, however, were not convinced by Trekson's fervent tales of the Oroko tree's powers. They saw the tree as nothing more than a beautiful part of their landscape, a silent witness to their daily lives. Trekson's claims of the tree's movement and supernatural abilities were met with skepticism and mockery. The villagers laughed at his stories, making a mockery of his deep-seated beliefs. They saw him as a dreamer, lost in his own world of fantasies.

Despite the ridicule, Trekson's faith in the Oroko tree remained unshaken. He passionately shared his experiences with anyone who would listen, his eyes shining with conviction. One day, he confided in a close friend, sharing the story of how the tree had granted his wish for love. His friend, who also struggled with undiagnosed dyslexia, found resonance in Trekson's words. He, too, began to see the tree through Trekson's eyes, believing in its mystical powers and movements.

Together, Trekson and his friend began to organize a group of followers. These individuals, drawn by the passion and sincerity in Trekson's voice, started to believe in the Oroko tree's supernatural abilities. Occasionally, one or more of their followers would experience what they believed to be the tree's movement, further cementing their faith. The Oroko tree became a symbol of hope and mystery, a focal point for those who sought something beyond the ordinary in their lives.

After their marriage, Trekson and his wife, Amira, shared many heartfelt conversations under the canopy of the Oroko tree. One day, while taking a walk, Trekson said to his wife, "Amira, every time I look at this tree, I am reminded of the day you said yes. I truly believe it was the Oroko tree that brought us together."

"I know how much this tree means to you, dear. Whether it has powers or not, it has certainly given you hope and strength. And for that, I am grateful," Amira said softly.

"The villagers still mock me for my beliefs. Sometimes, it feels like they will never understand," he said dejectedly.

"My love, people often fear what they don't understand. But remember, your faith in the tree has brought you happiness. That's what matters most," Amira responded deftly.

"Sometimes, I wonder if my mind plays tricks on me. I see the tree move, but others don't. Could it be that I'm just seeing things differently?" he voiced his confusion.

"We all see the world in our own unique ways. Your perception might make things appear different, but it doesn't make your experiences any less real. Your perception is part of who you are, and I love you for it," she reassured him.

"I want to share the story of the Oroko tree with our children one day. I want them to know the magic and hope it brought into our lives," he said promisingly.

"And we will. We'll tell them about the tree, about how it brought us together, and about the power of belief. It's a beautiful story, one that deserves to be passed down," she responded, her answer a comforting balm.

"Sometimes, I just like to sit here with you, in the shade of this tree, and listen to the leaves rustle. It feels like the tree is speaking to us," he said.

"It's peaceful here. Whether it's the tree or just the wind, I feel a sense of calm and connection when we're together under its branches," she retorted approvingly.

Their conversations reflected the deep bond between Trekson and Amira, their mutual respect for each other's beliefs, and their shared hope for the future.

As they spoke, a sudden gust of wind swept through the village, causing the branches of the Oroko tree to sway dramatically. They looked up, startled by the intensity of the movement. Just then, a small, intricately carved wooden box fell from one of the higher branches, landing softly at their feet.

"What is this? It looks like it was hidden in the tree," Amira questioned, her eyes widening with curiosity and a hint of trepidation.

Trekson picked up the box, examining its delicate carvings. It was adorned with symbols and patterns that seemed ancient and mysterious, each groove telling a story of its own. With a sense of reverence, he opened the box to reveal a collection of old, yellowed letters tied together with a faded ribbon.

"These must be very old. I wonder who they belonged to," he said, his voice tinged with surprise and wonder.

They carefully untied the ribbon and began to read the letters. Each one was a love letter, written by a young man to his beloved, expressing his deepest feelings and dreams for their future together. The letters spoke of secret meetings under the Oroko tree, where the couple would share their hopes and fears away from the prying eyes of the village.

"These letters are beautiful. It's like we're reading a piece of history, a love story that was hidden away for so long," Amira said, her voice soft and filled with emotion.

As they read through the letters, they discovered that the young man had also believed in the tree's mystical powers. He wrote about how the tree had brought him and his beloved together, just as it had for Trekson and Amira. The parallels between their stories were striking, and Trekson felt a deep connection to the couple from the past.

The discovery of the letters deepened Trekson and Amira's bond with the tree. They felt as if they were part of a timeless story, one that transcended generations. The tree, with its ancient roots and sprawling branches, had witnessed countless tales of love and faith, and now, their story was woven into its history.

"It's incredible, Amira. This tree has been a witness to so many love stories, including ours. It's like it's a part of something much bigger than we ever imagined," Trekson said, his voice filled with awe and reverence.

The discovery of the letters became a significant event in their lives, reinforcing Trekson's belief in the Oroko tree's supernatural powers and deepening their bond. They decided to keep the letters safe, preserving them as a testament to the enduring power of love and the mystical presence of the Oroko tree and the magic that exists in the world.

From that day on, Trekson and Amira felt an even stronger connection to the tree, knowing that it had been a silent witness to love stories across generations.

As the belief in the Oroko tree's supernatural powers grew, so did the number of its followers. The village Chief, a pragmatic and cautious leader, began to worry about the increasing obsession with the tree. He noticed that more villagers were spending their days under the tree, praying for miracles and attributing everyday occurrences to its mystical influence. The Chief feared that this growing craze could disrupt the harmony and productivity of the village.

In a village council meeting, the Chief voiced his concerns. "The Oroko tree has become a distraction," he said. "Our people are neglecting their duties and placing too much faith in a tree. To restore order, I propose we cut down the Oroko tree." His words were met with gasps and murmurs of disapproval, but the Chief stood firm, believing it was the best course of action to quell the growing frenzy.

News of the Chief's proposal spread quickly through the village, igniting a wave of anger and unrest among the believers. They saw the tree as a sacred symbol, a source of hope and divine intervention. The thought of losing it was unbearable. Riots broke out, with believers gathering around the tree, chanting and holding signs that read, "Save the Oroko Tree!" The village, once peaceful, was now divided and tense.

The situation reached a boiling point when a large group of believers, led by Trekson, marched to the Chief's residence. They demanded an audience, their voices filled with passion and desperation. The Chief, seeing the intensity of their conviction, agreed to meet with them. In the village square, under the watchful eyes of the entire community, the confrontation took place.

Trekson stepped forward, his heart pounding. "Chief, I beg you to reconsider," he began, his voice trembling with emotion. "The Oroko tree is more than just a tree to us. It has brought hope and happiness into our lives. It granted me the love of my life, and it has given many of us a sense of purpose. Cutting it down would not only destroy a part of our heritage but also shatter the faith of those who believe in its power."

He paused, looking around at the faces of his fellow villagers. "I know not everyone shares our belief, but the tree has become a symbol of unity and hope. Please, let us find a way to coexist, to respect each other's beliefs without resorting to destruction."

The Chief, moved by Trekson's heartfelt plea, took a moment to reflect. He saw the sincerity in Trekson's eyes and the unwavering support of the believers. "I understand your feelings," the Chief said finally. "Perhaps there is a way to address both sides. We will not cut down the Oroko tree, but we will establish guidelines to ensure that our daily lives and responsibilities are not neglected."

The villagers agreed to the compromise, and a sense of relief washed over the crowd. The believers promised to respect the guidelines, and the non-believers agreed to tolerate the faith of their neighbors.

In the days that followed, Trekson often sat under the Oroko tree, reflecting on the events that had transpired. He realized that the true power of the tree lay not in its supposed supernatural abilities, but in its profound ability to bring people together, to inspire hope and unity. He understood that belief, whether in a tree, a symbol, or in each other, had the power to transform lives and communities.

The Oroko tree became a metaphor for the myriad of beliefs that shape societies. Just as the tree had united the villagers of Axum, symbols and beliefs across the world serve to bring people together, providing a sense of purpose and communal identity. Whether it is a revered monument, a flag, a religious symbol, or a cultural tradition, these elements hold the power to inspire collective action, resilience, and shared values.

Trekson's journey taught him the importance of understanding and compassion, of respecting different perspectives and finding common ground. He saw how deeply held beliefs, even those rooted in myth, could foster a sense of belonging and motivate positive change. The Oroko tree stood tall and proud in the heart of Axum, a testament to the enduring power of belief and the strength of community.

In the end, it wasn't the physical attributes of the Oroko tree that mattered, but what it represented: unity, hope, and the transformative power of collective faith. The tree reminded Trekson and the villagers that by embracing and respecting each other's beliefs, they could build a stronger, more cohesive society. It underscored the idea that in every community, there is something or someone that brings people together, ignites their spirit, and propels them toward a common goal.

Through this metaphor, the Oroko tree highlighted a universal truth: that the symbols and beliefs we hold dear can profoundly influence the fabric of our societies, guiding us through challenges and celebrating our shared human experience. The tree's legacy became a beacon of hope and unity, inspiring future generations to cherish the power of belief and the strength found in community.

Throughout the entire ordeal, a lecturer named Samson Arabe at a nearby university investigated the myths surrounding the Oroko tree. He discovered that while the tree's roots might have some medicinal uses, there was no evidence to support the belief that the tree could move. In fact, the tree that Trekson saw in Sambi was simply another tree of the same species growing in that part of the country. Samson also found that the myths about the tree had been passed down from one generation to another, reinforcing the belief in the tree's supernatural abilities. Not wanting to shatter the hope and joy that the tree brought to its followers, he chose to keep his findings to himself. Instead, he wrote a poem to capture the drama and mystique surrounding the tree:

The Legend Of The Oroko Tree

In Axum's heart, where legends grow,
   Stands the Oroko tree, a tale.
Beneath its boughs, young Trekson's woe,
   For love to bloom, his heart set sail.

The leaves would dance, the breeze would sing,
   A promise of the magic near.
In Sambi's fields, another spring,
   A twin in form, yet not so clear.

Yet myths endure, from old to new,
   A sacred bond, a faith so true.
For in their hearts, the tree did move,
   A symbol of the love they knew.

For sometimes faith, though blind it seems,
   Can light the path of lovers' dreams.
And so Oroko stands, a guide,
   In every heart where love abides.

12

Scars Of Tradition

The continent of Africa, with its breathtaking landscapes and abundant resources, still lags behind its counterparts—Europe, Asia, and the rest. The reasons for this disparity are well-documented: the scars of slavery, the wounds of colonialism, the chains of imperialism, and the turbulent political climates within African nations. Yet, despite these profound impacts, many Africans have clung tenaciously to their culture, those cherished practices and traditions passed down through generations. Some argue that this adherence has stifled potential, while others believe it has preserved a rich heritage that might otherwise have been obliterated by colonial forces eager to impose their own cultures.

The adherence to African traditions profoundly shapes the lives of its people, for better or worse. The role of women, often relegated to subordinates in many relationships, has long held them back, despite their proven capabilities. Their roles are frequently reduced to childbearing and catering to their husbands' whims. Even educated women are haunted by the specter of male domination, expected to cook, maintain their homes, and care for children, even as they work as hard or even harder than their husbands. This pervasive expectation hangs over them like an unshakeable shadow, darkening their potential.

In modern societies, parents are expected to raise their children and then let them forge their own paths. Yet, in many African cultures, children are seen as investments, akin to retirement accounts to be cashed in during old age, or social safety nets for their parents during their later years. Every piece of guidance, every instruction subtly reinforces this notion, especially for young women and some men. In some African societies, it is considered taboo to defy one's parents, whether or not the advice or expectation is contrary to the interests of the children.

Some parents even instruct their daughters to bring their husbands' earnings back to their families. This creates a dichotomy in African marriages, with parents often ending up in the same households as their children, seeking to exert control. This is a recipe for conflict, as parents who once ruled their own households must adjust to being subordinates in their children's homes—a difficult transition, especially when cultural differences between the husband's and wife's families come into play. This struggle is akin to a vine, once free to grow, now being forced into the confines of a small pot, its roots tangled and stifled.

Take Sulay Sulaimon, for instance, a man from West Africa who married Yele, a woman from the same region. They met while studying at the University of Texas in Austin. Under pressure from her parents, Yele brought them to live with her family in Texas. It wasn't long before problems started to rain in their household. Yele's mother, who had long obeyed her own husband's every command based on their long-held traditions, now criticized her son-in-law at every turn. The very behaviors she had accepted from her husband, she now told her daughter to reject. It was a lesson in contradictions. She couldn't see that her daughter's heart belonged to the man she loved, not to her parents. Her criticism was like a relentless storm, wearing away at the foundation of Sulay and Yele's marriage.

One Sunday evening, after dinner, as his in-laws retreated to their room, the weight of their presence bore down on Sulay like a heavy shroud. The atmosphere was thick with unspoken tensions, each breath a struggle under the oppressive expectations. Unable to endure the constant criticism and disrespect, he pleaded with his wife to consider renting a house for her parents. He explained that this would give them a chance to build a future for their own family, a future filled with love and affection for their children. He even offered to share the expenses, his voice tinged with desperation and hope. But Yele refused. "I cannot have my parents living away from us. It is against our tradition, and you know it," she remarked, pointing a finger at him, her face stern and unyielding. Her words were like cold iron, unbending and final. Sulay's pleas fell on deaf ears, and his desire to build a life free from in-law interference went unheeded.

Yele's unwavering commitment to her parents' expectations led to a bitter divorce. The indoctrination she had endured as a child under her parents' tutelage came at the expense of her happiness. She later married another man suggested by her parents, but recently confided, "I regret my decision to leave my former husband. I wish I had listened to him and supported his plan for our lives. He truly loved me, and I miss his affection. I cannot say the same about my current husband." Her regret was like a lingering shadow, a constant reminder of the love and happiness she had forfeited.

In many instances, the influence of African parents on their children is far from subtle. Take the tale of Jane Johnson, a bright young woman from West Africa. Her parents had poured their hard-earned savings into her education, sending her off to Great Britain with dreams of a bright future. Little did they know, their plans for Jane would soon be challenged.

While in college, Jane met Jesse Mathenge, a charming gentleman from East Africa. Jesse was everything Jane had ever dreamed of—sweet, loving, and devoted. One evening, beneath the twilight sky in a lush campus garden, Jesse proposed. The garden was a living symphony, with vibrant flowers in full bloom and the intoxicating scent of jasmine dancing on the breeze. The stars above twinkled as if to bless the moment, casting a gentle glow on the couple's beaming faces. It was the happiest day of Jane's life, and she couldn't wait to share the joyous news with her parents.

The next morning, as the sun's first rays painted the skies, Jane called her father. Her heart swelled with happiness as she shared her engagement news, but her father's response was cold and calculating, like a courtroom judge weighing evidence. He questioned Jesse's background and status with relentless precision. Jane's descriptions of Jesse's sweetness and love fell flat, failing to sway her father. In his eyes, Jesse was not good enough. When her mother joined the call, she reminded Jane of the sacrifices they had made for her education and vehemently opposed the marriage. Defiantly, Jane declared, "I will marry him." Her mother's ominous reply, "Mark my words. If you marry him, you will never be happy," hung heavy in the air.

A few months later, with graduation on the horizon, Jane and Jesse moved into an off-campus apartment. Their home was filled with laughter and love, the walls adorned with reminders of their shared dreams. But their happiness was short-lived. Jesse fell gravely ill and was admitted to the intensive care unit. Jane stayed by his side, holding his hand as he slipped into a coma and passed away. The sterile hospital room, once filled with the hum of machines, now echoed with the silence of profound loss.

Heartbroken, Jane called her parents, seeking comfort. Her father answered but quickly handed the phone to her mother. After Jane tearfully recounted her sorrow, her mother coldly replied, "Didn't I tell you that you'd never be happy with him? Focus on finishing your studies. From now on, you will do as I tell you." Jane was shattered. The lack of empathy from her parents added a chilling sting to her grief.

Despite her heartbreak, Jane completed her studies and secured a job in the US. In time, she met George, a handsome and successful man from West Africa. On their second date, as candlelight flickered softly, Jane expressed her longing for her parents' approval. George, a man of integrity, vowed to earn their acceptance and prove his love for Jane. However, he underestimated the powerful influence Jane's parents wielded over her.

George and Jane's wedding was a fairytale affair on a warm summer day. The sun bathed the world in a golden glow, and the air was fragrant with blooming flowers. The church, adorned with white lilies and roses, echoed with the harmonious notes of a choir. Jane, radiant in a flowing white gown, walked down the aisle, while George's eyes glistened with tears of joy.

Their reception was a scene from a dream, with twinkling lights and elegantly set tables. Guests mingled, laughter and music filling the air. Amidst the celebration, tension crackled like a live wire as Jane's mother confronted her husband, catching him flirting with an old flame. George, witnessing the spectacle, questioned whether he had made the right choice in joining this family.

Despite the challenges, George loved Jane deeply and did everything to make her happy. He cooked dinners that filled their home with the comforting aroma of home-cooked meals and took care of the house while Jane worked. Their love was a delicate dance of give and take. But soon, Jane's mother began to interfere, calling constantly with "advice" that often pulled Jane away from her own interests. Jane feared her mother's supernatural influence, convinced that her mother's power had a hand in Jesse's tragic demise.

Their marriage became a battlefield of love and control, with Jane caught in the middle. The once happy home was now filled with tension, and George struggled to navigate the web of influence that Jane's parents had woven. Their love, once a beacon of hope, now flickered like a candle in the wind, threatened by the shadows of the past.

During Mrs. Johnson's visits to their home, George did everything in his power to ensure she was comfortable. He responded to her every request, whether it was running errands or preparing her favorite dishes. He even acted as her chaperone on visits to local attractions, making sure she experienced all the beauty and culture their area had to offer. George was the perfect host, but he could see how his mother-in-law's presence influenced his wife. Jane's adoration of her mother was palpable, but it went beyond respect—it was tinged with fear. She was careful to avoid anything that might arouse her mother's wrath, a shadow that loomed over their marriage.

George, who typically poured his heart into love poems for his wife, once wrote about the strain Mrs. Johnson placed on their relationship. The poem, titled "The Shadow's Whisper," reflected his feelings:

The Shadow's Whisper

In our dear home, where love should bloom,
A muted echo, casting gloom.
Her words, though soft, disrupt our peace,
Turning our joys into unease.

She questions choices, perturbs space,
Her presence felt in every place.
My dearest, torn between two loves,
Struggles as the grim tension grows.

In quiet times, we find our way,
Holding on tightly, come what may.
Our love, a beacon in the night,
Guiding us through the shadow's blight.

For in the end, our love will stand,
Together, we'll reclaim our land.
Building love's walls where shadows fade,
In our dear hearts, a home we've made.

Unfortunately, Jane shared this poem with her mother, who saw it as an affront to her pride. Quietly, she vowed to show George who was in control.

Mrs. Johnson soon convinced Jane that George wasn't the right man for her, primarily because she couldn't bend him to her will. George, loving, principled, and firm, did not yield to Mrs. Johnson's whims and influences, much to her dissatisfaction. Her ambitions, like sandcastles crumbling against a relentless tide, were thwarted by George's steadfastness. Despite all George had done for Jane—the love, care, and concern he showed—Jane divorced him on her mother's advice. "I know my mother's capability. I have no desire to cross her," Jane told George. She ended up marrying a cab driver who was easily manipulated by her mother, enduring her influence without protest. George was left heartbroken, a casualty of his mother-in-law's machinations.

In another poignant story, Ade, a man from Africa, married Francine, a young lady from his home country, and they settled in the US. While raising three children, Ade sponsored Francine's parents and siblings to join them in America, lifting them out of dire straits. Initially, things went well. The in-laws helped with the kids while Ade and Francine worked, and their home was filled with laughter and warmth. To meet the financial demands of his in-laws, Ade picked up an additional job, often working late into the night.

But soon, the harmony was shattered. The in-laws' expectations grew, and despite all Ade had done for them, they were dissatisfied. Their once harmonious home became a battleground of arguments and misunderstandings. The love that had anchored their lives now felt like a distant memory, lost in the waves of discord.

One evening, Francine left her phone on the kitchen island, bathed in the soft glow of the evening light. Ade picked it up and discovered a lewd text from Francine's former boyfriend, a man close to Francine's father, Tom. Ade's heart sank as a wave of anger and devastation washed over him. He confronted his in-laws, his voice trembling with emotion. Unbeknownst to Ade, Tom was aware of the clandestine relationship.

The house erupted with raised voices and accusations. Ade and Francine blamed each other for the rift in their marriage. Tom, his voice cutting through the tension like a blade, said, "What is the issue here? This is no big deal because they've known each other since childhood."

Ade, dejected, asked, "So you knew about this and approve of it?"

Tom replied sarcastically, "Perhaps if you had shown love and respect to your in-laws, your life would be different."

Ade's voice rose, filled with frustration and hurt. "Love and respect? I delivered you from poverty, loved and cared for your daughter and your children, and this is how you repay me?"

That same year, Francine moved out of their marital home, leaving Ade to care for their kids. The house, once filled with the sounds of family life, now echoed with silence. Since her departure, Francine rekindled her relationship with her ex-boyfriend, the man her father preferred. Moreover, she was seen with another ex-boyfriend, who also had close ties with her dad. A family friend recently observed that Tom only sought to comfort himself through the means of others, including his daughter's boyfriends. He cared not for the well-being of his children. The family friend dubbed Tom a pimp!

Lest one should think that African women are the only ones yielding or succumbing to the whims of their parents, consider the life of Turay, a friend of mine from Guinea. He was raised mostly by his mother, as his dad had to leave their village in search of employment. After graduating from college in Guinea, Turay gained a scholarship to study in France, which had controlled Guinea during the colonial era. Later, Turay emigrated to the US, where he met and married Marie, a lady from the Ivory Coast, also a former French colony. Their marriage was one of much love and joy. I admired their passion for life, the quality time they spent together, the affection they displayed at public gatherings and their plans for the future, which included building an orphanage in Africa as a way of giving back to their homeland.

Their detailed plans were derailed from the day Turay's mum joined them in the US. Jardine, Turay's mum, always wore a scowl. Even on the most pleasant day, with the sun at its peak and not a cloud in the sky, the best one could expect from her was a neutral expression; otherwise, she wore her scowl as a badge of honor. Beneath this scowl lay a woman disturbed. Her eyes, dark and piercing, seemed to hold a storm of unspoken grievances, like a tempest waiting to be unleashed.

One day, after Turay and Marie returned home from a hard day's work, Jardine scolded them for abandoning their African roots. The house, usually filled with the comforting hum of daily life, now echoed with her sharp words. When Marie inquired about her accusation, Jardine replied that they were "too American." When Marie pressed her for an explanation, Jardine, with her well-worn scowl, said, "You no longer wear African garb, you have stopped cooking African dishes, and when you do cook them, they do not taste as great like they do in our village, and your child cannot speak the language of our village." Marie was aghast, her face flushing with a mix of anger and disbelief. She wanted to scream, but her husband stepped in. Seeking not to anger his mother, he agreed with her that perhaps they had become too Americanized, bending with the wind of her displeasure.

One evening, as the sun set, draping their home in the long fingers of encroaching shadows, Turay's mom asked him a shocking question: whether Marie satisfied him sexually in bed. The room fell silent, the air thick with tension. Marie walked in on their conversation, her eyes blazing with fury and her hands trembling. She was livid at Jardine for interfering in their marital affairs. Turay sided with his mom, explaining to his wife that his mom was only asking out of concern. This incident, along with others that intruded into the couple's privacy, led Marie to request that her husband send his mom back to Africa. In her opinion, Jardine, after years of being subjugated to her husband's wishes, sought to assert control, a power that had eluded her for many years. She was like a seedling frozen in the snow, seeking to burst out in the spring. Marie was firm in her conviction that Jardine had overstayed her welcome.

Turay refused to honor his wife's request, and after many years of marriage, Marie could no longer endure the problems created by Jardine and Turay's lack of spine to stand up to his mother. Marie retorted, "He has become worse than a mama's boy. He might as well marry his mother and be happy for the rest of his life. He has lost his charm and lost his way. Therefore, he has lost me." Her voice was filled with a mixture of sorrow and resolve. A few months later, Marie filed for divorce from Turay.

Prior to their divorce being final, Turay lost his mother after a brief illness. The grief of losing her was compounded by the realization of his failing marriage. He tried to reconcile with Marie, but sadly it was too late. She had moved on, her heart hardened by the years of conflict.

She saw him not as the man she once knew and wasn't willing to take a chance again.

Some argue that there are significant benefits to African parents preparing their children for the challenges of future relationships. They point to several instances where, due to their parents' training, men and women remain in their marriages, regardless of their personal happiness and fulfillment. For example, some couples stay with their partners despite infidelity, citing their parents' traditions.

A friend of my brother, who lives in Virginia, has been married to his wife for over fifteen years. During their life together, he has fathered two children with another woman outside their marriage. Although she is aware of her husband's indiscretions, his wife has vowed never to leave him, citing her upbringing and traditions.

To be fair, there are many relationships involving African parents that have withstood the test of time. However, the influence of some African parents on their children continues to impact their lives. Their stories paint a vivid picture of the complexities and emotional turmoil that arise when traditional expectations clash with modern aspirations. The imagery of blooming gardens, twilight proposals, and sunlit days contrasts sharply with the shadows of manipulation, betrayal, and cultural conflict. Through it all, the young Africans grapple with love, loyalty, and the desire for autonomy, their lives a testament to the enduring impact of familial influence.

I wrote this poem to capture the impact of African traditions on people's lives:

Tradition's Embrace

In ancient lands, where time stands still,
Traditions weave their threads of will.
They hold us close, like mother's hand,
Guide us through life, in world so grand.

Tradition's beacon, bright at night,
Light up our path, with wisdom's might.
Binds to our roots, a lineage strong,
A tune of custom, sacred song.

In festivals and rites, in dances free,
It breathes its life, in every tree.
Drives us to honor, cherish, care,
Revere in every whispered prayer.

Yet, in its shadows, casts a pall,
A weight; a silent, heavy thrall.
It binds with chains, the mind confined,
A prison of progress maligned.

In its dear name, dreams oft are stilled,
Voices silenced, goals unfulfilled.
The roles we play, the masks we wear,
Can stifle will, make us unfair.

Its every light, a shadow cast,
A dance of joy and sorrows past.
Its sword, both blessing and a curse,
Of love and struggle in each verse.

Children do not choose to be born; it is the parents' duty to nurture and care for them so they can thrive and support future generations. African children should not feel constrained by traditions that limit their freedom, marriage prospects, and potential in order to repay their parents. Parents should not have children with the expectation that they will be repaid for their efforts in their later years.

The stories of Jane, George, Ade, Francine, Turay, and Marie illustrate the deep and lasting scars that can result from adhering to traditional African expectations at the whim of their parents. The lives of these individuals were profoundly impacted by the weight of family influence, often leading to heartache and strained relationships. While the children often sought to satisfy their parents' desires, they found themselves trapped in a web of manipulation and control, unable to forge their own paths.

The pressure to conform to their parents' wishes often came at the cost of personal happiness and fulfillment. The influence of parents, sometimes well-meaning but misguided, can steer their children into decisions that ultimately hurt their lives. The manipulation and control exerted by parents for their own gain create a legacy of emotional turmoil that is hard to erase.

These stories paint a vivid picture of the complexities and emotional struggles that arise when traditional expectations clash with individual aspirations. The scars left by these experiences serve as a poignant reminder of the profound need for a delicate balance between honoring cultural traditions and allowing children the freedom to pursue their own dreams and happiness. The journey to self-discovery and fulfillment should be guided by love, support, and mutual respect, rather than the heavy hand of parental control. In the end, it is this balance that can lead to a legacy of mutual understanding and enduring bonds, where both parents and children can find true contentment.

13

Snow Ville's Christmas Miracle

Nestled in a valley surrounded by snow-capped mountains, the small town of Snow Ville looked like it had been plucked straight out of a Christmas card. Each December, the town transformed into a winter wonderland, with twinkling lights adorning every tree and lamppost. The air was filled with the scent of pine and cinnamon, the aroma from nearby bakeries and the sound of carolers singing in harmony echoed through the streets. Snow Ville's charm lay in its simplicity and the warmth of its community, where everyone knew each other by name and greeted each other with smiles and holiday cheer.

A kind-hearted single mother, Emma Michelson worked as the town of Snow Ville's librarian. She had a gentle demeanor and a smile that could light up the darkest of days. Her love for books was only surpassed by her love for her son, Lucas. Emma's eyes sparkled with a quiet strength, and her laughter was a soothing melody that brought comfort to those around her. She wore her chestnut hair in a loose bun, often adorned with a festive ribbon, and her attire was always cozy and inviting, much like her personality. Readers who frequently visit the library consider Emma a gem, a special soul with the mind and demeanor of an archaeologist, often searching for more knowledge when others have given up.

At eight years old, Lucas was a bundle of curiosity and imagination. His bright blue eyes were always wide with wonder, and his cheeks were perpetually rosy from the cold. Lucas had an insatiable appetite for adventure, often found with his nose buried in a book or exploring the nooks and crannies of Snow Ville. He had a knack for finding joy in the simplest things, whether it was building a snowman or discovering a hidden path in the woods. His laughter was infectious, and his boundless energy brought life to every corner of the town.

Living about half a mile from the Michelson's home in a quaint, ivy-covered cottage at the edge of town is Mr. Edward Thompson, an elderly man with a mysterious past. His silver hair and weathered face told tales of a life filled with both joy and sorrow. He was often seen tending to his garden, though he rarely ventured beyond his property. The townspeople spoke of him in hushed tones, curious about the secrets he kept. Despite his reclusive nature, there was a kindness in his eyes that hinted at a heart full of untold stories. Mr. Thompson's presence was like the first snowfall of the season—quiet, yet profoundly impactful.

One chilly afternoon, as snowflakes danced outside their window, Emma and Lucas decided to venture into the attic to retrieve their Christmas decorations. The attic was a treasure trove of memories, filled with old trunks and forgotten keepsakes. As they rummaged through the dusty boxes, Lucas's eyes lit up when he found a particularly old and ornate box tucked away in a corner.

"Look, Mom! What's this?" Lucas exclaimed, his voice echoing in the attic's stillness.

Emma brushed off the dust and carefully opened the box. Inside, they found a collection of vintage Christmas ornaments, each one more beautiful than the last. But what caught their attention was a beautifully crafted, antique snow globe. It was unlike any they had seen before, with intricate details and a serene winter scene inside with a horse.

As Lucas gently shook the snow globe, they noticed something unusual—a small latch at the base. With a click, the hidden compartment opened, revealing a yellowed envelope. Emma's heart skipped a beat as she read the faded handwriting: "To Edward Thompson."

Lucas's curiosity was piqued. "Who's Edward Thompson, Mom?"

Emma explained that Mr. Thompson was their elderly neighbor, a man shrouded in mystery. Lucas, ever the adventurer, insisted they deliver the letter to him. Emma agreed, sensing that this could be the start of something special.

They bundled up and made their way to Mr. Thompson's cottage. The path was lined with snow-covered trees, and the air was crisp and filled with the scent of pine. When they arrived, Mr. Thompson answered the door, his eyes widening in surprise at the sight of the letter.

"May we come in?" Emma asked gently.

Mr. Thompson nodded, his voice barely a whisper. "Of course."

Inside, the cottage was warm and inviting, filled with the soft glow of a crackling fire. Mr. Thompson carefully opened the letter, his hands trembling. As he read, tears welled up in his eyes. He looked at Emma and Lucas, his voice choked with emotion.

"This letter... it's from an old friend during the war," he began. "I thought I'd never hear from them again."

Over the next few weeks, Emma and Lucas visited Mr. Thompson regularly. He shared stories of his youth, revealing that he was once a talented musician. He spoke of the war, the family he lost, and the music that had once brought him joy. His eyes would light up as he recounted the melodies he used to play, but there was always a shadow of sorrow, a reminder of the life he had left behind.

Through these visits, a bond formed between them. Mr. Thompson found solace in their company, and Emma and Lucas discovered a deeper connection to their own history. The snow globe, with its hidden letter, had not only unlocked a secret but also opened the door to healing and friendship.

One snowy evening, as Lucas was admiring the snow globe once more, he noticed something peculiar. The base of the globe had a small, almost invisible latch that he hadn't seen before. With a sense of excitement, he carefully opened it, revealing another hidden compartment. Inside, there was a second letter, this one addressed to Emma's late grandmother, Margaret.

"Mom, look! There's another letter!" Lucas exclaimed, his eyes wide with wonder.

Emma took the letter, her heart pounding with curiosity. She gently unfolded the delicate paper, revealing a message written in elegant handwriting as the first. As she read, her eyes filled with tears.

"Dearest Margaret," the letter began, "I hope this letter finds you well. The war has kept us apart for far too long, and my heart aches for the day we can be together again. I dream of the life we could have had, the music we could have shared. Until then, know that you are always in my thoughts and prayers. With all my love, Edward."

Emma's hands trembled as she finished reading. "Edward… Mr. Thompson," she whispered, the realization dawning on her.

The next day, Emma and Lucas visited Mr. Thompson, the letter clutched tightly in Emma's hand. When they arrived, Mr. Thompson welcomed them with a warm smile, but his expression changed when he saw the letter.

"Mr. Thompson, we found this in the snow globe," Emma said softly, handing him the letter.

Mr. Thompson's eyes widened as he recognized the handwriting. He read the letter in silence, his face a mixture of shock and sorrow. Tears streamed down his cheeks as he looked up at Emma.

"Margaret was your grandmother?" he asked, his voice breaking.

Emma nodded, her own eyes filled with tears. "Yes, she was. She never spoke much about the war, but she always kept this snow globe close."

Mr. Thompson took a deep breath, his voice trembling as he began to speak. "Margaret and I were deeply in love during the war. We planned to marry once it was over, but circumstances tore us apart. I was sent on a mission, and when I returned, she was gone. I searched for her, but I never found out what happened."

Emma listened, her heart aching for the love story that had been lost to time. "She must have loved you very much to keep this snow globe all these years," she said gently.

Mr. Thompson nodded, a sad smile on his face. "I never stopped loving her. Knowing that she kept this snow globe gives me some peace. Thank you for bringing this to me."

The revelation brought Emma and Mr. Thompson even closer, their shared history creating a bond that transcended generations. As they sat together, sharing stories and memories, the snow globe sat on the table between them, a symbol of love that had endured despite the odds.

Meanwhile, a young girl named Lily, a close friend of Lucas who attended the same school and lived down the street, lost her beloved horse, Bella. The town rallied together, organizing search parties to scour every corner of the town and the surrounding mountainsides for weeks, but Bella remained missing. Two years, prior, the horse had been a cherished Christmas gift from Lily's grandmother, making the loss even more poignant. Understandably, Lily was heartbroken, yet she never lost hope that Bella would return.

As Christmas approached, Emma and Lucas decided to organize a special concert in the town square, hoping to uplift the community's spirits. They knew the highlight of the event would be Mr. Thompson playing his violin, something he hadn't done in decades. With a mix of excitement and nervousness, they approached him with the idea.

"Mr. Thompson, would you play your violin at the Christmas concert?" Lucas asked, his eyes shining with hope.

Mr. Thompson hesitated, his hands trembling slightly. "I haven't played in so long... I'm not sure I can."

Emma placed a reassuring hand on his shoulder. "You can do it. Your music is a gift, and it would mean so much to everyone, especially to us."

Moved by their encouragement, Mr. Thompson agreed. The news of the concert spread quickly, and the townspeople eagerly anticipated the event.

On a cold Saturday, Lucas sat on Santa's lap at the town's center. "Hello, young man. What is your name?" Stetson Klausen, playing the role of Santa, asked Lucas.

"My name is Lucas," the little boy said.

"And what would you like for Christmas, Lucas?" Santa asked.

"Well, this year, I have a friend, Lily who lost her horse, Bella, and I would like nothing more than for her to get Bella back," Lucas said earnestly.

Shocked by the boy's request, Santa asked, "Is that all you want for Christmas?"

"Lily is my dear friend, and I will be happy if Santa can make her happy for Christmas by bringing back her horse," Lucas pleaded.

"Well, I'll see what I can do for you, Lucas," Santa said, admiring the boy's humility and kind heart. When Emma returned to pick Lucas up, Santa said to her, "Your son is a remarkable young man with a kind heart. You ought to be proud of him."

"Thank you for your kind words, Santa," Emma said, brimming with pride.

That evening, when Stetson Klausen returned home to his wife, he told her about his encounter with Lucas, how the boy had declined to ask for anything for himself, but wished only for Bella to return to Lily. "I have never met a kid with such humility, such selflessness," he said. "We must do everything to find Bella. Lily needs Bella for Christmas!" he urged.

That same evening, Lucas retrieved the snow globe. As he stared at the horse at the center of the globe, he thought about Bella and said a prayer. "Dear God, please let Bella return home to Lily. Let your stars shine bright and guide Bella home for Christmas day. Thank you." As he finished his prayer, there was a sparkle in the globe, perhaps a sign that his prayers will be answered.

On the night of the concert, the town square was transformed into a magical scene, with twinkling lights, a towering Christmas tree, and the scent of hot cocoa filling the air. As the concert began, the townspeople gathered, their faces glowing with anticipation. Emma and Lucas stood by Mr. Thompson's side, offering him support as he took the stage. The crowd fell silent as he lifted his violin and began to play.

The melody that filled the air was hauntingly beautiful, a piece Mr. Thompson had composed for Margaret all those years ago. The notes seemed to carry the weight of his love and longing, weaving a tapestry of emotion that touched the hearts of everyone present. Tears streamed down the faces of the townspeople as they listened, moved by the depth of feeling in the music.

The concert rekindled the Christmas spirit in Snow Ville, bringing the community closer together. Mr. Thompson found peace and closure through the music, his heart finally healing from the wounds of the past. The friendship he had formed with Emma and Lucas became a source of joy and comfort, filling the void that had once been in his life.

As the Christmas concert in the town square drew to a close, the townspeople were filled with a sense of joy and unity. People were hugging each other. Lucas gave Lily a hug and reassured her that Bella would return. He said, "Santa promised that Bella will be back." Just as everyone continued mingling and thought the night couldn't get any more magical, a commotion arose near the edge of the square.

Lily ran towards the base of the mountainside and suddenly cried out in delight. "Bella! It's Bella!" she exclaimed, pointing towards the snowy path leading into town.

The townspeople turned to see the beautiful chestnut horse trotting towards them, her mane glistening under the twinkling lights. The sight of her now, returning felt like a miracle.

Lily ran to Bella, tears of joy streaming down her face as she embraced her beloved horse. The townspeople cheered, their hearts warmed by this unexpected reunion. Mr. Thompson, who had been watching from the stage, smiled and began to play a joyful tune on his violin, celebrating the miraculous return. Stetson Klausen, dressed as Santa for the occasion, shed a few tears of joy, knowing that Lily and Lucas would have a truly joyful Christmas.

The crowd was exuberant, their hearts swelling with happiness. The snow globe, which had already brought so much magic into their lives, seemed to shimmer even more brightly, as if acknowledging the miracle that had just occurred.

The return of Bella not only brought joy to Lily and her family but also reminded the entire town of the magic and wonder of Christmas. It was a night of miracles, where love, music, and the spirit of the season brought everyone together in a way they would never forget.

The snow globe, once a simple decoration, had become a symbol of enduring love and the power of music to heal and unite. As Christmas Day approached, the town of Snow Ville celebrated with a renewed sense of joy and togetherness, their hearts warmed by the magic of the season and the timeless story of love that had brought them all closer.

As the days passed, Mr. Thompson's transformation became evident to everyone in Snow Ville. No longer the reclusive figure he once was, he began to actively participate in community events and gatherings. His warm smile and gentle demeanor endeared him to the townspeople, who welcomed him with open arms. He shared his musical talents, often playing his violin at local events, bringing joy and a sense of unity to the town.

Emma and Lucas felt a profound connection to their family history, having uncovered the beautiful love story between Mr. Thompson and Margaret. The snow globe, with its hidden letters and memories, had become a cherished family heirloom, symbolizing the enduring power of love and the importance of preserving one's heritage. Emma often found herself reflecting on the true meaning of Christmas—love, forgiveness, and the bonds that tie us together.

On Christmas Eve, the town square was once again filled with the festive spirit. The townspeople gathered around the towering Christmas tree, its lights twinkling like stars against the night sky. The air was filled with laughter, the scent of freshly baked cookies, and the sound of carolers singing beloved holiday tunes.

In the center of it all stood Mr. Thompson, his violin in hand. He began to play a familiar melody, the same one he had composed for Margaret. He shared the lyrics with the crowd so they can sing along:

A Christmas Melody for Margaret

In the heart of winter's night,
Underneath the stars so bright,
We gather 'round the Christmas tree,
With love and joy, our hearts are free.

Chorus:
Oh, sing with me this melody,
A song of love and harmony,
For Christmas time is here again,
Bringing peace to every friend.

The snowflakes dance upon the breeze,
Whispers of the memories,
Of times gone by and love so true,
A gift from me, a gift for you.

Bridge:
Though years may pass, and seasons change,
Our hearts remain, they still exchange,
The love we share, the dreams we weave,
On this magical Christmas Eve.

So hold your loved ones close tonight,
Beneath the tree's soft glowing light,
And let this song forever be,
A Christmas gift for you and me.

The music flowed through the crowd, touching the hearts of everyone present. Emma and Lucas stood by his side, their faces glowing with pride and happiness.

As the final notes of the melody lingered in the air, the townspeople erupted into applause, their faces beaming with joy. Mr. Thompson's eyes sparkled with tears of gratitude, overwhelmed by the love and acceptance he had found in Snow Ville.

The evening culminated in a heartwarming scene of the entire town celebrating together. Families exchanged gifts, children played in the snow, and friends embraced, their hearts filled with the magic of the season. Emma and Lucas looked around, feeling a deep sense of contentment and belonging.

The snow globe, now a symbol of unity and love, sat proudly on a table in the town square, its intricate details with the horse at its center reflecting the twinkling lights. It had brought together not only a family but an entire community, reminding everyone of the true spirit of Christmas.

As the night drew to a close, Emma whispered to Lucas, "This is what Christmas is all about—love, family, and the magic that brings us all together."

Lucas nodded, his eyes shining with wonder. "And the snow globe helped us find it."

With hearts full of joy and a renewed sense of togetherness, the people of Snow Ville celebrated a Christmas they would never forget, united by love, music, and the timeless magic of the snow globe.

One evening, as they sat by the fire, Emma read aloud a letter from Margaret to Mr. Thompson, written during the war. "My dearest Edward, though we are apart, my love for you remains as strong as ever. I dream of the day we can be together again, and until then, I hold you in my heart."

Mr. Thompson listened, his eyes filled with tears. "She never forgot me," he whispered, a smile breaking through his sorrow.

Emma squeezed his hand. "And now, thanks to you, we can keep her memory alive."

In the days that followed, Emma and Lucas continued to explore the snow globe, discovering more letters and mementos that pieced together the love story of Margaret and Mr. Thompson. Each discovery brought new insights and a deeper understanding of their family's history.

14

The Medicine Man

In the heart of remote and secluded communities across the globe, the legacy of their forebears' sagacity is intricately interlaced with the existence of the community. This profound knowledge, a mosaic of life's many facets, is lovingly handed down from one generation to the next. It encompasses the gentle art of using roots and plants not just as medicine, but as a sacred balm during surgery, transforming pain into relief. It includes the cherished recipes for teas that comfort and cure, and the tender remedies that soothe a child's tummy ache under the watchful eyes of caring parents.

These communities also hold the time-honored secrets of the wilderness, where hunting and herding are not mere acts of survival, but rituals that honor the bond between man and nature. They possess the ancient techniques of manual therapy, where hands that work the earth also bring healing to the body's aches.

Such customs, rich with emotion and steeped in tradition, have been the heartbeat of many societies since time immemorial. They are the legacy of the elders, a gift of love and wisdom to their children, ensuring that the rhythms of the past gracefully dance into the future.

In a secluded corner of Asia, there was a village cradled by the whispers of ancient trees, where an herbalist lived—a sage of the woods, a healer of hearts. He was not just a man of medicine, but a beacon of hope, a spiritual compass guiding his people through the storms of life. His hands, steeped in the wisdom of the earth, brought forth remedies that whispered of forgotten times when nature and man spoke the same language.

This herbalist, a guardian of his community's well-being, was a bridge between the old world and the new. His village, a jewel nestled in the embrace of the wild, shone brighter than its neighbors, a testament to his profound skill. Seekers of solace and healing journeyed from distant lands, drawn by tales of a man whose words could weave wellness into existence.

Through the years, his legacy bloomed like the very herbs he cherished, saving countless lives, both young and old. Each dawn, he would wander into the embrace of the forest, a silent sentinel in search of nature's cures. His wisdom, a river flowing from the wellsprings of his ancestors—his father, his grandfather—village herbalists of renown, whose spirits still danced among the leaves.

Esteemed and beloved, his counsel was pure gold in a world of base metals. In a village where many ultracrepidarians spoke beyond their knowledge, his voice rang true—clear, resonant, and trusted. Tirelessly, he toiled, a devoted steward of his people's health, forever striving to fulfill the sacred trust they placed in him. His was a life woven from the threads of service, a tapestry of devotion that would span the ages.

On a day fated to be etched in the annals of the village, the herbalist, bearer of ancient wisdom and healer of woes, felt a stirring within his soul. It was a secret, tender and true, that had long nestled in the quiet chambers of his heart. He believed the time had ripened, like the fruit of a rare bloom, to unveil this hidden chapter of his being to the community he cherished.

So it was, under the soft glow of twilight on a Friday eve, that he summoned the soul of the village—the elders, the young, the dreamers, and the doers—to the time-worn square with its statues of erstwhile chiefs, defenders and elders of the village, where countless stories had unfolded. There, amidst the hush of expectant hearts, he stood, a solitary figure of courage, and spoke of love—a love that mirrored his own essence, pure and unbidden.

The herbalist's revelation fell upon the village like a sudden storm, stirring waves of shock and dismay that rippled through the hearts of many. The village chief, swift to act, bound the herbalist and his partner, casting them into the shadows of confinement as the village's pulse quickened with uncertainty. The initial shock had barely settled when the village chief, a man of stern countenance, approached the herbalist's dim cell.

"Speak," he commanded, his voice a mix of authority and concealed dread.

The herbalist, bound yet unbroken, lifted his eyes, their gleam unwavering. "Chief, we've done no wrong. Love, in its essence, cannot be shackled by tradition. I love him, and he loves me. It's as simple as that."

A murmur arose among the villagers outside, their whispers like leaves in the wind. "They speak of love," one voice said, soft as a secret. "Yet, what cost to us? What about our traditions? Are they of no consequence?"

A young voice in the crowd, brave and clear, cut through the clamor. "Let them live, let them love!" It was the blacksmith's daughter, her eyes alight with fervor, her words like a beacon of hope amidst the gathering storm. The villagers turned to look at her, their expressions a mix of shock and curiosity.

An emergency conclave of the village council was summoned, a gathering clouded by the absence of Elder Joe, whose keen insight lay dormant in the depths of a coma. The hall was thick with tension, the air almost crackling with the weight of unspoken fears and judgments. Amidst the council, the oldest elder, a lean figure with a furious gaze, rose. His garment ripped asunder, a dramatic symbol of the fractured tradition, and with a voice like a hurricane, he roared, "Retribution," the word slicing through the tense air like a blade. "Our ancestors demand it!"

The scribe, his quill poised over parchment, met the elder's fiery gaze with a steady calm. "And what of compassion? Our laws are silent on matters of the heart. Must we then answer silence with blood?" he questioned, his voice carrying a quiet but powerful conviction.

Voices clashed like thunder, the hall filling with a cacophony of opinions. Some called for harsh judgments, their faces twisted with anger and fear, while others, more measured, spoke of mercy and understanding. The scribe, a pillar of influence amidst the chaos, urged adherence to the laws that had long bound them together. "In the absence of written edicts on love's many forms, exile should be the remedy," he proposed, his words resonating with reason.

Yet, the collective heart of the elders beat to a different rhythm, one more attuned to the cries for vengeance than to the pleas for leniency.

In a decision marred by dissent and fraught with the weight of tradition, they chose a path of severity, marking a day for the herbalist's fate to be sealed. The decision hung in the air like an ominous cloud, casting a shadow over the village and its future.

In this pivotal moment, the village stood at a crossroads, its soul weighed down by the gravity of its choices. The threads of tradition and compassion tangled in the hands of time, creating a tapestry of uncertainty. As dawn's first light crept over the horizon, painting the sky with hues of hope, a miracle unfolded—Elder Joe, the village's beacon of wisdom, emerged from the silent grip of his coma.

The room fell silent as he entered, his presence commanding attention. With the weight of impending sorrow heavy upon his shoulders, he gathered the council with a sense of urgency that brooked no delay. The air was thick with anticipation, each breath held as if the world itself was waiting.

"Fellow guardians of our cherished traditions," he began, his voice a blend of frailty and firm resolve, each word trembling with the weight of his recent ordeal, "I stand before you, bewildered by the shadows that have clouded your judgment. Have we become so estranged from the very essence of our humanity that we would extinguish a life that has been a font of healing and hope?"

His plea was a clarion call to the soul of the village, reverberating through the hearts of those gathered. It was a reminder that the life they sought to end was a sacred gift, not theirs to take. "This man, whom you cast out, has been the healer of our kin, the mender of our brokenness. Can we, in good conscience, repay his service with such a grave injustice?"

The council members shifted uncomfortably, the weight of Elder Joe's words sinking in. His eyes, once dimmed by illness, now blazed with fervor, casting a light on the path they had strayed from. The villagers outside, drawn by the gravity of the situation, listened in hushed whispers, the tension palpable.

Moved by Elder Joe's impassioned entreaty, the council's heart swayed. Faces softened, and eyes that had once burned with the fire of retribution now shimmered with the possibility of mercy. They chose exile over execution—a decision that, while still harsh, was a testament to the power of compassion. The village, in that quiet dawn, found a glimmer of hope, a chance to weave a new thread into their tapestry—a thread of mercy and humanity.

When the morning sun rose to its zenith, casting golden hues across the village, the two men, with nothing but the packs on their backs and the taste of bittersweet farewells, were led through the village. The drums tolled not for celebration but for a somber farewell, a dirge for what was lost. It was the kind of procession reserved for the death of the village's elders. This procession bore the weight of irony—a man who had breathed life into so many now cast away in a spectacle of scorn.

As the sun rose on a day of reckoning, the village streets swelled with a sea of faces, some etched with the early light of judgment. The morning mist lingered, adding a touch of melancholy to the scene. Those who once stood in awe of the healer's grace now gripped stones with intent, their praises turned to venomous jeers. The guardians of peace, the village guardsmen, stood firm against the tide, their batons raised not in anger, but in a desperate plea for order.

From the fringes, a teacher of great esteem, who knew both men and their families, watched, his heart heavy with the unfolding tragedy. His eyes were filled with sorrow as he observed the scene, every detail imprinting itself on his soul. With a poet's quill, he painted the scene in verses of sorrow:

The Death Of Compassion

The village square's drums did beat,
A somber march, a grim defeat.
The healer's hands, once raised in care,
Now bound and led to who knows where.

With stones in hands, the crowd awaits,
To cast their fury, seal their fates.
But in this act, what do we see?
Death of mercy and empathy.

For he who cured with gentle touch,
Is met with hatred, far too much.
And wisdom's voice, once strong and clear,
Is drowned by anger, pain, and fear.

So let us pause and think again,
Of what we lose, of what we gain.
For in each stone, a choice is cast,
To free our future, chain our past.

With heavy hearts, the village elders decreed an exile, a sentence that severed ties and banished hope. The two men, once cherished, now forsaken, embarked on a journey beyond the familiar. Over fifty miles they trekked, through the unforgiving embrace of nature's wild. The path was rugged, lined with ancient trees whose branches seemed to whisper tales of sorrow. As they walked, the weight of their exile pressed heavily upon them until they found solace in a distant village, where anonymity became their silent sentinel.

Meanwhile, the village that had cast them out found itself in the throes of celebration turned sour. The echoes of the outcasts' departure haunted the empty spaces they once filled, leaving a void that no festivity could fill. The families of the men left behind bore the brunt of a shame not their own, ostracized by most in the village. They self-exiled in their homes, the laughter and joy of past days now replaced by whispers of disdain and regret.

Time passed, and with it came the cruel hand of irony. The absence of the healer's touch brought forth a cascade of loss, a stark reminder of the life-giving force they had so hastily discarded. Crops wilted, illnesses spread unchecked, and even the chief's lineage was not spared. The village was left to reckon with the cost of its choices—a price paid in the currency of human lives. Each day without the healer deepened the villagers' realization of their grave mistake.

In the village where trust had once been broken, a gathering of troubled souls convened. Their hearts were heavy with the weight of past decisions, the air thick with the heat of debate. The elders grappled with the consequences of their actions, their voices rising and falling like the tide. It was Elder Joe, the venerable voice of reason, who pierced the cacophony of pride and prejudice. He stood, his presence commanding respect, and proposed a humbling reversal—to extend an olive branch to the exiled herbalist and his partner.

A trio of brave souls, versed in the language of the wild, was summoned by the elders and given a mandate to search for and return the outcasts to the village. They set forth on a quest to mend what was torn asunder. Through valleys deep and mountains high, they traversed, enduring the harsh elements and the whispers of nature. Each step was a testament to their determination to make things right.

In Sai Kung, amidst the whispers of the eastern winds, they found the herbalist. His eyes mirrored the pain of betrayal, a deep well of sorrow and resilience.

"Surely, you've come to seal our doom," the herbalist spoke, his voice a blend of fear and defiance, suspicious that they were being flimflammed out of their hiding place to be executed by their visitors. But the messengers, with trembling hearts, spoke of loss, of a village bereft of its healer's touch. Moved by tales of sorrow and the innocent eyes of a child now lost, the herbalist and his companion chose the path of forgiveness, and agreed to return to the place that had once forsaken them.

As they journeyed back, fate dealt a cruel hand when one of the men from the village fell ill, his body succumbing to the relentless march of an unseen ailment. The herbalist, with hands that whispered secrets to the wild herbs, sprang into action, retrieving cures from the bosom of the forest. Under the light of a crescent moon, they kept a watchful eye on the sick man, whose strength seemed to be slightly rekindled by the touch of nature's balm.

In the quiet of the night, as the men rested under a canopy of twinkling stars, a confession broke the silence. "I must apologize," began his colleague, his voice a low murmur of guilt and remorse. "I was given secret orders by an elder to poison you." The revelation hung between them, a specter of betrayal. The men's eyes lit up, and the sick colleague's frail body, lying on the grassy bed, straightened with shock. Yet, the herbalist, ever the beacon of hope, forgave the deceit, understanding the tangled webs woven by the hands of desperation.

The herbalist examined the contents of the poison mixture and discovered a twist of fate—the Rosy Periwinkle, toxic yet a healer in disguise. With wisdom and care, he transformed the intended poison into a cure for the diabetic man. The irony danced in the moonlight, an unspoken observer of forgiveness's restorative grace. The following day, the sick man fully regained his strength, his vitality returning under the herbalist's watchful care.

As the sun rose, they continued their trek towards the village, their steps lighter with the newfound hope and resolve.

Back in the village, the herbalist's hands weaved miracles once more, breathing life into the ailing, mending the fractures of a community on the brink of despair. His touch was a balm to the weary, a beacon of light in the darkness. Yet, beneath the surface of healing, the waters of doubt still churned. Whispers of past betrayals and the scars of mistrust lingered, casting long shadows over the village's path to redemption.

Time unfolded, revealing truths hidden in plain sight. An elder, once a herald of punishment, now stood bare, his own heart's secret laid open for all to see. He too had a partner like him. The revelation sent ripples through the council, a mirror held up to their own judgments. The once stoic faces of the elders now mirrored shock and introspection, the weight of their hypocrisy pressing heavily upon them.

Faced with this new test, the elders chose to lay the decision at the feet of the people. The village square buzzed with a mixture of curiosity and tension, the air charged with anticipation. But before the verdict could be cast, the perspicacious Elder Joe rose, his words a storm of righteous fury, chastising the elder for his duplicity. "You, who cast stones, harbor the same love in your heart. How dare you betray our trust and hide behind the veil of deceit?" His voice rang out, echoing through the crowd like a clarion call.

An apology was demanded, and it came—a confession of fear and a claim of newfound bravery in the wake of acceptance. The elder's voice trembled as he spoke, tears welling up in his eyes. "I feared the judgment of our people, but now I see the strength in standing by my truth. Forgive me."

In the heart of the village, voices rose and fell, a chorus of opinions and pleas. The herbalist, once a victim of scorn, now stood as a beacon of compassion, his words urging the villagers to see beyond the veil of imperfection. "We are all flawed," he began, his voice gentle yet firm. "But it is our humanity that binds us. Let us not judge harshly, but embrace each other with the understanding that love, in all its forms, is sacred."

His plea for understanding resonated, and the crowd, moved by his grace, roared their approval. The collective breath of the village seemed to sigh in relief, the tension dissolving into a newfound sense of unity.

In the end, the vote was cast, and the decision was clear—the elder and his partner were to live among them, not as outcasts, but as equals. In this moment, the village found a new beginning, a step towards a future where every soul was valued, not for their conformity, but for their contribution to the tapestry of life.

As the sun set, casting a golden glow over the village, there was a palpable shift in the air. The once fractured community began to heal, each member playing their part in weaving a story of acceptance and love. The herbalist's compassion had sown seeds of change, and the village, now united, looked forward to a future where differences were celebrated and every heart, no matter how imperfect, had a place.

15

The Price Of Choices

Nestled amid rolling fields and open skies, Polk City, Iowa, was a charming small town where everyone knew each other. The gentle hum of daily life in the town was punctuated by the warm greetings of neighbors and the rustle of leaves in the cool breeze. Each morning, the sun would rise over the golden cornfields, casting a soft, warm light that made the dew-kissed grass sparkle like tiny diamonds. The town's picturesque streets, lined with neat, white picket fences and blooming gardens, and cozy homes with their welcoming porches, were a testament to the simplicity and beauty of midwestern life. The scent of fresh-baked bread and the sound of children playing in the distance were constant reminders of the peaceful rhythm that defined Polk City.

Sheila Cockerill was the epitome of charm and success. With her sun-kissed blonde hair cascading in waves like a golden waterfall, and a smile that could brighten the gloomiest of days, she could light up any room she entered. Her presence was electric, her laughter a melody that resonated with everyone around her. As a top real estate agent selling million-dollar homes, she was the darling of Polk City's elite, her name synonymous with luxury and excellence. Her radiant smile and magnetic energy drew people to her like metal filings to a magnet, making her a force to be reckoned with in the real estate world. In every handshake, every confident stride, Sheila exuded an aura of success and sophistication.

In stark contrast to Sheila's exuberance, Brady Tucker was a serene presence, the calming counterpart to her vibrant energy. He was her high school sweetheart, an introverted soul who found joy in the quiet moments that life offered. Brady's dark hair and thoughtful eyes reflected a depth of character and kindness that was apparent to all who knew him. He was content to stand in Sheila's shadow, always playing the supportive partner, his quiet strength and unwavering support providing a solid foundation for their relationship. His gentle demeanor and soft-spoken nature were the bedrock of their bond, a calm harbor in the midst of Sheila's whirlwind of activity. Together, they were a perfect balance, complementing each other's strengths and weaknesses with a profound and enduring love.

Their engagement was a beacon of joy, celebrated by everyone who knew them. The memory of Brady's proposal still lingered in Sheila's mind like a cherished dream. They were planning a beautiful future together, their dreams intertwined with the promise of a life filled with love and happiness. Visions of a sun-dappled wedding, surrounded by family and friends, danced in their minds. They envisioned a ceremony in the heart of their beloved Polk City, a celebration of their enduring love against the backdrop of their hometown's serene beauty. The future lay before them, a tapestry of shared hopes and endless possibilities.

The news of Sheila's pregnancy was like a radiant sunrise, bathing their lives in newfound hope and excitement. When Sheila discovered she was pregnant, it felt as if the universe had gifted them with a precious new beginning. Brady's heart swelled with joy, his face lighting up with a smile that seemed to reach his very soul. His happiness was infectious, spreading like wildfire through their family and friends. Every conversation sparkled with his excitement, each word brimming with pride and anticipation. The prospect of becoming a father tugged at his heartstrings, filling him with dreams of a future resplendent with the laughter and love of their child. He envisioned gentle nights rocking a crib under the soft glow of a nursery lamp, and sunny days filled with playful giggles echoing through the house.

However, as the weeks passed, the once-unblemished surface of their relationship began to crack. Sheila started spending more and more time with Sean Jackson, a flamboyant millionaire client who had been a part of her professional life for many years. Sean's extravagant lifestyle, with his flashy cars and lavish gifts, became a dazzling lure that pulled Sheila into his orbit. The constant attention he lavished upon her created a rift between her and Brady, widening the emotional chasm between them.

Brady could feel the growing coldness from Sheila, a stark contrast to the warmth they once shared. The love that had once flowed freely between them now felt like a frozen stream, its icy surface impenetrable. Evening meals together that were once filled with intimate conversations and shared dreams became lonely dinners for one. The familiar sound of her laughter was replaced by the deafening silence of an empty chair.

Sheila's defensiveness and evasiveness became a wall that Brady couldn't breach, no matter how hard he tried. He felt isolated, left out in the cold by the woman who had once been his closest confidante. Brady's heart ached as he watched the woman he loved drift further away, each day feeling more like a ghostly presence at their once warm and loving dinner table. The memories of shared meals and whispered dreams now haunted him, transforming their home into a shadowy relic of lost love. His eyes often lingered on the empty seat across from him, a poignant reminder of the emotional distance that now separated them. Their love, like sun-poor flowers, was wilting in the darkness of her absence.

On a balmy summer evening, Brady's heart pounded in his chest as he drove to a property Sheila had listed for sale. The sky was painted in hues of crimson and gold, but all he felt was a growing dread. Upon arrival, he spotted Sean Jackson's sleek Mercedes Benz Maybach parked discreetly under the shadows of an ancient oak tree. Approaching the car, his breath caught in his throat as he peered through the tinted windows. There, entwined in a compromising embrace, were Sheila and Sean. The sight was a knife to his heart, twisting and sharp, leaving him breathless and broken.

Brady's devastation turned to a cold, hard anger as he confronted Sheila later that night. The moonlight cast a ghostly pallor over their faces as they stood in the doorway of the home they had once shared with so much love. Sheila's eyes, once warm and inviting, now held a steely detachment.

"You're boring, Brady. I've outgrown this monotonous life," she spat, her words like daggers piercing the fragile remnants of their relationship.

Brady's voice trembled with a mix of hurt and desperation, his eyes searching Sheila's for any flicker of the love they once shared. "We were supposed to start a family. You're carrying our child, Sheila."

The air between them felt heavy, charged with the weight of unspoken emotions and shattered dreams. Unapologetically, Sheila replied, her voice cold and unyielding, "This baby was never meant to be. I'm ending this, Brady."

Her words hit him like a physical blow, knocking the breath from his lungs. Brady felt as if the ground had shifted beneath his feet, leaving him teetering on the edge of a precipice. His heart, already bruised and battered, now splintered into a thousand irreparable pieces. The finality in her tone was a death knell to their future together, a brutal end to the life they had envisioned.

The reality of her decision bore down on him like a crushing weight, the room around them shrinking into a suffocating void. Memories of shared dreams and whispered promises swirled in his mind, now tainted by the harsh truth of her words. The thought of losing not only the woman he loved but also the unborn child they had created together was more than he could bear. Tears welled up in his eyes, but he fought to keep them at bay, not wanting to give Sheila the satisfaction of seeing him broken.

"Sheila, please," he whispered, his voice a raw plea filled with anguish. "We can still make this work. We can be a family."

But Sheila's gaze remained distant, her resolve unshaken. "No, Brady. This is over. I need something more than what we have. I'm moving on."

As she walked away, the door closing softly behind her, Brady stood frozen, his heart shattered beyond repair. The silence that followed was deafening, a stark contrast to the life and laughter that had once filled their home. He sank to his knees, overwhelmed by a tidal wave of grief and despair. The love they had shared, the future they had planned, all vanished in an instant, leaving behind only the cold emptiness of loss.

With a final, cold glance, Sheila packed her bags and moved into Sean Jackson's opulent mansion, leaving behind the life she once knew. The echoes of their shared laughter and dreams now haunted the empty rooms of the home she deserted, marking the start of her new chapter with Sean.

Brady was a shattered man, his heart lying in pieces like broken glass. Nights were the hardest, filled with agonizing memories of happier times. He spent long, sleepless hours in the dimly lit bedroom, staring at pictures of their high school prom, vacations, and engagement ceremony. Each image was a ghost, a cruel reminder of the joy that was now out of reach. Doubts gnawed at him relentlessly, especially about the paternity of the unborn child that Sheila had decided to abort. The silence of their once vibrant home echoed his sorrow, deepening his despair.

Meanwhile, Sheila adjusted to her new life with Sean, basking in the luxury and attention. Yet, it didn't take long for her to notice Sean's lack of interest in settling down. Despite her dreams of building a family and expanding their success in the real estate industry, Sean remained noncommittal. His wealth and charm masked a deeper disinterest in the stable life Sheila yearned for.

As the seasons changed, Sheila began to see the cracks in her new life, like fractures in the facade of a grand but decaying mansion. The initial thrill of luxury and excitement gave way to a stark reality. Sean's affections wandered like a wayward breeze, never settling in one place for long, like a sparrow fluttering restlessly. Sheila found herself competing with other women for his attention, a bitter pill to swallow for someone used to being the center of adoration. The sting of realization pierced her heart, yet she remained determined to secure her place in Sean's life.

Desperation drove Sheila to devise a plan, a fragile hope to bind Sean to her. She became pregnant, believing the prospect of fatherhood would anchor his wandering heart. The weeks passed in a haze of nervous anticipation, each day a delicate thread in the tapestry of her fragile hope. However, her plan took a tragic turn when she suffered a miscarriage three months into the pregnancy. The loss was a devastating blow to her dreams and hopes, shattering the fragile peace she had tried to weave.

The cold autumn air mirrored the chill that settled in Sheila's heart as she dealt with her grief alone. Sean, detached and engrossed in his latest affair with a beautiful blonde, Gloria Mesner, offered little comfort. His indifference was a knife that twisted in her heart, deepening her sorrow. Sheila's grief was compounded by her isolation, each day a lonely echo of the unfulfilled dreams that haunted her.

In the wake of her devastating miscarriage and Sean's continued indifference, Sheila found herself at a crossroads. Desperation gnawed at her heart, the pain of loss and unfulfilled dreams a constant shadow over her days. One evening, with a resolve borne of despair, she reached out to Jeff Holman, Sean's lifelong friend and mentor. Jeff, a man of quiet wisdom and steady influence, listened as Sheila poured out her heart, her voice trembling with unspoken fears and hopes.

"Jeff, I don't know what to do anymore," Sheila confessed, her eyes glistening with unshed tears. "Sean is slipping away, and I feel like I'm losing myself in this fight to keep him."

Jeff, with his calm demeanor, placed a reassuring hand on Sheila's shoulder. "Sheila, I've known Sean for a long time. He needs to be reminded of his responsibilities, of the life he's risking to throw away. I'll talk to him."

True to his word, Jeff confronted Sean with the gravity of his actions. However, Sean's allure for the wild life and Gloria Mesner's beauty led him astray. One autumn evening, Sean and Mesner had plans to meet for dinner. The restaurant buzzed with the hum of evening chatter, its ambient light casting warm hues over their table in the corner.

As they sat together, the door swung open and a man stormed in, his face a mask of rage. He marched straight to Sean and Mesner, declaring himself as Mesner's fiancé. This revelation was a jolt to Sean, who had been unaware of Mesner's engagement. The air grew thick with tension as their argument escalated, voices rising above the clatter of cutlery and murmur of other diners.

In a flash, the confrontation turned violent. A gunshot rang out, the deafening sound echoing through the bustling restaurant. Sean fell back, clutching his torso, his shirt staining crimson as he collapsed onto the floor. Mesner's fiancé fled, leaving chaos in his wake.

Sheila received the call and felt her world spin. Rushing to the hospital, her heart pounded with a mix of fear and hope. The sterile corridors of the emergency room seemed endless as she searched for Sean. When she found him, pale and weakened in the hospital bed, her breath caught in her throat.

Sean looked up at Sheila with eyes filled with remorse. "Sheila, I've been a fool. I promise, I'll change. I want to make this right."

The sincerity in his eyes, coupled with the near-death experience, marked the beginning of a transformation. Sheila set aside her real estate work to be with him, ensuring he had the support needed for a full recovery. Within months, Sean and Sheila stood together in a beautiful autumn ceremony, exchanging vows under a canopy of golden leaves, committing to a new chapter of their lives.

The next three years were a rollercoaster of hope and heartbreak for Sheila. Each month brought the painful reminder of her struggle to conceive. The sterile smell of doctor's offices became all too familiar as she went from one appointment to another, only to be met with repeated disappointments. Each negative test felt like a dagger to her heart, the dream of motherhood slipping further away.

Meanwhile, life had taken a different turn for Brady. After the heartache and betrayal, he found solace in the arms of Marcie Sussex, a woman whose warmth and kindness reignited the light in his life. Meeting Marcie was like stepping into a warm embrace after being lost in a storm. Her genuine smile and compassionate heart were the healing balm his wounded soul desperately needed. Their connection was instant, a breath of fresh air that slowly started to mend his shattered spirit.

They married in a quaint ceremony, surrounded by the love of family and friends, beneath a canopy of blooming flowers that symbolized new beginnings. The vows they exchanged were heartfelt, filled with promises of unwavering support and endless love. Marcie's presence brought a newfound stability and joy to Brady's life, allowing him to leave behind the shadows of his past.

Together, they built a home filled with love and laughter. Over the years, their family grew, blessed with four beautiful children who brought endless joy and chaos into their lives. The sight of his children playing in the yard, their faces lit with pure happiness and their laughter echoing through the house, was a symphony to Brady's ears. It was in these moments, watching them chase butterflies under the golden sun or build snowmen in the crisp winter air, that he found true healing.

The walls of their home were adorned with drawings and photos, each frame a testament to the love that bound them together. The once heavy burden of his past failures and hurts with Sheila began to lift, replaced by the warmth and comfort of his new life. Brady's heart, once scarred by betrayal, now overflowed with gratitude for the family he had built.

Marcie's gentle nature and unwavering support were the pillars that held their family together. Each day with Marcie and the children was a reminder of the resilience of the human spirit and the power of love to heal even the deepest wounds.

Brady's journey from heartbreak to happiness was a testament to his strength and capacity for love. As he watched his children grow and thrive, he felt a profound sense of fulfillment and peace. The scars of the past were still there, but they no longer defined him. Instead, they were reminders of a journey that had led him to a place of unimaginable joy and contentment.

Haunted by her failures and the emptiness of her once vibrant career, Sheila decided it was time for a change. She left the cutthroat world of real estate behind and found solace in volunteering at a nonprofit organization for disadvantaged kids. Here, amidst the laughter and challenges, she discovered a new purpose. The children, with their wide eyes and boundless energy, reignited a spark within her, a flame of hope and fulfillment. A friend of Sheila working for the nonprofit, who'd witnessed Sheila's love for children, penned this poem about Sheila's choices:

Her Imprudence

Her eyes much brighter than the morning sun,
   Her heart bequeathed with nice gardens of love.
   If charm's tall as skies, hers is miles above,
Her sheer elegance, any being would stun.
Her organ fruitless like the bare desert,
   Yet, this was ne'er her unique circumstance,
   Perhaps a quite imprudent comeuppance,
For she'd squandered that of her was a part.
Neath her gorgeous façade, a heart distressed,
   By the permanence of her act unwise,
   Since tried but failed had doctors in this town.
She cares daily for kids crushed and oppressed,
   Remaking them whole, her love she applies,
    Regrettably, none would e'er be her own.

With time, Sheila's reflections on her past actions led her to seek forgiveness. She reached out to Brady, the man she had once loved and hurt so deeply. Her apology was heartfelt, a moment of catharsis for both. Brady, ever the compassionate soul, accepted her apology and welcomed her back into his life, not as a partner, but as a dear friend.

Sheila's bond with Brady's children grew, and she became their godmother, a role she cherished deeply. The scars of the past began to heal as she embraced this new chapter with open arms.

Through her work at the nonprofit, Sheila eventually adopted three children, giving her the family she had longed for. Sheila's journey, fraught with pain and redemption, finally led her to the motherhood she had always dreamed of, transforming her sorrow into joy and purpose.

Sheila's decision to adopt came after many sleepless nights and quiet moments of reflection. The sterile white walls of the doctors' offices, the hopeful beginnings that ended in heartache—these memories weighed heavy on her. Yet, amidst the laughter and chaos of the nonprofit, she found herself drawn to three particular children. Each had their own story of loss and resilience, mirrored in her own journey.

The day she brought them home was filled with a mix of nervous excitement and overwhelming love. The mansion, which once echoed with emptiness, now burst with the sounds of laughter and little feet pattering across the floors. The children's wide eyes and infectious giggles brought a newfound light into Sheila and Sean's lives. Her heart, once scarred by pain and regret, began to heal with every hug and shared moment.

The mornings became a symphony of joyful chaos, filled with the scent of pancakes and the sound of playful banter. Sheila's life, which had seemed a barren desert of unfulfilled dreams, now blossomed into a garden of love and fulfillment. Each child's unique personality added color to her days, painting a vivid tapestry of family life. She reveled in the simple joys of bedtime stories, shared meals, and the warmth of their unconditional love.

As the years passed, Sheila found herself reflecting on the tumultuous path that had led her to this point. Sitting by the window, watching her children play in the yard, she felt a profound sense of peace and purpose. The mistakes, the heartbreak, and the moments of despair—they were all chapters in her journey, each teaching her lessons of resilience and strength.

Sheila often thought back to her time with Brady, the love they had shared, and the choices that had driven them apart. She acknowledged her faults and the pain she had caused, but she also embraced the woman she had become—stronger, wiser, and deeply compassionate. Her work with the nonprofit had not only filled the void in her heart but had also given her life new meaning.

In the quiet moments, when the house was still, and the children were asleep, Sheila would close her eyes and offer a silent prayer of gratitude. Her journey had been far from easy, but it had led her to a place of redemption and fulfillment.

Sheila's story was one of transformation—a testament to the power of hope, love, and the unwavering human spirit. Despite the twists and turns, she had found her way to a life of purpose and joy. Surrounded by her children, she felt whole, her heart finally at peace. The sense of redemption that came with each smile, each hug, each moment of shared happiness, was the culmination of her journey.

As the sun set on another day, casting a golden glow over the yard, Sheila watched her children chase fireflies, their laughter echoing in the twilight. She knew that, no matter what challenges lay ahead, she had found her place in the world. Her story was one of redemption, a journey from heartache to healing, and she embraced it fully, grateful for the love and light that now filled her life.

16
Threads Of Redemption

Clara Adelson stood at the pinnacle of her career, a beacon of success in the corporate world. Her name was synonymous with efficiency and excellence, yet behind the polished exterior lay a heart encased in ice. Years of relentless ambition had sculpted her into a formidable businesswoman, but at the cost of her emotional connections. Clara's office, perched high above the city of Lakewood, offered a panoramic view of the bustling metropolis below—a stark contrast to the solitude she felt within. The city lights twinkled like distant stars, a reminder of the world she had distanced herself from.

The city itself was a character in their story, a sprawling urban jungle teeming with life and energy. Skyscrapers pierced the sky, their glass facades reflecting the ceaseless motion of cars and people below. Amidst the chaos, pockets of serenity existed—parks where children played, cafes where friends gathered, and the Lakewood Community Center, a haven for those seeking solace and support. Yet, beneath the city's vibrant surface, personal struggles simmered, waiting to be unveiled.

Marcus Wison, once a promising employee under Clara's wing, had seen his dreams shattered by her ruthless decisions. A talented project manager, he had been dedicated and loyal, only to be cast aside when his ideas clashed with Clara's vision. The final straw was a project led by Marcus in which he gave his best. His painting of the Nativity scene was selected by three judges in a panel to be displayed at an upcoming exhibition, but Clara vetoed their idea and selected another painting as a favor to a friend of hers, denying Marcus the opportunity he'd long sought to be recognized by the art industry. Moreover, the financial reward from the display in the form of a bonus would have sustained his living for a while.

The betrayal left him disillusioned and struggling to rebuild his life. A month later, Marcus quit his job and started work at the small Lakewood Community Center, far removed from the corporate ladder he once aspired to climb, burying his talent under layers of hurt and disappointment.

Marcus opened his heart to his dark impulses, often hanging out with pals at parties, lighting up like a Christmas tree to hide his pain and disillusionment. The bright lights and loud music were a temporary escape from the shadows that haunted him. One Friday evening, he stopped at a local liquor store and purchased a Glenfiddich bottle of fine whisky, the amber liquid promising a brief respite from his inner turmoil.

Returning to his apartment, he pulled up a blank canvas, hoping to drown his sorrows in art and alcohol.

As the night wore on, Marcus poured glass after glass, the whisky burning a path down his throat. His brush moved erratically across the canvas, each stroke a desperate attempt to capture the chaos within. The room spun around him, the walls closing in as he drank more and more. In the middle of his living room, surrounded by empty bottles and scattered paint supplies, he passed out on the floor, the whisky bottle still clutched in his hand.

The next morning, Marcus woke up with a pounding headache, the harsh light of day piercing through the curtains. He groaned, pushing himself up to a sitting position. He prepared and enjoyed a jentacular feast of fresh fruit, eggs, bacon, yogurt, and granola, the meal seeming to quell his hangover. His eyes fell on the painting he had created in his drunken stupor. The portrait stared back at him, a twisted reflection of his own despair. The man in the painting looked lost, his eyes hollow and devoid of hope. It was a version of himself that Marcus detested, a stark reminder of how far he had fallen, a ghost of his former self haunting him with the harsh reality of his decline.

Determined to rid himself of the haunting image, Marcus grabbed the painting and headed for the dumpster outside his apartment building. The cold morning air bit at his skin, but he barely noticed. As he approached the dumpster, he heard a voice behind him.

"Are you about to throw that away? It is beautiful, can I have it?" The voice asked, gently.

Marcus turned to see Sharrod Cole, the head of a non-profit organization that helped little children. Sharrod's eyes were kind, filled with genuine admiration for the artwork. Marcus, feeling a mix of shame and surprise, handed over the portrait without saying a word and returned to his apartment.

That day, Marcus realized he had more to offer than he had allowed himself to believe. The encounter with Sharrod was a wake-up call, a reminder that his talent still had value. He understood that his drinking was a selfish and self-inflicting wound on his health and overall living. The whisky had been a crutch, but it was time to stand on his own and chart a new path.

With renewed determination, Marcus quit drinking and focused on his work at the community center. He poured his energy into helping others, finding solace in the smiles of the children and the gratitude of the community. His art flourished once more as he imparted his knowledge into the minds of fledgling artists, each one a testament to his journey from darkness to light.

Emily, Clara's younger sister, had once been inseparable from her. Their bond was forged in the fires of a tumultuous childhood, where they had relied on each other for strength and comfort. However, as Clara's career took off, her relentless pursuit of success created a chasm between them. Emily, feeling abandoned and overshadowed by her sister's achievements, harbored deep resentment. Clara's decisions, often made with cold pragmatism, had hurt Emily in ways she struggled to articulate. Their relationship, once a source of strength, had become a distant memory, marked by silence and unspoken grievances.

The community project, a beacon of hope and renewal, became the unexpected bridge between the estranged sisters. Emily, passionate about social causes, joined the initiative to make a difference. Clara, seeking redemption and a way to mend her fractured relationship with her sister, also became involved. Their paths crossed frequently, each encounter a mix of awkwardness and tentative steps towards reconciliation.

Their initial meetings were strained, filled with polite but distant conversations. Emily's guarded demeanor and Clara's guilt-laden attempts at connection created a fragile tension. The air between them was thick with unspoken words, each interaction a delicate dance of emotions.

As they worked side by side, their shared goals began to chip away at the ice-covered walls between them. The community project became a canvas where they could paint their hopes and dreams, each brushstroke a step towards healing. They found common ground in their dedication to the project, slowly rediscovering the camaraderie they once had. The laughter of children playing in the nearby park and the hum of conversations in the café provided a soothing backdrop to their efforts.

Late-night conversations over coffee, moments of shared laughter, and the occasional argument allowed them to confront their past. The dim light of the café cast long shadows, creating an intimate space where truths could be spoken. Emily voiced her pain, her words heavy with years of pent-up emotion. Clara listened, her heart aching as she truly understood the impact of her actions for the first time.

"You left me behind, Clara. I felt like I didn't matter to you anymore." Emily said, her voice trembling.

"I'm so sorry, Emily. I was so focused on my career that I lost sight of what really mattered. I never meant to hurt you." Clara responded, her eyes welling up.

The turning point came during a community event, where their combined efforts were celebrated. The air was filled with the scent of blooming flowers and the sound of joyous chatter. Emily, seeing Clara's genuine remorse and commitment to change, felt a shift in her heart. The anger and hurt that had defined their relationship began to dissolve, replaced by a tentative hope.

In a heartfelt conversation under the stars, Emily forgave Clara, acknowledging the changes she had seen in her sister. Clara, overwhelmed with gratitude, promised to be a better sister and friend.

"I can see you've changed, Clara. I forgive you." Emily said, softly.

"Thank you, Emily. I promise I'll never take you for granted again." Clara replied, her voice breaking.

Their reconciliation was not just a moment but a process. They continued to work together, their bond growing stronger with each passing day. The community project, a symbol of their renewed relationship, flourished under their joint leadership. The vibrant murals and thriving gardens were a testament to their shared vision and hard work.

Clara's journey of redemption was deeply intertwined with her reconciliation with Emily. Their renewed bond gave Clara the strength and resolve to continue her path of healing and forgiveness, transforming her life and the lives of those around her.

A month later, Clara's day started like any other, filled with meetings and deadlines. As she drove home late at night, fatigue began to set in. The city streets, usually bustling, were eerily quiet. The glow of streetlights cast long shadows, creating an almost surreal atmosphere. Suddenly, a car ran a red light, colliding with Clara's vehicle. The impact was severe, leaving her trapped and unconscious.

Marcus, who was walking home from the community center, witnessed the accident. Without hesitation, he rushed to the scene. Despite the danger, he managed to pull Clara from the wreckage just before the car caught fire. As the ambulance arrived, Marcus stayed by her side, ensuring she was safe before slipping away into the night. As the ambulance pulled away, Clara's car burst into flames, and the noise from the explosion could be heard for miles. A fire company was able to put out the fire without further incident.

Clara woke up in the hospital, disoriented and in pain. The sterile smell of antiseptic filled the air, and the steady beep of the heart monitor was a constant reminder of her fragile state. The doctors informed her that a good Samaritan had saved her life. As she recovered, Clara became determined to find and thank her savior. It wasn't long before she discovered that the man who had saved her was none other than Marcus, the former employee she had wronged. On the night she found out that Marcus had pulled her to safety, she was weeping like a broken faucet, her tears flowing unabated, reflecting her inner emotions. She could never imagine that a man whose dreams she had once shattered would muster the courage and forgiveness to stretch a hand of help, a bridge to safety towards her.

Clara, who often wrote poetry, penned one about her experience:

<u>From Darkness to Light</u>

In stillness of the night, a crash,
Ambition's life now turned to ash.
Trapped in metal, my own making,
Saved by a hand, past forsaking.

Eyes open to a sterile white,
A heart once cold now filled with fright.
A savior from the past revealed,
Guilt and remorse, emotions healed.

An artist whose dreams I shattered,
Saved me when it truly mattered.
A chance to mend, to right the wrong,
To find a place where we belong.

Through tears and words, we bridge divide,
In art of forgiveness, confide.
His brushstrokes vivid, heart laid bare,
Together heal, bond beyond compare.

My own dear, sister, lost in fray,
Now finds her voice in light of day.
Our paths converge in hope's project,
In threads of redemption, connect.

From darkness to light, journey one,
In life's tapestry, story spun.
Forgiveness, love, chance to renew,
In heart of Lakewood, dreams come true.

Overwhelmed by guilt and a desire to make amends, Clara reached out to Marcus. Initially, he was reluctant to meet her, still harboring resentment for the past. However, curiosity and a sense of closure led him to agree. Their first meeting in a quiet café was tense, filled with unspoken emotions and guarded conversations.

Clara, while nervously stirring her coffee said, "Marcus, I… I can't thank you enough for what you did. You saved my life."

"I didn't do it for you, Clara. I just happened to be there." Marcus said, sitting stiffly with his arms crossed.

Clara looking down, sighed and said, "I understand. Still, I owe you an apology. For everything. I was wrong, and I hurt you deeply."

"You think an apology can fix everything? You ruined my career, Clara. You took away everything I worked for." Marcus replied, his eye narrowing, gesticulating and almost knocking his drink over.

"I know. And I'm so sorry. I was blinded by ambition, and I made terrible choices. I can't change the past, but I want to make things right." Clara responded, her voice trembling.

"Why now? Why after all this time?" Marcus asked, his voice softening slightly.

"The accident... it made me realize how fragile life is. I don't want to carry this guilt anymore. I want to help you, if you'll let me." She said, meeting his gaze.

He paused, then sighed, "I don't know, Clara. It's not that simple. Trust isn't something you can just rebuild overnight."

"I understand. I'm not asking for your forgiveness right away. Just... give me a chance to prove that I've changed." She nodded.

"Alright. One chance. But don't expect me to forget everything." He said reluctantly.

"Thank you, Marcus. That's all I ask." She said, smiling faintly.

As they continued to meet, Clara's genuine remorse began to break through Marcus's defenses. She offered to help him in any way she could, and slowly, Marcus started to open up about his struggles and lost dreams. Their encounters were a rollercoaster of emotions, with moments of anger, sadness, and unexpected connection.

Marcus had always been an artist at heart. His sketches and paintings were once his refuge, a way to express the emotions he couldn't put into words. However, after his fallout with Clara, he had abandoned his passion, though he found joy in teaching young kids the intricacies of being an artist. The betrayal and subsequent struggle to rebuild his life left him disillusioned and creatively blocked.

Clara's relentless efforts to support Marcus began to bear fruit. She helped him reconnect with his passion for art, providing him with opportunities to showcase his work. Marcus, seeing Clara's sincere attempts to make amends, found it in his heart to forgive her.

In a pivotal moment, Marcus shared his own journey of pain and healing, encouraging Clara to confront her past traumas. He helped her see that her ruthless ambition was a shield against her own fears and insecurities. This mutual exchange of vulnerability and support led to a profound transformation in both their lives.

Clara's genuine remorse and Marcus's forgiveness became the foundation of their renewed relationship. They realized that their paths, though fraught with pain, had led them to a place of mutual healing and redemption.

The community project became a turning point for Marcus, though he didn't realize it at first. Clara, in her quest for redemption, spent time at the community center and stumbled upon some of Marcus's old sketches, tucked away in a forgotten corner. As she sifted through the dusty papers, her eyes fell upon a painting that took her breath away.

It was a portrait with a lady in a red dress at the center of a lively scene, dancing to music played by a band of men. The colors were vibrant, the brushstrokes fluid and expressive. The lady's dress swirled around her, capturing the motion and joy of the dance. The musicians, each lost in their own world of melody, added depth and harmony to the scene. It was a spectacular portrait and a remarkable representation of Marcus's talents.

Clara stood there, mesmerized by the painting. She could almost hear the music, feel the rhythm, and see the joy in the lady's eyes. The painting was not just a piece of art; it was a window into Marcus's soul, revealing a depth of emotion and creativity that she had never known. It was a stark contrast to the man she had wronged, a man who had once been full of life and passion.

"This is incredible. How could I have been so blind?" Clara whispered to herself.

Determined to make amends, Clara sought out Marcus. She found him in a quiet corner of the community center, working on a new project.

His face was a mask of concentration, but there was a hint of sadness in his eyes.

Approaching him cautiously, she said, "Marcus, I found some of your old sketches. There's one in particular that... it's amazing. The lady dancing with the band. It's beautiful."

Marcus looked up, surprise and a touch of wariness in his eyes.

"That was one of my favorites. I painted it during a time when I still believed in my dreams." He said, softly.

"You still have that talent, Marcus. You shouldn't hide it. Let the world see what you can do." She responded earnestly.

Clara was captivated by the raw emotion and talent in Marcus's artwork. She saw a side of him she had never known and felt a deep sense of responsibility for stifling his gift.

Marcus's defenses began to crumble as Clara's genuine admiration and encouragement broke through his walls. She arranged for his artwork to be displayed as part of the community project, giving him a platform to showcase his talent. The community's response was overwhelmingly positive. Marcus's art became a central feature of the project, drawing attention and praise. The recognition reignited his passion and confidence, leading him to create more and explore new artistic avenues.

On the first anniversary of Clara's recovery from the hospital, Marcus painted a portrait of Clara depicting her walking away from darkness into the light with her hand outstretched as if she was offering help to others. It was a gift he gave her. Clara was moved by the portrait, shedding a few tears when she first saw it.

A week later, Sharrod Cole, the gentleman who had received Marcus's discarded portrait, walked into the community center. The morning sun streamed through the windows, casting a warm glow over the bustling activity inside. Sharrod's presence commanded attention as he approached Marcus and Clara, who were engrossed in their work.

"I have been looking for you, but could not find you. Someone said you'd be here. I came to say thank you for the portrait you gave me. It fetched fifty thousand dollars at an auction for our organization. Your portrait has been a blessing to our children." Sharrod said, smiling warmly.

Marcus and Clara stared at each other, their eyes wide with shock and disbelief. The news from Sharrod Cole was unexpected, yet profoundly moving. Marcus felt a surge of emotions—gratitude, pride, and a deep sense of purpose. His artwork, once a symbol of his pain, had become a beacon of hope for those in need.

"Fifty thousand dollars? I... I can't believe it. Thank you, Sharrod. I'm so glad it could help." Marcus responded, his voice trembling with emotion.

Sharrod stepped forward and enveloped Marcus in a heartfelt hug, the embrace conveying more than words ever could. Clara watched, her heart swelling with pride and joy for her friend. The moment was a testament to the transformative power of art and the impact of Marcus's journey.

Sharrod releasing Marcus, from his bear hug, his eyes shining said, "Your talent is a gift, Marcus. Never forget that."

As Sharrod was about to leave, Marcus made him a promise, two portraits to his non-profit foundation to support the children each year was his donation. Sharrod was ecstatic, thanking Marcus profusely for his generosity and heart.

As Sharrod left, Marcus and Clara stood in silence, absorbing the magnitude of what had just happened. Marcus's journey back to art was not just about personal fulfillment but also about healing and redemption. As his career revived, he found a sense of purpose and joy that had been missing for years. His art flourished, and he began to gain recognition beyond the community project, opening doors to new opportunities.

Clara's role in Marcus's resurgence validated her efforts to make amends. Seeing Marcus thrive gave her a profound sense of accomplishment and reinforced her commitment to supporting others. Their shared journey of healing and growth brought Marcus and Clara closer. They developed a deep, respectful friendship, built on mutual support and understanding. Marcus's success as an artist symbolized the power of forgiveness and the possibility of new beginnings.

"You've come a long way, Marcus. I'm so proud of you." She said, smiling at Marcus, her eyes filled with warmth.

"I couldn't have done it without you, Clara. Thank you for believing in me." Marcus retorted, smiling back, his voice steady.

Their bond, forged through trials and triumphs, was a testament to the resilience of the human spirit and the healing power of forgiveness. Together, they looked forward to a future filled with hope, creativity, and endless possibilities.

As Clara and Marcus continued their journey of healing and redemption, the community project flourished, bringing together people from all walks of life. Among the volunteers was Emily, Clara's younger sister. Initially, Emily's involvement was driven by her passion for social causes, but as she spent more time at the community center, she found herself drawn to Marcus.

Emily and Marcus's paths crossed frequently during the project. Their shared dedication to the community and mutual respect for each other's talents created a strong foundation for their relationship.

On a warm sunny afternoon with the sun fully at the horizon, Emily walked into Lakewood community center where Marcus was busy creating his vision on a canvas. Smiling as she watched Marcus paint the mural, she said, "Your art is incredible, Marcus. It's like you bring the walls to life."

Marcus, grinning back replied appreciatively, "Thanks, Emily. Your energy and ideas have really transformed this place. It's inspiring to work with you."

Their conversations, initially centered around the project, gradually became more personal. They shared stories, dreams, and fears, finding comfort and understanding in each other's company.

Clara, observing the growing bond between her sister and Marcus, felt a mix of emotions. She was happy for them but also worried about the complexities their relationship might bring. However, she realized that her journey of redemption had not only healed her relationship with Marcus but also paved the way for new beginnings.

One day, Clara and Emily bonded while having ice cream at the local dairy. During a quiet moment, Clara leaning over, said to Emily, "You and Marcus seem to have something special. I'm glad you found each other."

Emily blushing slightly, said, "It's unexpected, but it feels right. Thank you, Clara. For everything."

As the project neared completion, Marcus and Emily's relationship blossomed into love. They supported each other through challenges and celebrated their successes together. Clara, the thread that had brought them together, watched with a sense of fulfillment and joy.

"I never thought I'd find someone who understands me like you do." Marcus uttered, holding Emily's hand, looking into her eyes.

"And I never thought I'd find someone who makes me feel so alive. I'm grateful for every moment with you." She replied, smiling warmly. They sealed their admiration with a kiss and a hug.

The community project culminated in a grand event, celebrating the collective efforts and achievements of everyone involved. Clara, Marcus, and Emily stood together, a testament to the power of forgiveness, love, and redemption.

During the celebration, Clara addressed the crowd saying, "This project has been a journey of healing and growth for all of us. It's a reminder that even in our darkest moments, there's always a chance for new beginnings."

As the crowd applauded, Clara looked at Marcus and Emily, knowing that their love was a beautiful outcome of the path she had chosen to walk. Their story was a testament to the transformative power of forgiveness and the unexpected ways in which life can bring people together.

17

Trust Shattered

Nestled in the heart of Texas, Lubbock was a town where conservative values ran deep, and the air was thick with the scent of blooming wildflowers in spring. The Thompson family home sat in a pristine neighborhood, its white picket fence and well-tended garden a testament to the simple, wholesome life they cherished. Inside, the walls were adorned with family photographs and mementos of a life well-lived, the air always filled with the warmth and comfort of home. Each room in the house told a story, from the cozy kitchen where Susan baked her famous apple pies, to the living room where the family gathered for Sunday dinners, their laughter echoing through the hallways.

Richard Thompson, known to everyone as Dick, was the second child and the notorious black sheep of the family. He was like bacon, with many vices, his excessive fat frying him up in his own skillet of life. With a rebellious streak that often led him into trouble, he was a constant source of worry for his parents, a shadow that darkened their days. His erratic behavior and poor choices were like dark clouds perpetually hanging over the family. Despite his charming smile and quick wit, Dick's life was a series of missteps and wrong turns that overshadowed the Thompson family's good name.

Susan, the matriarch, was a dedicated healthcare worker with a nurturing spirit that touched the lives of many. Her gentle hands healed countless patients, and her kind heart provided solace to her children. She had devoted her life to instilling values of hard work and compassion in her children. Her heart ached for her wayward son, Dick, and the worry etched lines into her face that no amount of time could erase. Every night, she prayed for him, hoping for a miracle that would set him on the right path, a divine lighthouse on the shores of his despair.

Gerald, the patriarch of the Thompson family, was a man of stern resolve and unwavering determination. He worked tirelessly in the oil industry, enduring long hours and grueling conditions as a rig operator. The scorching Texas sun beat down on him, and the relentless grind of the machinery echoed in his ears, but Gerald's spirit remained unbroken. His hands, calloused and weathered from years of hard labor, were a testament to his dedication to providing for his family.

Through his hard work, Gerald was able to educate his children, giving them the lifeline to a brighter future. He took immense pride in seeing most of his children become successful in their careers. Each achievement was a beacon of hope, a sign that his sacrifices were not in vain. But amidst these successes, there was a shadow that loomed over Gerald's heart—his first son, Dick.

Sadly, Gerald spent most of his life trying to fix his rebellious son, Dick, but to no avail. Dick's constant run-ins with the law were a source of endless heartache. Each arrest chipped away at Gerald's strength, his heart growing heavier with every bail and lawyer fee. Nights were spent at the police station, the fluorescent lights casting a harsh glare on his weary face as he waited to bring his son home, like a persistent nightmare haunting his dreams. Dick's quomodocunquizing behavior raised eyebrows within his family, as he seemed more interested in making money by any means necessary rather than adhering to the ethical standards set by his parents.

Despite the toll it took on him, Gerald never gave up on Dick. He believed that somewhere beneath the layers of mischief and defiance, there was a good man struggling to break free. Gerald's love for his son was unyielding, a steadfast flame that burned through the darkest times. He carried the weight of Dick's mistakes on his shoulders, each one a heavy burden that pressed down on his spirit.

"One day, you'll find your way," Gerald would say to Dick, his voice tinged with both hope and desperation. "I know there's more to you than this."

But with each passing year, the strain became more evident. Gerald's once strong frame grew frailer, his steps slower. The worry lines etched into his face deepened, and the spark in his eyes dimmed.

Carla, the oldest sibling, was a nurse whose caring nature and dedication to helping others were a reflection of their mother's influence. Often acting as the family's anchor, her steady presence was a source of strength for her siblings. Her nurturing spirit extended beyond her patients to her family, always offering a listening ear and a comforting hug when needed.

Lisa, the younger sister, was a dietician. Her calm and collected demeanor contrasted sharply with Dick's chaotic life. She found solace in helping others lead healthier lives, her work a sanctuary from the turmoil caused by her brother. Lisa's serene presence was like a balm to the family, her advice always delivered with gentle wisdom.

James, the youngest, was a park ranger whose love for nature and protecting the environment mirrored the family's core values of caring and responsibility. James always kept away from Dick, knowing his brother's ruthless nature. While the other siblings were more forgiving, James could not stand being in the same room as his brother, the pain Dick had caused their parents still a raw wound. The rustling leaves and chirping birds of the forest were his refuge from the discord at home.

Growing up, Dick was always drawn to the wrong crowd, gravitating toward the most seasoned criminals in town. The allure of danger and the thrill of rebellion were too intoxicating for him to resist. He spent his days in a haze of recklessness, drifting from one misadventure to another. His constant run-ins with the law were a stain on the Thompson family's reputation, casting long shadows over their otherwise respectable lives.

Dick's escapades became legendary in Lubbock, each story more harrowing than the last. From petty thefts to more serious crimes, his name was whispered with a mix of fear and disdain, though his cohorts admired his villainous image and ability to frequently stay one step ahead of law enforcement. Gerald's repeated efforts to bail him out and hire lawyers took a toll on his health. Each late-night call from the police station, every desperate plea for help, added another layer of worry to Gerald's heart. The weight of his son's wayward path was like a millstone around his neck, dragging him down into a sea of anxiety and sorrow.

The final straw came one bleak winter night when Dick was arrested for a particularly egregious offense. The strain was too much for Gerald. His heart, already weakened by years of worry, finally gave out. He collapsed in the family home, clutching his chest as Susan frantically called for help. Despite the paramedics' best efforts, Gerald passed away, leaving the family devastated. The family was left reeling from the loss, their grief compounded by the bitter realization that Gerald had died trying to save his wayward son.

After Gerald's passing, it appeared that Dick had turned over a new leaf. The guilt and grief that weighed on him seemed to spark a desire for redemption. He opened a small antiques store in Lubbock, claiming to have found a passion for collecting and selling treasures from Mexico. The shop was a quaint little place, filled with curiosities and relics that whispered tales of distant lands. Though his siblings rarely saw customers in his shop, they were relieved to see him seemingly on a path to redemption.

In 2006, Susan, now retired, received a surprise visit from Dick. He arrived at her doorstep with a warm smile, carrying bags of groceries and a handful of cash. The gesture was so uncharacteristic that it left her speechless. Susan's eyes welled with tears as she embraced her son, her heart swelling with a mixture of hope and disbelief.

"Dick, you have no idea how much this means to me," she said, her voice trembling with emotion.

Her son, who had once caused her endless worry, seemed to have finally found his way. The transformation was astonishing. The boy who had brought her so much heartache was now a man standing before her with a promise of better days. The sight of him, looking healthier and more determined than ever, filled Susan with a profound sense of hope. Her face showed the eternal optimism ingrained in a mother for her children. She believed that Dick had reclaimed his life and that he was on a path to success and redemption.

As the days turned into weeks, Dick continued to visit his mother regularly, each time bringing a little more light into her life like having a fresh bloom in the garden of her spirits. The change in him was evident to everyone who knew him. His siblings, though still wary, began to believe in his transformation. The once rebellious son seemed to be making amends, and for the first time in years, there was a glimmer of hope in the Thompson family.

A year later, the Thompson family's world was once again enveloped in grief as Susan passed away. The matriarch, who had been the bedrock of the family, was now gone, leaving her children to navigate the loss. The siblings gathered to honor her memory, each one wrapped in a shroud of sorrow and nostalgia. At the funeral home, the lachrymose atmosphere was palpable as they bid farewell to their beloved mother, tears streaming down their faces. Surrounded by his siblings, Dick stood with a solemn expression, holding a bright and beautiful diamond necklace.

"She deserves to wear this," he said, his voice cracking with emotion. "I bought it for her birthday. It's the least I can do for everything she's done for me."

Though surprised by the gesture, Carla, Lisa, and James agreed it was a fitting tribute. The necklace sparkled under the dim lights of the funeral home, a testament to their mother's unwavering love and sacrifice. It was as if the necklace was a final, glittering piece of their mother's legacy, encapsulating the love and hope she had always held for Dick.

Susan's funeral was a grand affair, held in the majestic Cathedral in Lubbock. The air was heavy with the scent of lilies and the soft murmur of condolences. The pews were filled with friends, family, and former patients she had cared for, each one a living testament to her kindness and dedication. The Cathedral's stained glass windows cast a kaleidoscope of colors over the gathering, their beauty a stark contrast to the sorrow in the room.

As the funeral procession made its way to the mausoleum, the diamond necklace lay gleaming on Susan's neck, a final token of love from her son. Her remains were gently placed in the mausoleum, the polished wood of the casket reflecting the somber faces of her children. The community gathered to pay their respects, their collective grief a silent tribute to the woman who had touched so many lives.

Six months later, Lubbock was rocked by a macabre event. The police investigated a break-in at the mausoleum, where several men had desecrated graves and stolen valuables from the dead. The news spread like wildfire, leaving the town in shock and disbelief. Among the stolen items was the diamond necklace that had adorned Susan's casket.

The police, upon arresting the culprits, traced the necklace back to Susan's grave. The investigation revealed a twisted web of crime that tainted the memory of the departed. When Carla was summoned to identify the stolen property, her heart pounded in her chest. The moment she saw the necklace, she knew it was the same one Dick had insisted their mother wear. She was arrested on suspicion of possessing stolen goods, a turn of events that rocked the Thompson family to its core.

At the police station, the truth began to unravel like a thread pulled from a tightly woven fabric. The necklace had been stolen during a robbery in which Maria Gonzalez, a matriarch in North Lubbock, was brutally murdered. Blood tests confirmed the necklace belonged to Maria, the remnants of her tragic end still etched in its crevices.

When Carla's siblings arrived, they were met with the grim reality of the situation. They explained to the police that Dick was the one who had placed the necklace on their mother. An APB was issued for Dick, the nefarious mastermind, and the search led authorities to Mexico, where he was eventually found and brought back for interrogation. The family's hopes for Dick's redemption were shattered, replaced by a painful new chapter in their ongoing saga of sorrow and betrayal.

Under the unforgiving glare of the interrogation room lights, Dick's resolve began to crumble. The walls felt like they were closing in, the oppressive silence only broken by the steady ticking of a clock. Each tick was a reminder of the time running out on his lies. The FBI agents, their eyes sharp and unyielding, bore into him with relentless pressure. Sweat beaded on his forehead as he finally broke, the weight of his actions crashing down on him like a tidal wave.

"I was the getaway driver," Dick confessed, his voice barely more than a whisper. "The necklace was my cut."

The room seemed to grow colder as he continued, the gravity of his words hanging heavy in the air. He revealed that the robbery had been meticulously planned, involving not just his criminal associates but also cemetery workers who had been part of a sinister ring. The ring specialized in stealing from caskets, desecrating the resting places of the dead for profit.

The agents exchanged glances, their expressions a mix of anger and determination. With Dick's cooperation, they began to unravel the dark web of crime that had infiltrated their town. To keep Dick's identity hidden, the FBI put him in a vehicle with a brown paper bag over his face, the edges crinkling with each breath he took. The drive to the cemetery felt interminable, the weight of his betrayal pressing down on him.

When they arrived at the cemetery, the night was heavy with a tense silence, the tombstones standing like silent sentinels in the moonlight. Dick, his face still concealed, pointed shakily towards an obscure corner of the grounds. The FBI agents moved swiftly, their flashlights casting eerie beams through the fog. They uncovered a hidden stash of stolen items, buried deep in the bowels of the cemetery's vaults. The macabre discovery sent shockwaves through the community, transforming the once-quiet town of Lubbock into a hub of scandal and betrayal. Several members of the gang were arrested on the spot, their secretive operations laid bare.

The news of Dick's confession hit the Thompson family like a sledgehammer. The siblings, who had dared to hope for his redemption, were now consumed by a searing anger. Carla, Lisa, and James felt a deep sense of betrayal, the brother they thought had reformed had dragged their family name through the mud. The bond they had once shared was now shattered, each shard a painful reminder of Dick's deceit.

"How could you do this to us?" Carla's voice trembled with rage and sorrow as she confronted Dick. "To Mom, to Dad, to all of us?"

Lisa's eyes, usually so calm, were filled with tears of hurt and frustration. "We trusted you, Dick. We thought you had changed."

James, who had always kept his distance, felt his anger boil over. "You've disgraced us all. I never want to see you again."

The siblings vowed never to speak to Dick again, their connection to him severed by the corrosive power of his actions. The once-tight family unit was left in tatters, their trust and love irrevocably damaged.

Facing a long prison sentence, Dick knew he had little choice but to broker a deal with the FBI. His nights were filled with the haunting thought of spending the rest of his life behind bars, a prospect that terrified him. He offered information about other low level individuals involved in the ring, hoping for some semblance of leniency.

At first, the FBI agents balked at the deal Dick proposed. "No deal," said the lead investigator, his voice a sharp blade cutting through the air. "You are a criminal." Just as the investigator was about to walk out of the room, Dick played his final card.

"What if I told you that some people higher up in this community were also involved in this ring?" he asked, his voice trembling with desperation.

The FBI agents sitting around the table, who were ready to wrap up, straightened. The lead investigator paused, considering Dick's words.

"Okay," he said slowly. "I'm not making any promises, but if you deliver someone of a high rank in this community, we will propose a lenient sentence for your cooperation."

Dick got into the FBI vehicle, his face once again obscured by the brown paper bag, and they drove to none other than the house of the sheriff of Lubbock. The house was cloaked in darkness, a silent witness to the unfolding drama. The agents served the search warrant to the sheriff's wife, who watched with a mixture of fear and confusion as they combed through their home.

Inside, they discovered more stolen items, the evidence of the sheriff's betrayal laid bare. However, the sheriff himself was not home. An APB was sent out for his arrest, and for an entire week, the search for him gripped the town. The sheriff's wife went on TV, her plea for him to surrender echoing through the homes of Lubbock's residents.

Unfortunately, the search ended in tragedy. The sheriff's dead body was found about sixty miles from Lubbock, hidden behind a shed on a property he owned. In the shed, the investigators found a suicide note expressing his regret for letting the community down. They also discovered cash and more stolen items, remnants of his criminal endeavors.

The community was shell-shocked by the turn of events. The sheriff, a figure of authority and trust, had been unmasked as part of a criminal conspiracy, plunging the town into deeper turmoil. The revelation was a bitter pill for the residents of Lubbock, who had placed their faith in those sworn to protect them.

The story of the Thompson family is one of heartbreak, betrayal, and the far-reaching consequences of misguided loyalty. Dick's actions not only cost him his freedom but also the trust and love of his family. His betrayal was a wound that cut deep, leaving scars that time could never fully heal. The siblings, though scarred by the events, found solace in each other, determined to rebuild their lives free from the shadows of their brother's crimes.

Carla, Lisa, and James leaned on one another, their bond strengthened by the trials they had endured. In the quiet moments, they reflected on their shared past and the lessons learned. The love and resilience they found in each other became the cornerstone of their healing. Lisa penned a poem about their experience which read:

Unbroken Bond

In the depths of sorrow, we found our way,
Three hearts entwined, forever to stay.
Through trials and tears, our spirits grew,
In the darkest of nights, the morning dew.

The weight of betrayal, a heavy stone,
Yet in each other's love, we were never alone.
From the ashes of pain, our strength did bloom,
A garden of hope in a world of gloom.

Our past, a tapestry of joy and strife,
Woven with threads of our shared life.
Each lesson learned, a beacon of light,
Guiding us through the endless night.

In quiet moments, our hearts would mend,
The bond of siblings, a love without end.
With each other's support, we stood tall,
Together we rose, we did not fall.

Through the storms of life, we held on tight,
Our love, a beacon in the darkest night.
And in that love, we found our way,
Three hearts entwined, forever to stay.

As the sun set over the rolling fields of Lubbock, casting a warm, golden glow over the Thompson family home, there was a palpable sense of peace. The orange and pink hues of the sky seemed to wrap around the house, embracing it in a gentle, healing light. Inside, the air was filled with quiet resilience, the echoes of laughter and love intertwining with the bittersweet memories of the past.

The shadows of betrayal and heartbreak still lingered, ghostly remnants of a time marked by pain and sorrow. But these shadows no longer defined the family; instead, they served as reminders of their strength and the trials they had overcome. Each sibling bore the scars of their shared journey and carried the unbreakable bond forged in those fires.

Carla, Lisa, and James stood together on the porch, watching the sun dip below the horizon. They reflected on the lessons learned, the love rediscovered, and the hope rekindled. Each moment of pain had brought them closer, each tear shed had strengthened their resolve. Together, they looked to the future with hope and determination, ready to build a new legacy free from the weight of betrayal.

Meanwhile, Dick faced the consequences of his actions. He was sentenced to five years in prison, with three years suspended for his cooperation with authorities. The reality of his sentence was a harsh reminder of the path he had chosen and the price he had paid for his misdeeds. As he looked out from his prison cell, he reflected on the choices that had led him here. There was a flicker of remorse in his eyes, a faint hope that one day he could find redemption.

For the Thompson family, the journey was far from over. They knew there would be more challenges ahead. But as they stood together, united by their love and resilience, they felt a profound sense of peace. They had faced the storm and emerged stronger, their spirits unbroken.

In the quiet moments, when the world seemed to stand still, they found solace in each other. The love that bound them was a light guiding them through the darkest times, a beacon of hope in an uncertain world. The Thompson family was ready to embrace the future, their hearts filled with the promise of new beginnings and the strength of their enduring bond.

As the stars began to twinkle in the twilight sky, they knew that no matter what lay ahead, they would face it together, their spirits intertwined and forever strengthened by the trials they had endured.

SONNETS

1. Burden Of The Past

In her muddled mind, her son's a vestige,
    Of a once-burgeoning romance turned bad.
The lad, now an unwelcome refugee,
    In the adults' loveless commotion—sad.
She'd whip him hard, scream at his every fault,
    Hurling insults to mask her failures' pain,
For in the lad, she saw her man, her past,
    Her love's missteps, driving her thoughts insane.
The lad had no nose in their withered rose,
    Nor sparked he the flame in their burnt candle.
Their vain hearts, quite sullen, chose to impose,
    On the fragile, their failures to handle.
He sent no charms, nor blew their tryst's kisses,
He mustn't bear the venom of their hisses.

2. Character: The Sculptor Of Spirits

She dwells deep in the human soul—virtues;
    Like honesty's fragrance, ever so pure,
    Or vices, like envy's acrid allure,
Guiding our stance on life's vast avenues.
She's the reckless driver in rage's storm,
    The wild girl whose words lash out like a whip,
    Yet, she's the balm for grief's unyielding grip,
With kindness, she can a raging heart transform.
Her influence might sculpt or scatter worlds;
    Molding hearts where her essence firmly resides,
        Imprinting her mark, she sways, and she guides.
Urging unity when discord unfurls,
    Or watching as the fragile earth backslides,
        In every heartbeat, her power abides.

3. Charisma's Betrayal

They are mouthpieces of mankind's ethics,
    Oft on His behalf, claiming divine frame,
Yet, one is left speechless by their antics—
    Their egos more than the vast oceans claim.
With charisma that can't be bought with gold,
    Silver, or e'en the rarest finds of earth,
They conjure the frail minds of cohorts—bold,
    Leaving trails of pain and gall in their path.
Living not by His divine words' plain truth,
    But by their deeds, become the golden calf.
Bearing the brunt of their dealings uncouth,
    Their helpless cohorts succumb to their craft.
'Tis sad that those with divine aptitude,
Would display such deceitful attitude.

4. Chasing Feathered Dreams

As dusk whispers, we chase those nests of hopes,
    With brazen wings, we soar through skies unseen,
A dance of light where moonlit silver glows,
    In realms where stars and whispered wants convene.
Through fields of gold, where dawn's first blush ignites,
    We follow their trails on gossamer wings,
In every breath, a promise that excites,
    A symphony of life that softly sings.
With hearts alight, we journey through the night,
    In search of visions that flap just ahead,
A tapestry of wonder, pure delight,
    Where every step by inspiration led.
In trips of fancy, our spirits take flight,
A boundless sky, where endless hopes unite.

5. Christmas - Jewel Of Yesteryears

Once the sparkling jewel in winter's crown,
     The bright snow globe of happy memories,
Guiding glow of joyful hope's true beacon,
     And twinkling lights, and stars across the skies.
Your garden of lights, a feast for my soul,
     And fabric woven with laughter and cheer,
With joys and comfort remaking my whole,
     You cast a magic spell on me each year.
Then life's dark deluge starts to cast its spell,
     Engulfing fine December's lovely cheer;
Of loss and anguish, tolling a glum bell,
     My aching heart yearns for its yesteryears.
Bring back the bright lights, gentle snowfall, kind,
And pledge my life you'll ne'er put in a bind.

6. Currents Of Bliss And Fear

I swam a cheerful fish within the sea,
     And faced new earthquakes in my consciousness.
Communal bliss of fishes I did see,
     Floating in a current of happiness.
Yet in this realm, this joy is much fleeting,
     Weaving through liquid maze of glinting blades,
For in the abyss, tyrants are lurking;
     Their menace turns life into peril's waltz.
A splash, a wave, the titans of the deep,
     Their mouths swallowing large spools of the weak,
Like their pals; wolves on land with might to keep,
     Their power to devour, making lives bleak.
Each realm, it seems, to tyrants' fears is prone,
Their vile terror in shadows still unknown.

7. Dreams Of True Love

In dreams, I wander through the twilight's glow,
Where secrets dance and whisper soft and low.
    A heart that yearns, a soul that seeks to find,
    The dear one, whose love will fore'er be kind.
Beneath the moon's embrace, I search the night,
For eyes that shine with love's eternal light.
    A touch, a smile, a bond time can't sever,
    A love that's true, lasting now and ever.
Through lonely days and nights of silent tears,
I hold the hope that love will calm my fears.
    For in the depths of longing, hearts entwine,
    And in that union, true love's light will shine.
Until that day when fate shall bring us near,
I'll cherish dreams and hold my longing dear.

8. Ebbing Morality

The world is mired in drought of righteousness;
    Its rivers, bone dry with harsh, darkened minds,
Oft in charge, wielding swords of wickedness,
    To scare and maim hearts preserving these lands.
Its streams of living waters are ebbing;
    Terror and tyrants parching its landscape
With deceit, blasphemy and mass killing,
    Ensuring the faultless have no escape.
His rain of love seized by tyrants with lies,
    Reaches not the hearts of those thirsty souls.
Those who once preached of Him are now allies
    Of tyrant's lies; their once pure hearts now ghouls.
Send Lord your virtues laden rain to drown,
Those soiled hearts, saving the world from its frown.

9. Echoes Of Poverty

With empty hands and hearts that barely beat,
　　The weary souls of many tread their path.
In places drear, where hope and light retreat,
　　They face the world's indifference and wrath.
Their dreams once bright now fade in hunger's grip,
　　As children's laughter turns to silent cries.
In homes where cold and sorrow see them weep,
　　The spark of life within their spirit dies.
Yet in the darkest night, a flame persists,
　　A will to rise above the harshest plight.
For in their hearts, a strength that still exists,
　　To fight for dawn and bring the morning light.
Though dearth and need may cast a cruel shade,
The human spirit's light will never fade.

10. Eternal Flame

Where passion's fire in hearts forever glows,
　　A flame ignites that time cannot subdue.
Through trials faced and each bleak storm that blows,
　　Its light endures, unwavering and true.
In tender whispers shared beneath the stars,
　　And gentle touches felt through fleeting years,
Its essence shines, unmarked by life's deep scars,
　　A beacon bright that conquers all our fears.
Though seasons change and youth may fade away,
　　Its unique warmth remains a constant guide.
In every moment, night, or brightest day,
　　Its flame persists, forever by our side.
Eternal is the fire which it ignites,
A timeless glow that warms the darkest nights.

11.   Façade Of Eloquence

He is a bombast with grand words flowing,
  Quite smoothly from glib lips, which echo false;   .
Yet consumed by his enthusiasts: fawning
  On his presumed firm grip on learning's pulse.
His counterpart, quite humble yet studious,
  Calm, thoughtful, and consistent with wisdom,
Better than most, voices nothing dubious,
  Yet poorly viewed through their chieftains' prism.
His speeches, each with flowery word and tale,
  Would stir up a tame hound, straining its leash,
His feigned lisps and gestures would impale,
  The keen eyes of rhetoricians in a flash.
Nonetheless, their world admires the player,
The allure: the upright, oft the loser.

12.   Golden Light Of Happiness

Beneath sunny skies, her sweet laughter blooms,
  Hearts dance to sweet melodies of delight,
A symphony of smiles in every room,
  Chasing sorrows away with golden light.
She is that jolly, gentle breeze that sings,
  Painting bright rainbows after life's gray rain,
Lifting our spirits on hope's fragile wings,
  Her canvas of broad smiles that knows no pain.
Her embrace, like a warm familiar hand,
  A friend to every heart, and not a quest.
Her treasure found in life's oft-shifting sand,
  And quiet contentment in mankind's breath.
Only fools would reject her warm embrace;
For without, sadness e'er their lonely place.

13. Haunted By Innocence

There in dark lands, where shadows steal their light,
　　Severed from nurture by man's forces vile,
Clipping their wings, so their futures won't take flight,
　　Through wars and menace stacked up in a pile.
Yet their pure love, the world can't comprehend,
　　Their dreams, like fragile glass, shatter and fall,
Their fading light, a glow that won't ascend,
　　And silent cries, a song of sorrow's call.
Wilting flowers, see them in their meekness,
　　Their voices haunt me—enduring spirits,
Spurning to be silenced by the darkness,
　　Of my prolonged and lonely sleepless nights.
O Lord, shield these little angels from harm,
Then will my nights in sleepy safety calm.

14. His Reckoning

On that day, after quite a long journey,
　　A bold book of his deeds in hand will bring.
For assent in home of the Trinity,
　　Ready he must, for his real reckoning.
Before His throne, he must present and show,
　　How his whole life was used, and in what wise;
His oft good works, perhaps bad, but a few,
　　In view of the angels of paradise.
He shall be alone, with those deeds alone;
　　No tributes, or rather proxy defense,
No erstwhile errs or near misses bemoan,
　　And Michael won't hear his pleas for redress.
It is a pure count of his erstwhile deeds.
He must hope for higher count of good seeds.

15. Humbled Arrogance

Within grand halls, where ego's banners fly,
    He stands, a stubborn fortress, built of self,
His walls adorned with boasts that touch the sky,
    Yet deep within, he crumbles like a shelf.
For his pride, though quite bold, is but a mask,
    A fragile shell against life's humbling blows,
Blinding the eyes to wisdom's gentle ask,
    And veils the heart from truths that freely flow.
Succumb ye not, but learn from his strong sway,
    To temper pride with grace and empathy.
For in humility, we find the way,
    To rise above our flaws and truly see.
Great minds shed oft the armor of conceit;
And seek the path where kindness and truth meet.

16. In The Depths Of Betrayal

Midst darkened depths, where trust once brightly shone,
    Her serpent coils, its poisonous intent.
It blew her kiss, a dagger to the bone,
    Unsheathed by hands that once were love's lament.
The vows we made, like fragile webs, now torn,
    As whispered secrets echo through the night.
Each uttered word a blade, each silence worn,
    Our once-entwined hearts, severed in their flight.
Such hate! Her fire consumes both heart and mind,
    A tempest raging 'gainst love's feeble shore.
The once-beloved, now foe, we seek to bind,
    Yet find no solace in this bitter war.
Mourn I what often was so pure and sweet,
For her cold venom's kiss has sealed our fate.

17. Integrity: True Estate Of The Soul

Among steadfast hearts that tell the truth well,
    Its majesty stands firm, a guiding light.
Through trials faced, its strength man cannot quell,
    A beacon shining through the darkest night.
No fleeting winds of change can sway its course,
    Nor enticements' whispers lead it astray.
For in its core lies an unyielding force,
    A moral compass that will never sway.
With every step, it walks the path of right,
    Unmoved by shadows cast by doubt or fear.
Its voice, a clarion call in dimmest night,
    To hold man's values ever close and near.
The world must treasure most this noble trait,
For in its grace, our souls find true estate.

18. Love Over Steel

Man's darkness cast by steel and powder's might,
    Where echoes of the past still haunt the day,
A world once bright now shrouded in the night,
    As lives are lost and dreams are swept away.
The promise of protection turns to fear,
    When man's quick quest for safety brings despair.
In homes and streets, the cries of pain we hear,
    A silent plea for peace hangs in the air.
Yet hope remains, a spark within the dark,
    That hearts can change, and minds can find a way,
To lay them down and heal each wounded mark,
    Forming a world where love and kindness stay.
In man's hands rest the power to create,
A future free from bloodshed, free from hate.

19. Moral Contradictions

There are those who oft keep His laws as writ,
    Yet now and then, stray from His holy script,
And justify their deeds with vain, wry wit—
    Their good deeds outweigh their ills by a lot.
Calm the seas of those needy recipients,
    Set on pedestals, parents, and spouses,
Pray oft, and with dove-like peace solve dissents,
    Yet like storms, menace, and heave harsh curses.
No one with a clear conscience should attempt
    To defend a galling and false compare;
Sin is lame, and moral deeds are upright,
    And there's no room for flouting His decree.
If your heart dons conflicting consciences,
Be fit to live with the consequences.

20. Navigating The Virile Sea

Her wisdom unequal to their shared minds;
    Surpassing even their rare, best efforts,
Wise and wonderful, her mind always finds
    Keys that elude their oft-heralded sorts.
Her counsel sought oft in times of need,
    Yet she's unlike them; they see not her brain.
Her pure charisma compelling indeed,
    Yet, "she is not like us," they oft complain.
Sadly, this is their ocean of egos,
    Where she must sail 'gainst the whims of their winds.
Arrogant, strong, and bold are their ethos,
    Yet, she too can weather their ocean's fiends.
She's forced to pilot in their virile sea,
Where her ship must e'er in conformance be.

21. Paradise Found

Those lands where golden sunlight gently gleams,
    And rivers whisper secrets to the trees,
A place exists beyond our wildest dreams,
    Where joy and peace are carried on the breeze.
Fields are emerald rugs, skies a sapphire dome,
    With laughter echoing through every street.
In every heart, a love that feels like home,
    Where strangers smile and every soul you meet.
No shadows fall, no tears you'd ever see,
    For kindness reigns and harmony is king.
In this fair land, all worries swiftly flee,
    And every day, new hopes and dreams take wing.
A paradise where happiness is found,
In this utopia, true love knows no bounds.

22. Shadows Of Insomnia

'Neath the cover of night, I lie awake,
    The specks on the ceiling shimmer and gleam,
My mind flowing like water in a lake,
    Caught in the web of an unending dream.
The clock ticks on, its hand a steady beat,
    A symphony of silence fills the air,
My thoughts, they race, a never-ending fleet,
    In the stillness, I find no comfort there.
The moonlight casts its shadows on the wall,
    A dance of light that keeps my eyes aglow,
I hear the whispers of the night's soft call,
    Yet you remain a distant, fleeting show.
O, restless sea, you are a friend and foe,
For in your firm grasp, the hours, they move slow.

23. Silent Tears

'Neath the sun's rays, our love once brightly burned,
    A flame that danced, then flickered, dimmed away.
The echoes of her laughter still return,
    A haunting melody that cannot sway.
The moon, our silent witness, wept for us,
    As promises, once certain, dissolved like dew.
The stars, like shattered dreams, grew ever sparse,
    And time, unkind, unraveled what we knew.
Yet, her fond smile resides within my heart,
    A bittersweet refrain that lingers on,
The ache of loss, a tear that will not part,
    As her sweet memories continue to dawn.
And here I stand, a sad man lost for words;
Forever bound by love's elusive cords.

24. Sorrow's Bond

I'm longing, but for it, a different peek,
    Yet wonder oft what that picture might be.
Would a glow be on me at my sun's peak,
    Granting views of the pleasant, vibrant sea?
Lately, my heart's been deluged by its rain,
    With my fond memories' treasure chest drowned,
By its vile reign of sorrow and of pain,
    Binding joys, splitting strong ties and bond.
A brother and another, its hands snatched;
    Their demise slow until it clutched their breath.
A mother and a sister, its pull drowned;
    Their descent—painful cries to reach its depth.
My tearful eyes cry out for better views,
Of life's great treasures, those of merry news.

25. The Creaking Silence

Rear door entry; one secret of our house,
    Front door keys to her heart slipped from my grip.
With chance to see once again my dear spouse,
    "I miss her dearly," my lonely heart quipped.
Creak! Creak! I heard from our lovely bedroom,
    Creak! Creak! Not my darling wife, she is meek.
Creak! Creak! Creak! Disgust I saw and the gloom,
    Creak! Now drowned by their silence—made me sick.
If I grab my gun, would it be self-defense?
    Barge I in on them? This I'm on the fence.
Fight I for her love? Yet this makes no sense,
    Grab I my phone, taping the evidence.
Creak! Creak! Hands shaking, standing on knees weak,
Creak! Creak! Creak! My once bright daylight, now bleak.

26. The Dark Angel Calls

Here he comes, quite happy in much fanfare,
    His mind on sensual lusts and his treasure.
Run here and there from affair to affair;
    Such profound pleasure for him to endure.
Yet it will beset him, living beastly,
    Outside His laws, without a heart contrite.
With pleasure, his heart, it will smite swiftly,
    And never consent, nor give him respite.
More, it sets not by means, gold or riches,
    Nor by emperor, king, sage, or princes,
But comes in stealth sternly and reaches
    For his worldly treasures, life, and seizes.
Once it besets, amends it cannot make,
For mercy and pity it does forsake.

27. The Folly Of Wisdom

Ignore his folly, act not in his play,
　　Or blindly, you'll be just as much a fool.
Respond to match his idiocy's display,
　　And he'll boast wisdom, though he's but a tool.
To trust him with your words is self-harm's choice,
　　Like maiming feet or sipping venom's kiss.
As useless as old legs that lost their voice,
　　Is truth in his mouth, where reason's amiss.
Like an archer who shoots without a cause,
　　Is he who'd prize such aimless, harmful skill.
As thorns grasped by a drunk, heedless of laws,
　　Are words from his lips, prone to hurt and kill.
See those who in their own eyes seem so wise?
More hope lies in the fool than in such guise.

28. The Gallant Gardener

He plays oft on the luscious onion fields,
　　Their blooms friendly to his frequent visits.
Like a busy bee, his vast pollen spreads
　　To young, pretty shoots, eyeing where he sits.
His mind oft restless, craving more delight,
　　Sets not on one bud, but seeks the many,
Yearning for his presence—the rapture's sight,
　　Of the one with special skills and savvy.
Spreading his wings over each onion bud,
　　No complaints or rifts are raised by patrons;
Perhaps he is quite good, a special stud,
　　Or a lucky bee, not without options.
If his luck runs out, he must be mindful,
Onions have the means to make one tearful.

29. Their Romantic Boat

Their romantic boat, steady in their stream,
    Flowed despite the storms; those spousal strains.
Jealous hearts who tried their love demean,
    Were stranded, soaked in futility's rains.
Rowing with the tides, they endured with joy,
    Their efforts joined in sweet marital bliss,
Against the flows, they paddled to employ,
    Ensuring no shared desire went amiss.
Then a black hole emerged upon their path,
    Dragging down their boat to murky depths,
Testing their commitment, seething their wrath;
    Dark coins soiled the pure love within their hearts.
Lost at sea, the silver capsized their boat,
Pulling them down, while virtue stayed afloat.

30. Veil Of Ignorance

Though knowledge fails in cloudy hearts to spread,
    Its petals bloom, a veil upon the mind,
With tendrils wrapped around those thoughts we dread,
    And truth remains elusive, hard to find.
Yet in this darkness, seeds of wisdom grow,
    For its strong chains, though binding, spur our quest;
To seek the light, to learn, to fully know,
    And break those chains that bind us to unrest.
Strive we must to pierce this veil of night,
    To question, seek, and challenge what we see.
Its stubbornness, when faced with curious might,
    Becomes a stepping stone to clarity.
Embracing knowledge, minds will truly see,
And banish its impact with truth's decree.

31. Whispers And Warnings

Without wood to fuel, a fire will fade,
　　Without a gossip, strife will quiet down.
A quarrelsome soul stirs conflict unswayed,
　　Like charcoal to embers, wood sparks a crown.
The words of a gossip, like choice morsels,
　　Traverse to a weary man's inmost parts.
Foes may disguise malice with their false lips,
　　But in their hearts, they hide deceitful arts.
Though speech may charm, be wary of the fool,
　　For hidden outrages taint their soiled heart.
Their malice, though veiled by deceit so cruel,
　　In time, their deeds will tear their guise apart.
Whoever digs a pit may fall within;
Gossips, in their pits, find their own chagrin.

32. Whispers Of Tranquility

Upon the tranquil meadows, she descends,
　　Where lilies sway and gentle breezes play.
The world a canvas painted soft with blends,
　　In hues of calm that chase the night away.
No clamor here, nor discord's bitter sting,
　　But whispers of the moon and stars above.
She, like a gentle dove with outstretched wing,
　　Alights upon our hearts, igniting love.
In quietude, we find our souls at rest,
　　The troubled seas of life now still and clear,
And in her hallowed space, we are quite blessed,
　　To dream of hope to banish every fear.
Her wings hover for all to find respite;
The humble, wise would her refuge see fit.

LOVE POEMS TO
WARM THE HEART

1. A Ballad Of Devotion

'Neath the moon's glow, he saw her face so fair,
    Her eyes, like stars, did light his darkest night.
He vowed to love her, always to be there,
    To guard her heart, to be her shining knight.
Through storm and strife, he'd stand by her with pride,
    No mountain high, no valley deep, he'd fear.
For her, he'd cross the seas, the world so wide,
    Her laughter was the song he'd always hear.
He'd give his life, his soul, enduring pain,
To see her smile, free her from purple rains.

2. A Ballad Of Love's Symphony

When nights appeared, our hearts began to soar,
With whispered dreams, we danced upon the shore.
Her eyes, like stars, ignited flames so bright,
Our love, a lighthouse in the darkest night.
With every touch, my soul was set aflame,
In passion's grip, we played a timeless game.
Our laughter echoed through the silent skies,
A symphony of love that never dies.
But fleeting time, it casts a shadow's veil,
Yet in my heart, our love will never pale.

3.   A Canvas Of Dreams

Her hair, like golden marigolds,
Cascades in waves, a sight to behold,
Each strand a sunbeam, pure and bright,
Illuminating the darkest night,
In her glow, my love unfurls.

Her skin, like lilies, smooth and hale,
A canvas where my dreams set sail,
Each touch a petal, soft and fine,
A fragrant bloom, a love divine,
In her embrace, I prevail.

Her kindness, like a gentle rain,
Nourishes my soul, eases pain,
Her laughter, like a songbird's tune,
Brightens my days, like the sun at noon,
In her love, I am sustained.

Her presence, like a fragrant breeze,
Brings comfort, puts my mind at ease,
Her love, a treasure, pure and true,
A blessing that I never knew,
In her arms, I'm truly blessed.

4.   A Pile Of Tenderness

1. Her sunshine face e'er makes me smile,
        While the whole world's a blur,
    Then suddenly, all seem worthwhile,
        Matters not that I'm poor.

2. She sets our pace in her own style,
     Yet keeps her love in store,
   For me and only me—a pile
     Of tenderness for sure.

3. Ecstatic that I can beguile,
     Her love with modesty,
   Romantic stitches, nothing vile,
     In her life's tapestry.

5. Congested Paths

1. Each man has faced his own traffic,
     Smooth, light, or oft congested lanes.
   I faced mine once, it was tragic;
     A time of deep, enduring pains.

2. For quite a while, her path was clear,
     With signs of love and joy in sight.
   Free flowing, with no tolls to fear,
     No drivers causing any plight.

3. Then her cold lips began to weave,
     Untruths about her winding ways;
   Congestion from her secret leave
     With drivers, led our hearts astray.

4. They had the means to pay her toll,
     Yet cared not for her winding road.
   I cherished every twist and roll,
     Yet was left helpless in the cold.

6. Crossroads Of The Heart

On the vast highway of love,
Two pathways I encountered;
One that restricted my load,
With her tolls, my pockets drowned,
Her sharp turns, my bright mind tensed,
Her rough paths, my body pained,
With oft exotic views lined,
And a roller coaster ride.
The next, welcome she displayed,
Her heart's yearn for me she bared,
Her nice views my mind conjured;
A stunning arrow-like road.
Of which path did my heart tread?
The answer may cause you dread;
I chose the path with pain dotted,
And still paying for that love.

7. Daylight Dreams

I long to see you in the morn,
    My dreams come true at dawn,
Your words, a golden sun reborn,
    My arduous day is won.

I crave your sweet, calm voice at noon,
    A melody in bloom,
That sways my heart, a fragrant tune,
    Love's pleasant, sweet perfume.

I yearn for your soft touch at night,
  Your fingers, pure delight;
Play my soul's strings in every part,
  Setting my heart aright.

8. Enduring Affection

I'll kiss your lips and stroke your hair,
  As we love day by day,
Hold your hands through gales fierce or fair,
  Treasure each word you say,
And hold you in my heart, my dear,
  Whene'er you are away.

Your love, a garden bright and fair,
  Where every bloom does sway,
In your soft touch, I find my care,
  Your heart, my guiding way.
Through every storm, your light does flare,
  And keeps the dark at bay.

You touch my heart, inspire my dreams,
  In each and every way,
And through your loving touch, it seems
  I'm happy, every day.
Our love will sail through golden streams,
  While shining every day.

9. Eternal Bloom Of Love

1. In her smile, a lovely flower,
   Stimulating as perfume,
   Like a field of rich lavender,
   Bidding me her gifts consume.
   In this garden, oft a shower
   Of her lovely, endless bloom,
   On my longing soul endower,
   Like those rains on open sea.

2. In her gaze, such deep emotion,
   Mirror of her purity,
   Through her wisdom, no commotion,
   Tree of knowledge, all can see.
   No wink of frail doubt or notion,
   Window of her soul's beauty,
   Jewel of her face's lantern,
   Brimming for the world to see.

3. In her arms, a cozy blanket,
   Even through my coldest night,
   Clothes my soul amidst the tempest,
   Keeping me from harm and blight.
   For her warmth kindles my comfort;
   Golden thread of hope and light,
   And eternally my consort,
   Ever in her arms will be.

10. Garden Of Her Face

In the garden of your face, I stand,
Awestruck by the blossoms so grand.
Your eyes, like bluebells, deep and blue,
Hold secrets in their morning dew,
A gaze that makes my heart expand.

Your lips, like tulips, bright and sweet,
A pleasant path where love's complete.
Their touch, a whisper in the breeze,
That brings me gently to my knees,
And in your presence, my heart beats.

Your smile, a field of daisies white,
Exudes with joy, so pure and light.
Each stem a promise, soft and true,
A meadow where my dreams come through,
In your laughter, my heart takes flight.

Your cheeks, like roses, soft and fair,
With petals kissed by summer's air.
A blush that warms the coldest night,
And fills my soul with pure delight,
In your beauty, I find my prayer.

11. Girl Of My Dreams: An Acrostic

Gleaming bright like the morning sun,
In every way, you are the one.
Radiant beauty that lights my day,
Love untainted, you guide my way.

One of a kind, loving and true,
Forever, I belong with you.

My dreams are filled with your embrace,
Your presence, a warm, resting place.

Dancing through this life, hand in hand,
Reaching those heights we never planned.
Every moment, a cherished theme,
As we live best our common dream.
My heart sings e'er a joyful song,
Since in your heart, fore'er I belong.

12. Harmony Of Hearts

In the lush garden of my heart,
    You are the rarest bloom,
Your fragrance lingers in the air,
    Dispelling all my gloom.
Your eyes, twin stars that light my heart,
    Brighten my darkest night,
Guiding me through the shadows dense,
    To world of pure delight.

Your touch, a gentle breeze that stirs,
    My yearning soul awake,
In your embrace, I find the peace,
    No storm can ever shake.
With every whispered word, you weave,
    A dazzling charm, so sweet,
In the symphony of our love,
    My heart finds e'er its beat.

13. I Could Never Say Goodbye

1. We can bring back our love, dear,
    To the way it used to be,
Like we were in our first year,
    Locking lips, just you and me.
I'll go away, knowing well,
    That my love can bring us through,
Cause loving you has my will.
    Yet my dear, it's up to you.

2. We can bring back our love, dear,
    Better than it used to be,
Like more cool nights on the pier,
    Arm in arm, just you and me.
You'll go away, though apart,
    Still between the love of two;
Even if he has your heart,
    All of mine will be on you.

I could never say goodbye,
  Thinking you just might get hurt;
Things he'd do to make you cry,
  Will gash you and crush my heart.
I deserve to know just why,
  You let him tear us apart.

1. We can bring back our love, dear,
      At least, let us try and see,
    Like budding lovers out there;
      Joyful, so will you and me.
    We'll go our ways with regrets,
      Knowing love can bring us through,
    If our hearts on love they set.
      Yet dear, it's all up to you.

14. I Wish To Be More Like You.

1. In your eyes, I see light so true,
    A beacon bright, guiding me through,
    Your kindness spreads like morning dew,
    In every act, in all you do,
    I wish to be more like you.

2. Your strength stouter than mighty oak,
    Standing tall, never to be broke,
    With every word, with every stroke,
    You stir buoyant dreams, you evoke,
    I want to be more like you.

3. Your heart is pure, your spirit free,
   A gentle soul, the calmest sea,
   In your presence, I find the key,
   To be the best that I can be,
   I wish to be more like you.

4. In your love's laughter, joy does bloom,
   Chasing away the darkest gloom,
   With every step, you fill the room,
   With love and sunshine, you consume.
   I wish to be more like you.

15. Love's Mournful Whispers

1. In love, we erred like shadows cast,
   A dance of choices, haunting past.
      In moonlit hours, whispers we share,
      Echoes of longing, hearts laid bare.

2. Promises broken, trust unbound,
   With silent tears on nights profound.
      Regret's refrain, a mournful song,
      Lost chances, echoes that prolong.

3. The touch we missed, the words unsaid,
   A love once vibrant, now misread.
      Plagued by the past, love's cruel jest,
      In quiet hours our hearts protest.

4. Though hope remains a flicker bright
   To mend the fractures of the night,
      Shadows remain; time has not healed
      The hurts in depth, our hearts revealed.

16. My Love, My Heart

1. Once, close to me you were,
   Wrapped in your arms, I found my safety there,
   But now, you choose to go elsewhere,
   Leaving me far behind,
   Knowing that without you, I'm so blind.

   Through our mirror, I can see, my love, my heart,
   All the ways you tried to hide; my love, my heart.
   Once my garden with full blooms,
   And reflection of blue skies;
   You'll always be my love and my heart.

2. I loved you day by day,
   Those sweet and tender words you'd always say,
   Yet, now you choose to go away,
   Putting me in a bind,
   Why do you have to be so unkind?

   Through our mirror, I can see, my love, my heart,
   All the ways you tried to hide; my love, my heart.
   Lone lighthouse in all my storms,
   And sanctuary of my peace;
   You'll always be my love and my heart.

3. You've left a hollow space,
   Where once your lovely smile lit up my face.
   Memories linger, time can't erase,
   In shadows, I now find,
   The echoes of a once loving bond.

Through our mirror, I can see, my love, my heart,
All the ways you tried to hide; my love, my heart.
Once my sunrise o'er calm seas,
And tapestry of my dreams;
You'll always be my love and my heart.

17. Passion Potion

O love that brings me endless bliss,
Your kiss, my mind intoxicates,
My heart inebriate dissolves,
Your spell, my longing soul conjures,
A passion potion must be.

O sweetest heart that calms my fears,
Your arms, a shelter in my storms,
Seeing me through the harshest rains,
And in your presence shed my pains,
Love's rainbows ever I see.

O dearest calmer of my doubts,
Your hands caress like gentle waves,
Over rugged rocks of my fears,
With peace and comfort through the years,
Your love's like a tranquil sea.

O crystal spring of humble heart,
Your eyes dispel my shades of doubt,
Your lips speak softly to my heart,
Through stressful storms, never apart,
Forever as one we'll be.

18. Romantic Tussle

'Twas an autumn eve in the garden,
The trees singing with sounds so clear,
A symphony for all to hear,
And my babe started to wrestle
Me in love, amidst life's daily bustle.
The leaves were going rustle, rustle,
As she pressed against my frame,
Feeling the taut of my muscle.
The cool wind began to whistle,
While a nearby brook flowed gurgle
Out of sight, as she grabbed me tightly,
In our romantic love tussle.
Then on the next gravel path, softly,
We could hear footsteps crunch, crunch;
Perhaps her dad, not sure, just a hunch.

19. Seasons Of Love

You are summer in my morning,
    Gentle dew of blossoms bright,
Your affection, garden blooming,
    Warms my heart with passion's light.

You are autumn in my evening,
    With eyes like the harvest moon,
Your fond laughter like leaves rustling,
    In their joy, my heart to croon.

Summer's sun and autumn's sunset,
    Your pure love leaves me in awe.
Coldness will our love ne'er upset;
    Winter finds no place at all.

20. Symphony Of Love

1. You are my song, symphony of my spirit,
    Harmonious tune of completeness and delight,
    Unwritten ballads, those full of words so right,
    Pure love, sweet and uplifting in its flight.

2. You are my sun, that brightens all my darkness,
    Sure as a clock ticks time, your love is endless.
    My dawn's first light and promise of my future,
    Earnest, far-reaching and precious your nature.

3. You are my sea of boundless hope and vision,
    A calming tide of peace in my emotion.
    Deep and profound, fulfilling is your mission,
    To make this heart a harbor of devotion.

4. You are my world, the essence of my being,
    A universe of love, forever seeing.
    In every breath, your presence I am feeling,
    With you, my heart finds daily its true meaning.

21. Through Storms And Shadows

If the world must fall before my eyes
Can make contact with yours,
I'll find the courage rare,
On my shoulders would bear
Its heft, while shedding my joyous tears,
Just to see your brown eyes.

If its waters flood the hills and plains,
Where your tender heart sits,
My sunshine and its heat,
The deluge will defeat.
My love chases away those storm clouds,
Only your joy remains.

If the night should cloak the world in dark,
And hide your face from me,
I'll light a thousand stars,
To guide me where you are.
My love, a beacon through shadows dark,
Forever sets you free.

22. Timeless Affection

As the moon smiles, so does your face,
A thrilling sight, my heart's apace,
Your bright light shines, filling this space,
With love and passion, yet no pace.
With time, we cuddle in this place,
Laden with laughter, joys at ease.
We see our love not as a race,
But prize our minutes, damn the days.

23. To Ends Of The Earth: A Ballad

In serene slopes where rivers softly flow,
    A love so strong, I'd cross the stormy seas,
Through nights and days, our hearts will always glow,
    No road too rough, your love my heart will seize.
When mountains rise and valleys fall below,
    Across the lands, through deserts wide and free,
No star too high, no dream too grand to show,
    In every breath, your love will always be.
So hand in hand we'll stand, our love's true worth,
To keep this bond, I'd tread to ends of earth.

24. True Worth

At you, I stare with admiration,
Yet, he's gazing at his own reflection.
I carry your to-do list with care,
While he drifts aimlessly like the air.
Waste not your precious time on him,
For his worth is quite paper-thin;
In me, you have all that you need,
Amidst bright flow'rs, he's a useless weed.

25. Whispers In The Night

My dimly lit bedroom, she entered,
And in a heartbeat, she disrobed.
In my amazement, I stuttered—
"Are you okay?" her lips whispered
Softly, sending shivers down my spine.
"Yes, yes, my dear, I am quite fine."
Then I stared at her velvet skin,
Her rare beauty, without, within.
We lay on the bed by the fire, crackling,
Our motion sent the bed creaking.
My heartbeat thumping—and lulling
Her fine frame into peaceful sleeping.
Then I pondered my fortuitousness,
Wishing my days with her would be endless.

26. Yearning In The Night: A Ballad

His absence like a chill, cold and profound,
My heart's lament, a mournful, lonely sound.
Without him, life's a weary, endless quest,
I yearn for his pure love; my soul can't rest.
His touch, my solace and my longing's peak,
His warm embrace, my soul and spirit seek.
His love, the balm my aching heart does keep,
In dreams, I find him where awake I weep.
I lie alone, in silent, restless night,
Yearning for his soft touch, my noble knight,
The void beside me whispers tales of pain,
A hollow bed where once our love did reign.

OTHER POEMS

1.   A Father's Betrayal

1. His father died, a mournful death,
       A trip through illness at an end.
    While his old man took his last breath,
       Plotting he was, as if a fiend.

2. Declared he then, his father broke;
       Their clan's open hands foot the bill,
    For his parting and for his cloak,
       A fond farewell through parting's hill.

3. Then found out they that he had swiped,
       His father's cash an hour before,
    The old man cashed-in—soul expired,
       Yet he put not a cent afore.

4. His loot obscene, more than enough,
       To sign the old man's grave, unmarked,
    Yet would not budge; his heart was gruff
       Like a vile, barren land—untouched.

5. How cold mankind, a father's son,
       How cold to boldly hurt his own?
    So poor a head in greed's prison
       That proudly wears an evil crown.

2. A Motherland's Lament

1. O dearest, glorious motherland,
    Your manias with powder and steel,
    Chagrins the faithful, overwhelmed;
    Carnage uncorked against their will,
    With blood and slaughter, everywhere.

2. Your children's anguish fills the air,
    Their halls of knowledge choked with fear,
    And broken bodies disappear,
    With steel and powder, front and rear,
    And nonage bloodshed everywhere.

3. In sacred halls where peace should reign,
    The echoes of barrage remain.
    Prayers mingled with cries of pain,
    Faith's pure sanctuaries now profaned,
    With much violence everywhere.

4. Some send fake pray'rs when steel sheds blood;
    Their anthem to drown out the cries,
    Of those that seek to put an end,
    To steel's sentinels and their lies,
    And halt the carnage everywhere.

5. Their spineless courage to endorse,
    Mindless metals, cold unfeeling,
    Wielded by silly whims of those,
    Who sing their praise is bewildering,
    With deep senselessness everywhere.

6. O dearest, it baffles the mind,
   That your galaxy of bright minds,
   Won't its steel clamor answer find;
   Lives of shadows behind the blinds,
   Their blood often spilled everywhere.

7. This foolishness must be deterred,
   And steel and powder e'er interred.
   For sanity, dear motherland,
   And for your children's peace of mind,
   An end to bloodshed, everywhere.

3. Awakening Daffodil: A Haiku

Fill me, Daffodil,
Past the winter of my mind,
With creative will.

4. Beneath The Mona Smile

1. Like fish dodging sandy prison,
       She was slippery and sly.
   She'll defraud you without feeling;
       Watch your lifeless frame lie.
   Oft her diseased soul infecting,
       Fragile men in her trail;
   Their once sterile hearts succumbing,
       Her schemes, devious and vile.

2. Like a rare, fine Mona Lisa,
    Her looks arouse your strife.
   To her shores grant you a visa—
    Though trip may cost your life.
   In her words, and through her crying,
    Open arms you'll offer,
   Only, she will have you reeling,
    When her ills you suffer.

3. Like a game of contradiction,
    Her deceits are at play;
   Light and dark, juxtaposition,
    Her contrasts in display.
   She has in same frame residing
    Beauty and betrayal;
   A soul gulling and alluring
    With abuse, upheaval.

4. Like wise men with moral leanings,
    You should ne'er yearn for her;
   There aren't rainbows in her dealings,
    She'll burn you with her fire.
   Only fools will trust her pretense,
    Whate'er her merits be,
   You'll be footing e'er the expense,
    For the allure you see.

5. Beyond The Treasure Chest

When endowed with the means to bless,
One must ne'er his sea of wealth press;
Clinking coins in his treasure chest.
He mustn't ignore hearts in distress,
Their cell of hardship dark, oppressed.
Instead, lend a hand to address,
And ne'er seek renown nor redress.

6. Brewing Betrayal

1. I hardly ever talk,
        About the things she put me through—
    The treacherous spousal walk,
        And wicked tea mutely she'd brew,
    Set up for me to drink.

2. And raging storms she brought,
        Into my calm, beckoning sea,
    Its vast treasures she sought;
        Her greedy heart yearned, but for me,
    Of true love was a naught.

3. See her not of mankind,
        But of a rare alien species—
    Devoid of grateful mind,
        Callous like rocks of the Rockies,
    Warm hearts, she'll coldly bind.

4. And what of her deceit?
   I'd say it threw me for a loop.
   My idiocy complete,
      When she feigned fertility's trip,
   Though bare as desert's street.

7. Captive To The Fading Day: A Villanelle

On cloudy days, with the sun's darkened ray,
In loneliness, walks paths of endless night,
His heart a captive to the fading day.

The stars above, in distant skies, display,
Their indifference quite icy to his plight,
On cloudy days, with the sun's darkened ray.

He wanders lost, with dreams that fade to gray,
A solitary soul, devoid of light,
His heart a captive to the fading day.

The echoes of his past, they softly play,
Reminders of a time when life was bright,
On cloudy days, with the sun's darkened ray.

No comfort found in dawn's first gentle ray,
For loneliness remains his constant fight,
His heart a captive to the fading day.

Yet hope persists, a spark that will not fray,
A whisper in the dark, a silent might,
On cloudy days, with the sun's darkened ray,
His heart a captive to the fading day.

8.   Cherish The Children

1. There are paths for little children,
    And the world must now embrace them;
    With love's fervor e'er maintain them,
    Walks that God rightly ordained them,
    That their lives fulfill, enrich them.

2. There are homes for little children,
    And the world must now sustain them;
    Hearts that hold love's true emotion,
    Their growth and solace environ,
    Nourishing their minds and passion.

3. There are songs for little children,
    Worldlings too must learn to sing them;
    Lullabies of peace and wisdom,
    Melodies of war's cessation,
    That the world, its rifts may spare them.

4. There are joys for little children,
    And the world must reassure them;
    End their tears from segregation,
    Racist taunts, humiliation,
    Ceaseless hunger and oppression.

5. There are dreams for little children,
    And the world must help them reach them;
    Visions bright of future splendor,
    Innovations they'll engender,
    Guiding stars, their paths to render.

6. Precious lives of little children,
   May the world, its wrath ne'er break them.
   Guide, uplift and encourage them,
   Love and nourish and protect them,
   So pure love fore'er enfolds them.

9. Cold Heart, Warm Joys

Cold, icy hearts delight,
    In freezing joys of the delightful,
With callousness, their blight,
    Their deeds will fore'er be distasteful.
No empathy, no light,
    No kindness, but hearts, spoiled and spiteful,
Chilling all souls in sight,
    With their horror quite grim and frightful.
Hold your joys thawed and bright,
    Keep farthest from those minds, unmindful
Of your ways—divine right
    To be free, prosperous, and joyful.

10. Deadly Hands: A Cinquain

Powder,
Iron and steel,
Hands of a loose cannon,
Shattering the human spirit,
Fatal.

11. Dialogues With Divinity

As he wandered the western shores,
With thoughts adrift on seas of blue,
He pondered realms where beauty soars,
And heard a whisper, soft yet true:
"How quickly you forget My might;
The Alpha and Omega, I am.
Ask your wish beneath this twilight,
And trust you'll hear a guiding psalm."

He dreamed aloud of golden roads,
A bridge to span the ocean wide.
The Lord replied with sorrowed tones,
"Such wishes stem from hollow pride.
To carve this path would scar the earth,
A folly in your heart's desire.
Seek a new wish of greater worth,
Let your soul to heaven aspire."

In time, he voiced a humble plea,
"Lord, grant me wisdom deep and vast,
To fathom women's mystery,
Their tears and joy, from first to last."
The Lord then spoke with gentle mirth,
"Would you prefer two lanes or four,
For bridges born of earthly girth?
Such paths reflect your wished-for worth."

12. Divine Assurance: A Sestina

1. Cheer up! My soul, don't be so sad,
    Your once relentless storms are gone.
    For He who made you knows your fears,
    In doubt, He steered you through the years.
    He'll ne'er forsake a soul at need;
    The humble one that ne'er was mean.

2. What do His oft tough trials mean,
    That leave you down, worried and sad?
    Has He not oft furnished your need,
    Ordered those horrid days, "Be gone"?
    How soon did you forget the years,
    He was your shield and calmed your fears?

3. Dread not, He understands your fears;
    Your refuge from storms that are mean,
    The timeless keeper of your years,
    And lifeboat from seas that are sad.
    In time, your worries will be gone,
    He knows your heart; He sees your need.

4. Blind trust in mankind, you don't need,
    For this would aggravate your fears;
    They'll break your heart and soon be gone,
    Like two-faced friends, they're vile and mean.
    You'd see them prancing proud, yet sad,
    Spinning their wheels throughout their years.

5. Your gift of three score and ten years,
    Be glad, indeed, in spite of need.
    Burdens and tears enthrall the sad,
    The skeptics will e'er keep their fears.
    Your heart, unique and never mean,

Like golden sunsets, those now gone.

6. Sorrow's rains and dark tears are gone,
   Murky clouds will ne'er see your years,
   Nor your heart mingle with the mean,
   For He has made plans for your need,
   That will e'er calm your doubts and fears,
   And rid your life of drab songs sad.

   Envoi
   My soul, embrace light, shed the sad,
   For in His love, He calms your fears,
   With faith, you will find every need.

13. Divine Intervention

Theirs was once a carnal garden,
   Where bustling bees and blooms collide.
A bud begat by a maiden—
   A bloom, her bee had fertilized.

Off was her bee on more exploits,
   She gravely mused, "Discard his bud."
But He above did calm her doubts,
   And the poor, fragile bud was spared.

Bloom and bee, eye to eye can't see,
   But for tryst in fertility.
In their garden, wide as the sea,
   That spared poor, fragile bud was me.

14. Dust to Dust: The Great Leveler

O place of rest! O place of rest!
Once was serene—communal bliss,
But now partitioned into cliques,
Of bronze, of silver, and of gilts.

The dirt, impartial to the frames,
Contrasts the undertaker's vain;
The exploitation wrought by zones,
Of frames entombed, their spirits gone.

Each sector peddles mortal greed,
Each view, the entombed's rank and class;
To shame the poor, the rich to prod,
And prolong vanity's morass.

Those frames seeking solace at last,
Yet care not for their class or clique;
Of bronze or silver or of gilt,
God bless them in the rest they seek.

15. Echoes Of A Fractured Soul

To shatter any soul
Requires a heart to spoil;
Oft, one pure and fragile,
And a heart breaker—cold.

Once fractured by his despair,
Tainted, with a conscience bare,
He serves quite a bitter fare;
A banquet of sorrow—bold,
Yet serves himself with it.

16. Echoes Of Expression

1. Just like swords that leave their imprint,
   They can cut deep and scar,
   Yet, with soft or soothing instinct,
   Make one feel like a star.
   In fertile soil of minds like seeds,
   Lovely flowers they grow;
   But like pungent, invasive weeds,
   Stinking minds cause a row.

2. Bridging gaps between vast cultures,
   Launching channels for minds;
   Yet like carcass-eating vultures,
   Be icon that offends.
   They unlock the doors to knowledge,
   Empathy, connection;
   Whether in a home or college,
   Bare truth in confession.

3. Like echoes bouncing off thin walls,
   Resonate in our hearts;
   With kind ones spreading love and joys,
   Unlike hot oil that spurts.
   Whether blurted or unuttered,
   They are mankind's defense,
   In a world where bullies slaughtered,
   Those that voice out their sense.

17. Ephemeral Beauty: A Ballad

How swiftly beauty fades like morning dew,
  On petals kissed by dawn's soft breath of light,
And love, too, oft is slashed like in a hew,
  From desire's fire and reason's sudden flight.
We grasp at stars, their distant glimmers near,
  Yet constellations shift, elusive, free,
And dreams, like sand, slip through our fingers here,
  As time's unyielding current sweeps the sea.
Savor then love's sweet moments, brief and bright,
For life itself is but a fleeting flight.

18. For The Love Of Words

1. My verses woven in love's silk,
    Free flowing like idyllic birds;
  Of truth, of wisdom and their ilk,
    For the love of words.

2. Words noble, some may not adore;
    Their minds impaled by nescient swords,
  My eloquence, they oft ignore,
    And my love of words.

3. In silent whispers, and loud cries,
    Words can't disguise but bind strong cords.
  In their plain truth, my spirit flies,
    For the love of words.

4. My verses sail on wisdom's breeze,
    Through storms of ignorance, they weave;
   With strength that never seems to cease,
    By my words in love.

5. As poignant as a lone lighthouse,
    Or fiddle playing striking chords,
   The choicest verses e'er I'll use,
    For the love of words.

6. The love of words would e'er endure,
    In this man's heart, playing love's chords.
   Those verses pure would e'er secure,
    For the love of words.

19. Fragile Light Of Hope

1. We indulge in wanton madness,
    With hearts encased in winter's frost,
   Claim to see, yet choose our blindness,
    Ignore their pain, despite the cost.

2. Brother seeking our acceptance,
    We scorn his gifts, his unique grace;
   Through foggy lens, our reluctance,
    To see his worth, to know his face.

3. Sister, once broken by the scourge
    Of spousal failure, not her own,
   Yet our hearts like dead stones won't budge;
    Her pain through foggy glass is shown.

4. This plague of human laziness,
      To grasp each other's pain and needs;
   Aloofness, poor excuse, confess,
      Our hearts lean on these poisoned seeds.

5. Yet, hope remains a fragile light,
      To melt the frost, to clear the haze;
   When we embrace each other's plight,
      Our hearts will bloom in brighter days.

20. From Despair To Divine

1. Waited for its sign every hour,
      But it did not oblige;
   For its huge deluge to dower,
      And my smiles to emerge.

2. Each day, my longing drew quite dour,
      My buoyant hopes beset,
   Leaving my tongue bitter and sour,
      A failing heart upset.

3. The nights grew long, the days were bleak,
      My spirit worn and frail,
   Each moment felt a mountain peak,
      A never-ending trail.

4. I pondered if He cared enough
      For this poor, wretched soul,
   Enduring pain and suff'rings rough,
      Overwhelming the whole.

5. Yet when the heavens opened wide,
     Its dams of fortunes kept,
   My doubts and fears were set aside,
     As did sad tears I'd wept.

6. Perhaps a lesson for my mind;
     Endurance in extreme,
   While suff'rings have me in a bind,
     His pure love reigns supreme.

21. From Grease To Grace

1. Looking back on my early days,
     Aching and drudgery were a bane;
   Toiling in hot and greasy bays,
     That nearly drove my mind insane.

2. My back arched from the constant toil,
     Forced by the golden arches' head;
   The foods to grill, floors to unsoil,
     And run eggs as patrons demand.

3. Daytime, I labored, fed their frames,
     Nightly, I strived to feed my mind;
   To change my state, improve my odds,
     And put my drudgery in remand.

4. Knowledge has been a precious key;
     Opened my doors to brighter days.
   Lifted my soul, my spirit's free,
     From menial tasks and weary ways.

5. Now, golden arches' trips I make,
    Recall those tough marathon days,
When dreams deferred once overtook
    Lunches, for hard-earned, meagre pays.

6. I wish I had the privilege
    Of means, like in ancestral wealth;
The softer catbird seat, or edge,
    For a real chance at enhanced worth.

7. Yet, grateful for my experience,
    In meekness, my garden tending.
Perseverance needs no science,
    To shape a better human being.

22. Garden Of Souls: A Haiku

Mummy's lily glows,
In garden of resting souls;
Blooms in perfect peace.

23. Glory Hill

1. I stand atop my glory hill,
     Where only I can see,
   A life that matches my own will,
     To be all I can be.

2. For long, I marched to their own beat,
     Locked in their puppet show,
   My bright mind bound, my joy replete,
     In shadows, I did grow.

3. The many joys I sadly missed,
     In conformity's rule;
   Those lovely lips I never kissed,
     Living in a bubble.

4. Behind their veil, I failed to see,
     The mirth in bygone days,
   And with my blindness, botched the sea
     Of gems my life entails.

5. What spell of sorrow and despair,
     Or mental dissonance,
   To heed their willful, false affair,
     As if lost in a trance.

6. Now, I peek at the world's vast ends,
     Places I could have been;
   Gardens of love, where joy transcends,
     Scenes their eyes may have seen.

7. Ready to soar, a bird unbound,
     From structures of remand;
   This freedom of the mind I've found,
     Saves me from sinking sand.

24. Grounded Love

Once in skies clear, now storm clouds reign,
Her dreams grounded, a love in vain,
Her heart, a broken aircraft's plight,
And wings clipped, no longer in flight.
His promises, like engines, failed,
Left her stranded with hope derailed.
Once soaring high, now lost in haze,
A love that's crashed in endless maze.
She yearns for skies where love once flew,
Yet now she's left with skies of blue,
A broken plane, her heart's despair,
A grounded love beyond repair.
A love that once reached higher skies,
In pieces on the ground now lies.

25. Hatred's Hollow Echo

1. She is a venom that corrodes,
        The human heart and mind consumes,
    And cherished bonds swiftly divides,
        Leaving some souls in shadowed rooms.

2. Her blazing wildfire singes life,
        Leaving their ashes in her wake,
    Her embers—never-dying strife—
        Torches the hearts she keeps awake.

3. She grows wild in the hearts of man,
        Like a cancer gutting a soul.
    Her awful isolations reign,
        And often overwhelm the whole.

4. She spreads quickly in humble hearts,
    　　Even those with resilience crowned,
    Infecting their once-sterile parts,
    　　Ensuring they are darkness bound.

5. She eats away at humble souls,
    　　Her diseased fangs leaving her scars,
    Their love, compassion she swallows,
    　　Their strength and confidence she bars.

6. Be sure to keep from her prison;
    　　An anger and resentment trap.
    Although, she'll present a reason,
    　　You should ne'er give in to her wrap.

26. Heart Of The Home: An Acrostic

Dearest heart of family life,
Endless well of patience divine,
Anchor of love in storm and strife,
Rock of our care, steadfast through time.

Maiden, queen of our castle, dear,
Of wisdom's wellspring, pure and deep,
The source of comfort in days drear,
Heart of the home, our warmth to keep.
Ever an angel, always near,
Radiant sun, a love's passion deep.

27. Hearts In The Dark

1. My mind confused and heart beset,
     By issues near and far;
   When conflicts flare and never rest,
     My peaceful days they bar.

2. Their promises are never kept,
     Yet still, I bear the load;
   Their burdens, saving hearts bereft,
     By fears that self-erode.

3. The coldness of some hearts chagrins,
     And complicates my mind;
   Their numbness to their neighbor's needs
     Shows hearts that are unkind.

4. Their empty words, a hollow sound,
     That echo through my mind;
   They promise peace, yet wars abound,
     And leave my heart confined.

5. In shadows where compassion fades,
     I search for light anew;
   For kindness in these darkened glades,
     Where empathy is due.

28. Her Silent Struggle

1. Don't tell her that the world is fair,
   Of male and female, equal share;
   Grant her privacy in her care,
   Her outright freedom can declare.

2. The world, its laws restrict her fire,
   Yet expects her the load to bear;
   In trades, a lower fare for hire,
   But then its families to rear.

3. In chambers where the laws are writ,
   Their script is veiled in justice's name,
   Binding her flesh and soul so tight,
   Her flame is dimmed, a silent shame.

4. Yet silence cloaks his massive sphere,
   In matters where her voice isn't near;
   No laws demand his equal share,
   In body's right—conceptive care.

5. Yet oft she rises, fierce and bright,
   Against the chains that bind her light,
   Her voice, a beacon in the night,
   For justice, freedom, and her right.

29. Hope Amidst Hatred

1. In place once grand, now shadows fall,
   They sought hands to rebuild the dream.
   Migrants answered, heeding the call,
   Their toil and hopes, a steady stream.

2. They fled from war, from endless night,
   In lands of strife, where shadows loom.
   Seeking a future bathed in light,
   On gentler shores, where freedom blooms.

3. Streets once silent, now buzzed with life,
   New shops and homes rose from the dust.
   Yet hums of hate, sharp as a knife,
   Turned gratitude to vile mistrust.

4. "They eat our pets," the bigots cried,
   Spreading vile lies to stoke the flame.
   Branded as filth, dehumanized,
   In smear campaigns, defiled their name.

5. Through threats and fear, they held their ground,
   Building bridges, sad hearts renew.
   In union's strength, new hope was found,
   A town reborn, with life anew.

6. 'Tis sad how hatred's fangs can tear,
   At those who sought a brighter scope,
   A wrecking ball to bonds once fair,
   Yet still they hold to love and hope.

30. Hunger's Grip

1. Her pains do not discriminate,
   Of young and old, and black and white.
   Oft gnawing at them like a rat,
   Endless like a bottomless pit.

2. Yet, she absolves her friends, the rich,
   Who could her pains' lifeline afford,
   While poor, empty wells try to breach,
   Their oft-parched and dry riverbeds.

3. Like famished desert wanderers,
   Her victims wade through torments, strong.
   Their minds constrained by tight borders,
   Of sustenance-free zones, quite long.

4. Wish she could spare the children, weak,
   Their gentle hearts need not her strife.
   So, full and strengthened, reach their peak,
   And fear not on her dreadful life.

31. In The Shadow Of Indiscretion

1. In shadows cast by party lights so bright,
   A friend observed a scene that chilled the night.
   Lewd acts by patrons, brazen and unkind,
   He feared their influence on his wife's mind.

2. Yet like a sealed vault, his lips stayed quite tight,
   Snubbing their imprudence, chose not to fight.
   But whispers spread like wildfire through the air,
   Accused of speaking truths he did not share.

3. Disgusted by the blame on righteous hearts,
   While those who sinned played their deceitful parts.
   He saw the world through eyes now clear and wide,
   Where virtue's scorned and vice is glorified.

4. In this odd tale of shadows, truth, and lies,
   He learned the cost of silence and disguise.
   For in a world where blame and sin entwine,
   The righteous often walk a thin, frail line.

32. Journey To Peace: A Cinquain

Hour comes,
Veil torn, breath fades,
To nature under stars,
Rise and shine with the trinity,
At peace.

33. Kneeling For Wheels

In his room, he knelt down to pray,
For a bicycle, bright and new.
Mummy said, "Great, but not this way,
He hears you, in a whisper, too."

"I know He loves us," said the boy,
"And all our prayers, He surely hears,
But grandma's ears don't bring her joy,
And she's the one who holds the purse."

34. Lanterns Of Language

1. In the quiet chambers of thought,
       Where silence weaves a fragile web,
    They emerge like stars in the night,
       Guiding hearts where emotions ebb.

2. Each, a brushstroke on existence,
       Paints meaning on canvas of time.
    Their letters dance, their warmth embrace,
       And sounds create rhythm and rhyme.

3. Their master's ink spills truth and dreams,
       Entwined like lovebirds in twilight.
    Their structure bridging vast chasms,
       Binding souls in warm glow of light.

4. When silence threatens to engulf,
       They glow like lanterns, show the way,
    Their essence true, ever enough,
       To guide us in life's grand ballet.

5. Cherish these fine vessels of thought
        In their magic of expression;
    The pow'r to heal, to love—convert,
        Their whispers hold our confession.

35. Love's Steep Hill

1. On nature's street was a hill, quite steep,
        With straight and rugged paths.
    And old secrets kept by some, quite deep,
        Intriguing in their myths.

2. On a side of that hill, it was said,
        Love's myst'ry was beheld.
    Two lovers, dead, entwined on a bed,
        A scene that caused some dread.

3. They jumped from the hilltop to the bed,
        When their dear love was barred,
    By those who sought to tear the head,
        Of love blooming ahead.

4. Others doubted, said their frames were placed,
        On bed by men aligned,
    With those who drank wine with hatred laced,
        And to envy confined.

5. The songbirds; ebony and ivory,
        Were once thriving in love,
    Perhaps their mingling caused an outcry,
        Only God knows above.

36. Melodies Of Memory

1. The songs we sang with hearts so light,
     Now echo with a somber tone.
   Once filled with joy, now lost in night;
     They remind me, I'm quite alone.

2. Each note that played a cheerful tune,
     Now whispers tales of days gone by.
   In the deep silence of the moon,
     I hear the echoes of goodbye.

3. The laughter that we used to share,
     Now mingles with a tearful sigh.
   In melodies that fill the air,
     I feel the ache of our goodbye.

4. Yet, these are songs I truly love,
     Like the friends and dear ones now gone;
   Their spirits sing in skies above,
     While I pine for love's bonds now torn.

37. Mirthless Below, Mirth Above: Epitaph Of A Courtesan

I lie here with many men,
But now without their semen.
The dirt having much more fun,
Than I had under the sun.
Judge not my days; crestfallen.

38. Mystery Of Contradictions

He lives a life contradictory;
A paradox of mystery.
That which he hears, his mind denies,
Like whispers lost in the wind's cries.
That which he hears not, he invents,
Crafting wild tales from silence dense.

That which he knows, his speech belies,
Truth tangled in a web of lies.
That which he knows not, he perverts,
Twisting facts till their meaning hurts.

That which he sees, his brain distorts,
Truth bent in crude mental contorts.
That which he sees not, he concocts,
Imagined visions, truth unlocks.

That which he speaks, confounds his heart,
Quite often, his words fall apart.
When he speaks not, baffling his acts,
A puzzle of unspoken pacts.

He is a man perhaps possessed,
By an oxymoronic fiend.
A soul in conflict, ne'er at rest,
In paradox, his fate is gleaned.

39. Nature's Dominion

1. I glanced the wood and stone structures,
   Erected by the hands of man,
   Firm, can withstand nature's tortures;
   Its torrent anger, unconcerned.

2. Bold and enduring, they outlast,
   The minds and bodies that designed,
   Their coves and spaces, cool and vast,
   Bringing comfort to all mankind.

3. Wonder I oft, how this could be,
   That stone and wood could dare outlast,
   Their crafter's grit, quite gracefully,
   While he's confined to eras past.

4. Yet nature's force, relentless, grand,
   Will claim both man and his design.
   In time, all yield to her command,
   Her pow'r, eternal and divine.

5. Of stone and wood and man the same,
   To nature will comply at last.
   Yet in their forms, they leave a name,
   A legacy that time can't blast.

6. Though man may fade, his works remain,
   A testament to dreams once cast.
   In stone and wood, his spirit's flame,
   Burns bright, a beacon from the past.

40. Nature's Love Asterisks: A Haiku

O happy Asters,
Asterisks of love, send I,
Your fragrant showers.

41. New Life: A Cinquain

Her head,
Frame emerges,
Sever her old lifeline,
First cry, tasting nature's air,
Her time.

42. No Place Is Like Home

Its meadows fair, ne'er nettle,
　　The hearts that call it home,
Despite the pout and prattle,
　　Our love for it has shown.

In the east, we may hustle,
　　Juggling tasks of our own,
In the west, show our mettle,
　　Though, still we'll think of home.

On seas where winds may wrestle,
　　And waters churn with foam,
Its secrets start to whistle,
　　Calling our tired hearts home.

Its fields of flow'rs and petal,
　　Bristling and fully grown,
Rife with beauty, not subtle,
　　Ignite our memory's comb.

A serene nest midst battle,
　　And anchor in the storm,
In its comfort, we settle,
　　Unlike those who e'er roam.

It remains our hearts' refuge,
　　Our shelter through the gloom,
And fortress of solitude;
　　No place can be like home.

43. Noble Blossoms: A Haiku

O purple tulips,
The royalty of your cups,
Seals my trembling lips.

44. Nostalgic Noel

O Christmas!
Once you were full of laughter near,
Yet now I shed your tears each year,
O Christmas!
My childhood fantasies now rare,
Your tinsels' glitter disappear,
O Christmas!
Your lights dazzled in joyful cheer,
Yet these days, sadness, I can't bear,
O Christmas!
Your jingling bells, I used to hear,
Are muffled by silence of fear,
O Christmas!
I think about those gone so dear;
Their love and gifts, no more to share,
O Christmas!
I find this loneliness quite drear,
Yet you can make love reappear,
O Christmas!
My heart's despair, answer my prayer,
And bring me joy and love this year,
O Christmas!
May your bells jingle loud and clear,
Once more, and shed I not one tear,
This Christmas!

45. Not Good Enough

1. From her ancestral home, once plucked,
   To drudgery's dungeons on their shores.
   Their alabaster cities raised;
   Her doggedness, success assures;
   Yet, was told, she's not good enough.

2. Her patience, a sight to behold,
   Turning straws and dust into gold,
   Through sweaty tears and courage bold,
   With pain and misery, much untold,
   Yet, was told, she's not good enough.

3. She pleaded with her God, above,
   With faith, and hope, that sustains life,
   For freedom's beacon and their love,
   To cleanse hearts that fuel her strife,
   And perhaps see, she's good enough.

4. She was set free, yet was not free,
   From chains and dungeons of the past.
   Blamed for their ills, hung on a tree;
   Their pent-up vengeance, quite aghast,
   Claiming her life wasn't good enough.

5. Yet, in time she carved out a space,
   To thrive and conquer mountains, nigh.
   Measures, they changed beyond a trace;
   Yet, she surpassed their benchmarks, high;
   They smirked and said, "Not good enough."

6. She ponders oft about her fate,
   In their vast alabaster land,
   Where oft they expect her to wait,
   On prodigies that would not land,
   Because "She's not quite good enough."

46. Ode To Maternal Love

1. O tender hands that cradle life,
   With ceaseless love, you ease our strife.
       In your embrace, we find our home,
       A haven where our hearts can roam.

2. From dawn to dusk, your care does shine,
   A beacon bright, a love divine.
       Through sleepless nights and restless days,
       You guide us with your tender ways.

3. With every smile and every tear,
   You teach us courage, quell our fear.
       In laughter shared and lessons learned,
       Your wisdom, like fresh bread, we yearned.

4. Like a swan, with its endless grace,
   You shape the world, you set the pace.
       In you, we find our strength, our song,
       To you, our hearts and praise belong.

5. Through trials faced and battles won,
   Your spirit shines, like morning sun.
       In every hug, in every kiss,
       We feel the depth of boundless bliss.

6. Ode to you, our nourishing rain,
    In your embrace, we find no bane.
        For in your love, we find our way,
        A beacon bright, both night and day.

47. Ode To The Morning Sun

O radiant dawn, with golden hue,
You paint the sky in shades anew.
Your tender rays, they kiss the earth,
Awakening life, inspiring mirth.
In fields and forests, light does play,
Chasing shadows of night away.
With every beam, a promise bright,
Of hope and warmth, of pure delight.
Light of the dawn, your glow so grand,
Spreads joy and peace across the land.
In your opus, the world does sing,
A hymn of love for joys you bring.

48. Paths of Freedom

1. It is clear like an open road,
       With endless miles to tread,
    A journey where our lives unfold,
       With choices undeterred.

2. Like a bird, it bids us to soar,
       With wings its good faith brings,
    Grants vigor to fly mountains o'er,
       And to explore new heights.

3. Like a flow'r in a lovely bloom,
       It bids a life to thrive,
    Through self-expression, grants us room
       To flourish and survive.

4. It unfolds like a butterfly,
       Breaking from its cocoon.
    To summits high, all hearts can fly,
       Then for their minds, a boon.

5. It's like a ship on open sea,
       Unhindered in its course,
    Its journey, new horizons see;
       A joy without remorse.

6. It is the breeze blowing through trees,
       With solace for the mind.
    Amidst life's challenges that squeeze,
       It remains loose and kind.

49. Puzzle Of Life: An Elegy

Life's a puzzle, pieces scattered wide,
We search for meaning, why we abide,
But sometimes, my friend, the portrait's clear:
The gaps we leave will truly endear.

50. Quintessential Voice

1. In a world of sorts, I stand alone,
   A tune of mine, a different tone,
   Not a faint shadow, not a clone,
   A spark of light, a heart of stone.

2. Their colors blend, but I remain,
   A splash of red in sea of plain.
   Whispers may fade, but I sustain,
   A voice that sings through joy and pain.

3. Oft paths diverge, I choose my way,
   A dance of night, a song of day.
   In the vast crowd, I sway and play,
   A rhythm wild, a bold display.

4. Their eyes may judge, but I don't mind,
   A soul unbound, a heart unlined,
   In the true mirror, my eyes find,
   A heart unique, a life designed.

51. Restless Beauty: A Haiku

O bed of roses,
Thorny and restless, thy sleep,
And beauty poses.

52. Rewarding The Wrong

1. A school, with tardy students rife,
   Decides to curb this daily strife,
   By offering bread as deterrent,
   To make learning dreams apparent.

2. Yet this reward, too good to miss,
   Had an effect quite unforeseen,
   The students lingered for their bliss,
   And fed well; bread's unforeseen sheen.

3. Soon teachers too were running late,
   The bread incentive sealed their fate,
   Proving one must never reward,
   Behaviors that should be abhorred.

53. River Of Strife: A Haiku

O river of life,
Your flow of suffering and strife
Are with my tears rife.

54. Scorched By Grief

1. Often, 'tis indiscernible,
    Whipping my mind, crushing my soul,
   Profound and unexplainable;
    A storm inside, troubling the whole.

2. Furious like a combustible,
    Lasting and raw, leaving me scorched,
   Like in ties once unbreakable;
    It taunts my heart, shattered and pained.

3. Its echoes, not consolable,
    Whispering woes that never cease,
   In my dreams, drab and damnable,
    Stealing my hope, denying peace.

4. They said to cope and be able,
    For mother and brothers bygone.
   Its burden, quite impossible
    To bear on this shoulder upon.

5. My spirit not inflatable,
    Drowned in its sea of sorrow—vast,
   Its strong sway not debatable;
    With woe and anguish will not rest.

6. Its cloud, dreary and palpable,
    Saddens my heart, breaching my tears,
   Confused and uncomfortable;
    My bane now and in coming years.

55. Secrets Of The Pen: An Acrostic

Luminous thoughts in every line,
Opening folk's hearts with prose divine.
Voices echo through the ages,
Enchanting minds with penned pages.

Oceans of wisdom, vast and deep,
Flowing freely, their secrets keep.

Wisdom that dance and sing with grace,
Orchestrating both time and space.
Revelations in every phrase,
Dreams and truths in an endless maze.
Soulful whispers, our hearts embrace.

56. Silenced Potential: A Lament

I cannot help but analyze,
The treasures man could realize.
Those geniuses of minds with size,
Choked off by man—marginalized.

The growth in know-hows like new drives,
Smart cures for ills that wreck our lives,
The union of humankind's hives,
Or social clues that jolt our vibes.

Perhaps these geniuses are locked
In the oft spurned and overlooked;
The dark-skinned scholars oft bypassed,
Those bright girls' minds that are suppressed,
The sharp tool fellows once enslaved,
And freedom's beacons oft confined.

We'll never know, we'll never know,
If fairness reigned; what minds could show.

57. Song Of The Heart

1. There is a song that brings me joy,
     One never felt from her before.
   Whenever love's pains do annoy,
     It lifts my heart, forevermore.

2. Mysteriously, it lures my mind,
     To sweet, flowery beds of ease;
   Those comforts that are always kind,
     And long hesitations release.

3. I wish she learns to sing that song,
     Its words and melody intact,
   Pledging to be my partner strong,
     Our hearts as one, our love compact.

58. Success Or Significance

My mentor once inquired of me,
Of which merits my heart would chance,
World of choices, wide as the sea;
Life's success or significance.

Surely, success was my retort,
A blacksmith's forge since early years;
Sowing the seeds, scaling new heights,
And find gold in my silent tears.

Yet, he recapped to me on those,
Casting stones in the ponds of change,
Lighting paths to man's true purpose,
Expanding their legacies' range.

Victory was ne'er their sole resolve,
Soaking up applause, ne'er their goal,
The world from failing did absolve,
Their names fore'er etched on history's wall.

A change of heart is ne'er too late,
Triumph is great, yet not ornate,
The walls of history are my fate.

59. The Absence Of Empathy

1. Said she loved me; I trusted her
   In concerns complex and quite fair.
   When our sun was hot, and days clear,
   She was quite happy, always near.

2. Her smiles were bright, her laughter loud,
   When these hands her lone heart caressed;
   Carried her chores, funded her food,
   And saved her from a life distressed.

3. Then dark clouds gathered over me;
   My brother's soul to heaven's shore.
   With grief as vast as any sea,
   Her presence might have reassured.

4. Yet subtly, she dodged and dithered,
   Callous to my pain, she uttered,
   Words so hurtful, my heart splintered,
   Like shattered glass, pieces scattered.

5. Of diverse worlds, she claimed we were,
   Hers, perhaps numb to grief and pain.
   Then sped off to a place, somewhere,
   While I endured grief's heavy chain.

6. Yet, I'm sure, sorrow knows no bound,
   Nor pays homage to culture's clans.
   Our love, like sun-poor flow'rs wilted,
   In the darkness of her absence.

60. The Fall Of Pride

1. He is a gifted musician,
    Who is oft their best physician;
        The sick stringed instruments and harps,
        And sore pianos with flats and sharps.

2. He could play with much grace and flair;
    Such sweet melody; bass, tenor,
        Treble, alto in harmony,
        All to the Lord's praise and glory.

3. Yet his arrogance bested him,
    Refused in church to play a hymn;
        Deprived the Lord of praises wrought
        By songs, his talents often brought.

4. Then, in a bitter twist of fate,
    By accident, all men would hate,
        He lost his eyesight, then his hand,
        And the nice wife he had just found.

5. Indeed, one could see from his flay,
    That God will always have His way;
        Employ your talents for His cheer,
        They will be evermore your dear.

61. The Power Of Discernment

1. Sometimes it's hard for folks to see
   Some things are just quite bad,
   For them and their future success,
   Which often leaves them sad.

2. Awed by the glamor of beauty,
   Their sight becomes quite veiled,
   With minds enamored by the ruse
   Those good looks often shade.

3. Others gravitate to the lure,
   Of pleasures, treasures bring,
   Yet oft those clad with such riches,
   Are worse than a vile king.

4. Some, charmed by aura of power
   Around a charming chief,
   May find they're fascinated with
   None other than a thief.

5. Pray that your eyes will always see
   Beneath the folks' façade.
   It takes discernment blessed by God,
   To distinguish what's flawed.

62. The Scoundrel

1. Nothing in this conflict can do
   This scoundrel any harm;
   His boldness and frank corruption,
   Ever his greatest charm.

2. Yet, far from really hurting him,
   Bringing him further shame,
   Talks only serve to amplify,
   And magnify his name.

3. He'll never try to be less vain,
   Don't bet your life on it.
   He treats the world with much disdain,
   His hubris will persist.

4. He will make mockery of the laws,
   Tarnishing those in charge;
   He will deflect, insult, and lie,
   And in their duties barge.

5. There's place for scoundrels just like him,
   Who tread beyond the pale.
   They all deserve to be restrained,
   And spend their lives in jail.

63. The Temptress

1. I've glimpsed myriad sides in her gaze,
       A medley of hidden hues;
   Her heart, a maze of winding ways,
       Where desires and secrets fuse.

2. Her knees, never with each other,
       But sadly, always apart,
   With her sensual ilk will gather,
       In trysts, playing well her part.

3. No picky taste guides her delight,
       Each man's touch a fleeting flame;
   Late or swift, their presence takes flight,
       Their names—echoes in her game.

4. As eyewitness from a distance,
       Her moral scope lost at sea;
   Sensual lust, her sole sustenance,
       Kindness shades this view I see.

64. The Things We Love The Best

1. In the snugness of friendship's glow,
        We find a bond that stands the test,
    A gift to share, to let love grow,
        The things we love the best.

2. In laughter's light, our spirits soar,
        A joy that spreads from east to west,
    A treasure shared forevermore,
        The things we love the best.

3. In kindness shown, a gentle touch,
        A heart to which love's passions cleave,
    A world made brighter, oh so much,
        The best of things we love.

4. In love we give, in love we share,
        A bond that warms, ignites our zest,
    A light that shines beyond compare,
        The things we love the best.

5. In dreams we chase, in hopes we hold,
        A future bright, a life well blessed,
    Our glorious stories yet untold,
        The things we love the best.

65. Trust And Tremble

1. He tightroped oft 'tween deep craters,
        High above prairies spread below.
    The crowds adoring with loud cheers,
        As he pleased them, his skills on show.

2. He asked if they believed his walk;
        He'd cross the rope, so firm and taut,
    E'en with a human in a cart,
        A thrilling trip at such a height.

3. "Yes, we believe," his patrons said,
        "You are the best at what you do.
    So ask our help in what you need,
        With all our hearts, we trust in you."

4. So then he asked for one amongst,
        The joyous crowd to volunteer;
    Across the crater in his cart,
        While he would push the cart and steer.

5. A hush fell over the whole crowd,
        No courage in their time to shine.
    Men who boasted quite loud and proud,
        Now trembled at the risky line.

66. Unity In Diversity: A Villanelle

In every heart, a story yet untold,
Embracing differences, let love ignite,
For in our unity, we break the mold.

Through varied paths, our destinies unfold,
Each soul unique, a beacon in the night,
In every heart, a story yet untold.

With open arms, let kindness take its hold,
Acceptance blooms, a garden of delight,
For in our unity, we break the mold.

No judgment cast, no prejudice to scold,
In every face, a spark of purest light,
In every heart, a story yet untold.

Together strong, in harmony are bold,
A tapestry of colors shining bright,
For in our unity, we break the mold.

So let us cohere, let our hearts be bold,
In every soul, a chance to make hearts bright,
In every heart, a story yet untold,
For in our unity, we break the mold.

67. Unspoken Goodbyes

1. I saw her face at the café,
   Her rosy cheeks and piercing eyes.
   Our eyes contact without delay;
   She was gone in between my sighs.

2. I stretched my hand towards her way,
   The air was still, an empty space.
   She disappeared ere I could say,
   Miss you dearly, my love and ace.

3. I guess it will e'er be this way,
   Her shadows cast oft in my path.
   Her absence, now a stronger sway,
   On this mind with dearth of her mirth.

4. In my dreams, her voice softly calls,
   A whisper in the silent night,
   Her memory, a shadow falls,
   A guiding star now out of sight.

68. Unquenchable Fire

1. Her heart was bound by trinkets' trap,
   Like gold's alluring gleam.
   Her head immersed in greed's firm grip,
   And never-ending stream.

2. Her mind infected by the lure,
   Of silk and velvet's awe.
   To swindle others was her cure,
   To rid her of this plague.

3. Her eyes on others' gifts were fixed,
   In her perpetual void.
   Her endless maze could not be nixed,
   Nor her excess avoid.

4. Her lips spoke words bereft of truth,
   Like an unending beat.
   Devoid of conscience and uncouth,
   With her grace in retreat.

5. Her soul, a prisoner to desire,
   In chains of want, confined.
   No peace could quell the inner fire,
   That burned within her mind.

6. Though in her dark, a whisper came,
   A voice of truth and light,
   She could not break her bonds of shame,
   To guide her through her night.

69. Valley Of Despair

1. We drove the mountains, plains, and hills,
   Throughout the landscape o'er,
   Then reached a place beneath the hills;
   The valley of despair.

2. In an instant, we were approached
   By children traumatized;
   Quite pale and hungry, bruised and drenched,
   In excreta and mud.

3. Devoid of shelter, food, or drink
   For half a month and more,
   Unhinged and tormented to think,
   About their horrid core.

4. Decaying bodies strewn around
   Like grass on a green field,
   Filling each inch of naked ground,
   Most with their bones unsealed.

5. As we set out to feed the weak,
   The cries grew loud and strong,
   With painful tales, cruel and bleak,
   Of carnage, vile and wrong.

6. With long guns hushed and shelling done,
   Their hopes in swift retreat;
   For grace and dignity were gone,
   Once suff'ring harsh defeat.

7. These children handicapped by war,
   At bleak futures they stare,
   Because of mankind's warlike flaw,
   Are condemned to despair.

70. Veiled In The Wild: A Haiku

She's a daisy, pure,
In wild garden, where they dwell,
Yet, one could ne'er tell.

71. Velvet Heart: A Sestina

1. In their romance, she had no say,
   On their roadmap, or things to do.
   He called the shots and had his way,
   She was quite sad, and had no hope;
   His mind, a locked door to her needs,
   And deeds quite callous to her heart.

2. A smooth touch, velvet is her heart,
   No ills—critics on her can say.
   She cares for all, bridges their needs;
   Their distraught, sudden asks she'll do.
   Her smile, a beacon, emits hope,
   To worried comrades on her way.

3. His guiles and deceits strewn her way,
   Which sadly, oft distress her heart,
   Unlike the days she once had hope,
   For love with clasped hands, equal say,
   In all they think, or speak, or do;
   His love well runs dry to her needs.

4. Claiming she meets none of his needs,
   A shipwreck chanced, he went his way,
   Contrary to his vow, "I do,"
   Another dame did steal his heart.
   To this demise, what can one say,
   When man's deceit destroys love's hope?

5. Through torrent storms, she's garnered hope;
   A light in darkness to her needs,
   And songs with melody that'll say,
   'Tis well, my God will have His way;
   In time, love's bells ring in my heart,
   And guide my days in all I do.

6. Her dreams fulfilled, she said, "I do,"
   To a fine, new lighthouse of hope,
   That lights her days, brightens her heart;
   A key to the lock of her needs.
   Hopeful, yet thrilled on her new way,
   Where she will have an equal say.

Envoi
In love, partners must have a say,
That brightens hearts and lights the way,
And sing songs which fulfill their needs.

72. Walking Dead

1. Last week, his fingers were playing,
   Chords on the organ, rewarding;
   His mind intact, smiles yet charming,
   A sandcastle with tides rising,
   He was a walking dead.

2. She cooked a sumptuous, lovely fare,
   For all her friends and household dear,
   She joked and mingled with all there,
   Burst like a bubble in the air;
   She was a walking dead.

3. Today, we prance, and we frolic,
   Rest up, get up and endeavor;
   Eat luscious fares 'til we colic,
   Then spend our days to recover,
   Yet, we are walking dead.

4. A dream at dawn, we'll discover,
   A dear soul is gone up yonder,
   With weary hearts, weep and wonder,
   The shudder that makes us ponder;
   That we are walking dead.

5. So cherish each moment, dear friend,
   Embrace the dawn, let joy extend;
   For life is fleeting, let's transcend,
   Before our days come to an end;
   We are the walking dead.

73. Weathering Love

He said, "You're the sunshine of my life,
Without you, clouds roll in with strife.
You are the rain in barren lands,
Giving my heart all it demands."
With a playful smile, his partner quips,
"Is that a proposal or weather on your lips?"

74. Where Fences Meet: A Villanelle

In close abodes, where fences meet,
A bond, unbreakable, takes root,
Good, gracious neighbors, kind and sweet.

They lend a hand when storms compete,
Their laughter echoes resolute,
In close abodes, where fences meet.

From garden blooms to things discreet,
They share their stories, absolute,
Good, gracious neighbors, kind and sweet.

A surprise gift, a friendly greet,
A helping hand, a shared pursuit,
In close abodes, where fences meet.

Through seasons change, their hearts entreat,
A woven fabric, strong, acute,
Good, gracious neighbors, kind and sweet.

When life's harsh burdens weigh, they treat,
With empathy, they execute,
In close abodes, where fences meet,
Good, gracious neighbors, kind and sweet.

75. Whispers Of The Silent Stones: An Epitaph

Tread lightly and keep quiet,
    And you may just hear some sound.
For 'tis writ in Book of wit,
    "The stones will then cry out loud,
If you are still, and quiet."

76. Whispers To The Void: A Lament

1. My lament for my dear brother,
   In its shadow, he called for me.
   Promised him strength like none other;
   His voice reached out, "Please set me free,"
   But I was absent, lost in dread,
   "Brother, where are you?" his soul said.

2. Its hand, cold and unforgiving,
   Knocked at his door, I was not there.
   Its ghost, cruel—unrelenting;
   Breathed lies, "Despair, for care is rare."
   In the dark ward, his soul did cry,
   "Brother, where are you, as I die?"

3. At dawn, I came, full of sorrow,
   He whispered, "Lift me from its grip."
   My heart broke, no hope to borrow,
   Helpless to change fate's awful script.
   He wept, "Can't you halt my fading?"
   "Brother, I'm here,"—it's not waiting.

4. He faced life's woes, oft victorious,
   But 'gainst it, even aces fall.
   I, his ace, arrived too porous,
   To its decree, we must all crawl.
   With tearful eyes, I watched him part,
   My dear brother, e'er in my heart.

77. Xmas: The Lost Name

1. In glow of twinkling lights so bright,
   We gather 'round the tree each night,
   With hearts aglow, we feel the cheer,
   The magic of this time of year.

2. Yet in the rush of modern days,
   A precious word begins to fade,
   "Xmas" they write, to taint in haste,
   A sacred name, they now erase.

3. For Christmas holds a deeper grace,
   A story time cannot replace,
   Of love and hope and peace—the heir,
   Born to bring us God's joy and cheer.

4. Let not the "X" obscure the light,
   Of Christmas Eve, so pure and bright,
   For in that name, a promise lies,
   Of peace on earth, beneath the skies.

5. Now, let us speak with reverence true,
   Of Christmas, and its meaning too,
   For in each word, we find the way,
   To honor Christ on Christmas Day.

78. You'll Never Get It Back

1. If her soul had sought my heart, then
   I'm sure she would have seen;
   All the plans I had for us,
   Despite lies that her other tells,
   Trips round the world; to Venice and the sea,
   Trevi fountain and things she'd like to see.

2. If her soul had sought my heart, then
   Indeed, she would have seen;
   That my thoughts were always on her,
   In spite of her deceitful cheer,
   Caring on her health, her cares and welfare,
   Gladly giving my all, for us to share.

3. If her soul had sought my heart, then
   Certainly, she would've known;
   She seemed much like a stranger,
   Since her tryst with her paramour,
   Yet I, in love, worked hard to bring us back,
   She said, "My love, no way it's coming back."

79. Zebra Stripes Of Life

1. In the savannah's golden light,
    A zebra stands, a striking sight.
    Its stripes, a dance of black and white,
    Reflect the journey of a life.

2. Each line, a path we choose to tread,
    Some filled with joy, some tinged with dread.
    The dark and light, they intertwine,
    Like those life's moments that define.

3. The black stripes show trials we face;
    The challenges, the hurried pace.
    Yet, in the white we find our peace;
    The moments our sore worries cease.

4. Together they enhance a soul,
    A tapestry that makes us whole.
    For life, like stripes is never plain;
    A blend of sunshine and of rain.

5. So as the zebra roams the land,
    With stripes that nature's hand has planned,
    'Tis certain our lives too will blend,
    Both joy and sorrow till the end.

LIMERICKS

1. A Dancing Cop

Charm City had a cop with a grin,
Who loved to dance and twirl in a spin.
He'd direct traffic with flair,
Doing pirouettes in the air,
Charmed drivers didn't mind being stuck in a bin!

2. A Landsman's Rhyme

Fred was a man from the coast,
Who feared in the water to post.
He'd flail and he'd flip,
With each wayward trip,
Yet on land, he would proudly boast!

3. A Slip Of Fury

Flighty Matt Schlapp caused a flipping flap,
When he flipped out and slugged her a slap.
Her finger, she'd flipped,
Causing him to slip,
So his slipping fury fueled his flap!

4. A Quirky Friendship

There was once a man from Shendo,
Who was quite lonely and blue,
He bought a pet snail,
To join him for ale,
Now they both share a pint or two.

5. Bon Mot

A wordsmith who hailed from Provence,
Used bon mot and wit in response.
With each clever phrase,
He'd set minds ablaze,
And at parties, he was the renaissance!

6. Boomerang Bride

Thelma was a wife who did part,
Thinking single life was an art.
But the grass wasn't greener,
Since no man was keener,
So she returned to her husband's heart.

7. Dinner Date Disaster

Don was out with Dana on a date,
His friend, Danny was with his own mate.
Their paths crossed at the pub,
Where they each had their grub,
But Dana's filet fell from her plate.

8. Frolic And Frisk

She was all over me like antsy ants,
And frolicked and frisked in playful taunts.
She yanked down my pants,
And saw its contents.
She said, "Darn, what a creature in your pants!"

9. Grandma's Joy

A lovely grandma named Jane,
Had antics never quite plain.
She danced in the rain,
With a hat and a cane,
And sang like a bird on the plains!

10. Her Cooking

Elsa was a spouse from Peru,
Whose cooking was quite a to-do.
Her soup was quite bland,
Her roast was like sand,
And her loaf tasted quite like glue!

11. Her Flight Fright

In Clayton was a dame named Claire,
Who dreaded the thought of the air.
She'd cling to her seat,
And declined any treat,
While dreaming of travel by mare!

12. His Dear Wife

In Brighton was a man named Brad,
Whose spouse had quite a stubborn side.
She'd argue all day,
He'd just nod and say,
"Dear, you're always right," he'd confide.

13. His Endless Feast

From the east was a man named Ernie,
Whose appetite was quite the journey.
He'd eat foofoo with soup,
And all he could scoop,
Yet still have room left for a tourney!

14. His Odorous Odyssey

A very odd fellow named Clyde,
Whose smell was quite hard to abide.
He'd clear out a room,
With his pungent perfume,
And folks would scurry far and wide!

15. His Stunning Slip

A lonely fellow named Kip,
Once went on a leisurely trip.
He stumbled and fell,
When stunned by a bell,
Now he's known for his comical slip!

16. Love's Awkward Moment

For a time, she was his guiding light,
Together, their love shone so bright.
But while at the park,
Hoping to keep their spark,
Her ex appeared, causing a fright.

17. Man From Brent

O'Brien was a man from Brent,
Whose spouse had a penchant for vent.
She'd nag and she'd scold,
Till his patience grew old,
And he hid in his shed, quite content.

18. Man From The Coast

A man from the coast named Oreilley,
Loved to dance and oft would dilly-dally.
He slipped on a snail,
Yelled out as he fell,
"Now I'm late, and I've ruined the rally!"

19. Relief And The Commode

He had something that churned him inside,
His tummy spun like a top on a ride.
It was tight and swirling,
With loud growls unfurling,
On the commode, farting relief he did find.

20. Roar And Silence

Lurking around the stark, dark park,
Was a lion and a loud lark.
When the lion growled,
The poor lark was cowed,
And silenced its song with a stark mark.

21. Scratch Their Heads

In their church was a pastor named Ned,
Whose sermons were quite off the thread.
He'd preach about squirrels,
And moonwalking turtles,
Till the congregation scratched their heads!

22. The Dove And Blue Jay

A dove and Blue Jay in a feud,
Over seeds, they did greedily brood.
They pecked and they cooed,
In a manner quite rude,
Till the seeds were all gone—how shrewd.

23. The Flying Fibber

At work was a fibber named Fred,
Whose tall tales were spun from thin thread.
He claimed he could fly,
But feet stayed quite dry,
When he jumped off the roof, he turned red!

24. The Frog In A Coat

A frog in a bog, quite astute,
Found a science book in his commute.
He read about genes,
And what DNA means,
Now he croaks in a lab coat and suit!

25. The Philly Man And The Bridge

In Philly was a man quite contrite,
Who drove o'er a bridge, such a height!
His knuckles went white,
Heart filled with much fright,
But made it across, to his delight!

26. The Singing Miner

A local coal miner named Jack,
Once worked with a pick and a sack.
He'd sing country tunes,
Under bright mining moons,
And dream of a break and a snack!

27. The Stuttering King

Tuta was a king with a stutter,
Whose diction would clutter and flutter.
He'd say, "In my re-realm,
I'm at the he-he-helm,"
And his court would just melt as in butter.

28. The Thief

A very sly thief named Peter Lou,
Stole socks from each house he'd pass through.
He'd tiptoe at night,
Snatch socks left and right,
Yet had mismatched pair for each shoe!

29. The Thief And The Cop

An old, clever thief named Lee,
Was quite quick like a cat in a tree.
But a cop named McGraw,
With a doughnut in paw,
Caught him stuck in a branch on a tree!

30. The Yawning Lion

A lion, quite regal and dawning,
Was known for his mighty big yawning.
With each gaping wide,
The mice would all hide,
And the jungle awoke every morning!

31. Urgent Love

Making love was on my partner's mind,
Because she was going bedroom wild.
She pinned me on the bed,
And then stubbornly said,
"Take me now, my thoughts are in a bind!"

32. Witty And Wild

My slippery sitter gave me a sit,
Smiling quite slyly with her wry wit.
She opened my flap,
And sat on my lap,
My innocence buried deep in her pit!

33. Yapping Amber

Kate's friend was a girl named Amber,
Whose yapping, they'd all remember.
She talked to her pup,
'Til the sun was up,
Her folks wished for silence in December!

Printed in the United States
by Baker & Taylor Publisher Services